Born Donald McCain in 1930, Ginger began his career as a trainer in 1953, with a small stable behind a car showroom in Southport. He trained the legendary Red Rum to three Grand National victories and runner-up twice. Amberleigh House gave him his record-equalling fourth National win in 2004. He now operates from a yard set in almost 200 acres on the Cholmondeley Castle Estate in Cheshire.

Malcolm Folley, with whom Ginger McCain collaborated on this book, is Chief Sports Reporter for the *Mail on Sunday* with 30 years' experience on national newspapers. A former Sports Reporter of the Year, he has written *Borg Versus McEnroe*, a celebration of their epic 1980 Wimbledon final, and *A Time to Jump*, the authorised biography of Olympic champion Jonathan Edwards. He also co-authored Jason Robinson's acclaimed autobiography *Finding my Feet*, and worked with Hana Mandlikova on her autobiography *Hana*. He lives in Surrey with his wife Rachel and daughters Sian and Megan.

My Colourful Life

From Red to Amber

GINGER MCCAIN

WITH MALCOLM FOLLEY

headline

First published in 2005
by HEADLINE BOOK PUBLISHING

First published in paperback in 2006
by HEADLINE BOOK PUBLISHING

2

ISBN 978-0-7553-1373-0

Typeset in Perpetua by Avon DataSet Ltd,
Bidford-on-Avon, Warwickshire

Printed in Great Britain by
Clays Ltd, St Ives plc

Headline's policy is to use papers that are natural, renewable and
recyclable products and made from wood grown in sustainable forests. The
logging and manufacturing processes are expected to conform to the
environmental regulations of the country of origin.

HEADLINE BOOK PUBLISHING
A division of Hodder Headline
338 Euston Road
London NW1 3BH

www.headline.co.uk
www.hodderheadline.com

To Red Rum:
Thanks for the memories, old lad

CONTENTS

ACKNOWLEDGEMENTS

I wish to thank all those friends who stood behind me in bad times as well as good, too numerous to name but too precious to forget.

I will be eternally grateful to Noel Le Mare – the Guv'nor – for having the faith in letting me buy Red Rum in his name when I had no track record, used Southport beach as a training gallop and stabled my horses in a cobbled yard behind my second-hand car showroom. To suppose that we might one day share the joy of winning the world's greatest and most formidable steeplechase once, never mind three times, required a giant a leap of imagination on the Guv'nor's part.

I am similarly indebted to John Halewood, who entrusted me to try to repeat the trick and gave me permission to invest a significant amount of money in that quest. Without the boldness of these two men, my life would have taken a vastly different course. Sean Byrne is also deserving of my thanks for not only helping me find Amberleigh House for John, but for being my daft Irish friend who has been with me through thick and thin.

But my gratitude stretches to all those who have given me horses to train, good or bad. I hope they share my view that we had some fun along the way. In writing this book I have been made aware of all the friends and acquaintances who are no longer with us. They may be gone, but they are not forgotten.

My life would not have been the same without my wife Beryl – quieter, yes, but not the same. She has had much to put up with, but then I was worth it, wasn't I? Beryl's belief in me never wavered, and she has to take her share of credit for whatever success we have had. She also deserves praise for bringing up our children Donald and Joanne.

I would also like to express my sincere gratitude to Malcolm Folley, Chief Sports Reporter for the *Mail on Sunday*, for his professional contribution to the writing of this book. He did an awfully good job of assembling my memories and thoughts into a readable account of my life, in between travelling the world for his newspaper. Surprise, surprise we had some good *craic* along the way!

Without the *craic*, nothing has much meaning. So, finally, thanks to all those who have made my journey through life so enjoyable; and thanks to Sports Publisher David Wilson and all at Headline for believing it was worth printing.

Ginger McCain, Bankhouse, August 2005

In the crisp light of a Cheshire morning, Ginger McCain can be found watching his horses coming uphill on the all-weather gallop at his stables set in the idyllic acres of the Cholmondeley Estate. His faithful old springer, Tilly, will be at his side. It is a timeless scene from the autumn years of his long and eventful life. In these moments, McCain is in his element.

His love of horses has defined his existence, and he will make believe that they have been his pleasure and his pride above all else. Quite possibly this is true. But McCain is also a man with a rare capacity to make people smile; friends and strangers alike. During our collaboration in writing this book I witnessed from close quarters the affection McCain engenders wherever he goes. At every racetrack we visited, from Aintree to Hereford, persons unknown greeted him like a long-lost friend. We tried some recording sessions in local hostelries, but they never really progressed beyond the second glass of red wine as people came to our table to talk over old tales with McCain or plot new ones. Tapes were wasted; time was not.

He admits in the pages of this book that over the years he has been on occasion too blunt, to the detriment of his business. Of course, McCain would not know the meaning of political correctness and he has exhibited a nodding acquaintance with chauvinism!

His story is like him – larger than life. To win the Grand National three times with a horse trained on the beach and living in a stable behind a second-hand car showroom is preposterous. But to win the race again twenty-seven years later is nothing less than a fairytale. I feel privileged that McCain and his wife Beryl, a match for her man, have allowed me to chronicle their extraordinary tale and treated me like a friend.

I must also thank their son Donald, daughter Joanne and daughter-in-law Sian for their assistance. Thanks are due also to John and Judy Halewood, jockey Graham Lee, and all the other friends of McCain who showed such a generosity of spirit. I am grateful to some vintage BBC film and commentary, led by the incomparable Sir Peter O'Sullevan, which enabled us to relive Red Rum's imperious years of dominance of the Grand National. Mike Dillon from Ladbrokes was a source of rich memoir. I'd like also to thank Cara Sloman from the *Mail on Sunday* for her tireless editorial support and I am indebted to my Cheshire landlady Jan Dilworth, who made her delightful bed and breakfast farmhouse a welcome retreat.

I am most grateful to my agent Jonathan Harris, the inspiration and driving force behind this book, and I am fortunate to have had such enthusiastic and skilful editing from David Wilson and Juliana Foster, and the support of all the team at Headline. Lastly, I would like to express my appreciation to my wife Rachel and daughters Sian and Megan who forgave me my absence.

Malcolm Folley, West Horsley, August 2005

ROYAL SEAL OF APPROVAL

'I have two very important announcements to make. I know you will want to know the winner of the Grand National. It was Hedgehunter . . .

' . . . Having cleared Becher's Brook and The Chair, the happy couple are now in the winner's enclosure.'

The Queen, speaking to guests at the wedding reception she hosted at Windsor Castle for Prince Charles and his bride Camilla, now the Duchess of Cornwall, 9 April 2005

I CHUCKLED WHEN I read that Her Majesty had begun her speech at Prince Charles's wedding reception by announcing the winner of the 2005 Grand National to her guests. I have always respected royalty and the Royal Family, and it was only right and proper that the Queen, as an important woman of the Turf, should have had her priorities in order.

In getting married on Grand National day, Prince Charles certainly backed my own judgement, though I can't imagine what his grandmother, the late Queen Mother, would have made of having her focus on the Grand National compromised by a family wedding. The Queen Mother came heartbreakingly close to becoming the first member of the Royal Household to win the most famous steeplechase in the world when Devon Loch, ridden by Dick Francis, fell spreadeagled when in sight of the winning post in 1956. It was she who gave her daughter – our Queen – her love of horses and horseracing.

The Grand National is like a river running through my life. I became engaged on the day of the 1959 Grand National – won by Oxo – and two years later I married on the morning of the National, taking my bride from our reception in Southport to watch the race at Aintree that afternoon. It was enough in those days for a Jack-the-lad taxi driver like me to marvel at the courage of the horses and the men riding them. It was enough to appreciate the spectacle and to be involved in the craic happening on the sidelines. Never for a moment did I imagine that one day I would stand in front of television cameras and be asked to tell how I had trained the winner of the Grand National.

But then, never did I suppose that I would meet a horse like Red Rum. He changed the course of my life as no man or woman or child could ever do. Red lived with me for twenty-three years, an irascible character and a loyal friend. He won the Grand National three times and finished second twice, trained on the beach at Southport and living in a stable in a small, cobbled yard behind my second-hand-car showroom in Upper Aughton Road. It was simply my privilege to be the person most closely associated with him. He had a gift that I was able to exploit: that's all.

And that gift extended into retirement, a decision taken on the eve of the 1978 Grand National. From that moment, he became more than ever the horse of the people. In his racing career, Red was a champion; in retirement, he became a national treasure. His engagements diary was filled twelve months in advance. He brought joy wherever he visited, because the old lad was a showman until the day he died.

Red's death in 1995 was big news: a story told in every national newspaper and broadcast on television. And in recognition of what he achieved, of what he did to revive the fading fortunes of the Grand National, we were invited to bury him beside the winning post at Aintree.

I like the idea of him at rest where he made his legend, where he was at his happiest. Whenever I go to Aintree I never fail to have a word with him or to take him flowers. It's the least I owe him. Never a day goes past without Red being mentioned or some memory of him flashing through my mind. Red Rum has been central to all I have in life, and in the years after he retired there were some extremely hard times to endure when the job was difficult and my debts high.

But I never lost faith; nor did the woman I married on Grand National day in 1961. My wife Beryl – or Conk, as I call her – is a quite remarkable person, really she is. Without her I would have been brilliant. I would also have been dead. She's been my greatest critic, but you would never get someone to battle harder for you or be a truer friend than she is. She has so many, many good points, they nearly outweigh the bad 'uns! She's been a star, actually. I can't think of any two people who argue so much and who have stayed together for so many years as us. She has left me once or twice, but she always found her way home. I have never been brave enough to leave her. To be honest, I never had any inclination to do so – I'm too scared.

Beryl's had a fair bit to put up with from me, I suppose. Perhaps the run-up to the Grand National this past spring topped the lot. Certainly she thought so; not that I really understood the fuss. Actually, I've never felt so relaxed before a National as this time around. To tell you the truth, I was surprised how switched off I was.

On the morning of the race, I awoke sometime after six-thirty without a care, which is probably not something Prince Charles could say. As usual these days, my good friend Sean Byrne was over from Ireland for the Aintree meeting and was staying with us at our training yard on the Cholmondeley Estate in Cheshire – a part of England undisturbed by the passing of time. It was partly because of Sean that I'd found myself, against almost everyone's (except mine and Beryl's) expectations, back in the winner's enclosure at Aintree twenty-seven years after Red Rum won it a third time for me and his owner, a lovely old gentleman called Noel Le Mare. Mr Le Mare was – and always will be – the Guv'nor to me.

Around 8 a.m., Sean and I went out to the all-weather gallop, a few minutes' uphill walk from our house with its dramatic views of rural Cheshire, to watch the first two lots work. As always, I harrowed the gallop. Amberleigh House – whose home is the same stable where Red Rum lived in retirement – was brought out for a leg-stretching walk. My son Donald felt we had him as fit as we could possibly get him. His wife Sian placed a lock of the old horse's hair into Amberleigh House's bridle as she 'dressed' him. At 9.15 a.m., Donald, Sian and Wizard, my travelling head lad, left the yard with Amberleigh to make the drive to Aintree, a journey that takes around an hour and fifteen minutes in a horsebox. Sean, Beryl and I had a cooked breakfast and changed before we set out for Liverpool in my Rover. I drove: I much prefer driving to being a passenger, and that way I can make sure we are where we need to be on time.

I just love everything about the Grand National – and Liverpool. Those Scousers do go out to enjoy themselves. I love their witticisms, and I love the way the women go to have a good time and wear next to nothing in their attempt to show off their figures or their tan, even if it has come out of a bottle. You can keep Cheltenham or Ascot; this is the People's Race. The day before the National is Ladies' Day at Liverpool – attracting a crowd of 55,000 people to Aintree these days – and one of the features of the programme is what amounts to a beauty competition to find the best-turned-out 'filly'. This year several women came wearing bikinis – even though it was bloody freezing. The compère asked one of the girls if she felt cold. She replied that she had earlier, so he asked her what she had done about it. 'I put on another thong,' she replied, totally deadpan. I had to laugh. The first prize was a Jaguar and I heard the woman who had won trying to convince her husband on her mobile phone that she had been given a car. She told him she was standing near Ginger McCain, and clearly he asked to speak to me, as the next thing I know she has given me her telephone. I say his wife is telling the truth, she has won a Jaguar. I also tell him that, if he wants, I'll give him a price for it. Once a motor trader, always a motor trader, I suppose.

That was Friday.

On Saturday I discovered I was the one under an unforgiving spotlight – as Beryl had warned I would be. As soon as we arrived at the owners' and trainers' car park at Aintree, one of the security fellows said to me: 'Ginger, if that girl wins, they'll be queuing to kick your arse all the way from Aintree to Anfield.' That did make me think a little bit.

Let me refresh your memories. Eighteen days earlier I'd happily gone to Liverpool for the Grand National Media Lunch to lend my support – after all, the race has been the making of me. I'd been asked to take Amberleigh House as well. I had refused to do that, as I felt that it was too close to the National to disturb my little horse's routine. But, willingly, I was pictured and filmed standing beside Red Rum's grave. As I answered some questions, Carrie Ford cantered up the course on the horse that she was going to ride in the National, Forest Gunner.

'What do you think of Carrie riding in the National, Ginger?' someone asked.

I replied: 'Carrie is a grand lass, but she's a brood mare now and having kids does not get you fit to ride in Grand Nationals. Good luck to her, and they have a very good horse, there's no question of that. But to go four and a half miles around Aintree you have to be a top-class professional. We will discount Forest Gunner.'

Well, how was I to know what would follow? Now, Carrie and Richard Ford, who trains Forest Gunner, happen to be friends of mine and Beryl, and they live just eight miles or so from us, near Tarporley. They know me – and they would know that I had my tongue in my cheek when I said what I said. Mind you, I meant it when I said I felt it was impossible for a woman rider to win the National; but, certainly, I didn't mean any offence or insult. It seems lots of people took it that way, though.

But I really should have kept my mouth shut instead of saying that if Carrie did win I'd bare my backside to the wind for all and sundry to kick. It was all a bit of a wind-up on my part -- and if truth be told, I think the Fords enjoyed it as much as I did. It didn't harm the race, did it? The story was running almost every day, and Carrie gave interviews all over the place. But Beryl and Donald were decidedly unamused, as she will tell you:

'The last couple of weeks were awful. I was fielding calls about Carrie every day. Of all the things Ginger has said, this proved the most provocative. We do like Carrie and Richard and they were very understanding when I called to tell them how upset I was, and that Donald was as well. They didn't take offence. Young Donald had said to me that he wished his dad wouldn't upset people for no reason and I was getting very conscious of this. I was just fed up with my husband.

'We had already been concerned whether jockey Graham Lee would be available to ride Amberleigh House as his boss, trainer Howard Johnson, had a potential runner in the National in top-weighted Grey Abbey. Graham has a great relationship with our horse, having won last year's Grand National on him, after finishing third the year before that. Ginger had said some stuff in the press about Graham needing to make up his mind, and to show some loyalty. In desperation, I sent Graham a text and asked him to give me a ring. He did. I said that I hoped he was not being upset with what was being said, and that Ginger only wanted what was best for Amberleigh House and all of us.

'Graham said, "Look, Beryl, don't worry; it's only a horse race, there are much worse things going on in the world." I really appreciated that. The next day Donald and Sian were in our kitchen and I repeated what Graham had said about it being only a horse race. Sian turned round and said, "Not in this house, it isn't." She was right!

'Had Graham been able to commit to Amberleigh earlier than nine days before the Grand National – and we understood his position and Howard Johnson's need to do his best by his owner – we had prepared a press release for the Racing Post. We were going to inform them that Carrie was riding Amberleigh House and

Graham was on standby to ride Forest Gunner. The Fords were in on it. And the plan was to send it to the Post for publication on 1 April – April Fool's Day.

'But Graham could only let us know he was available the afternoon before, so it was too late to try to show the world that the McCains and the Fords were not at loggerheads over what Ginger had said about Carrie. Usually, it's quite good fun getting a horse ready for the National if his preparation is going without a hitch. And it was – it was Ginger causing the stress in our house. I went to the golf course one day and the lady captain said, "Beryl, I don't know what's the matter, but go out and enjoy yourself." I had to laugh.

'It got so silly – every day a variation of the story was in the papers. I was on a bit of a downer, really. I am probably more self-conscious about what people think of Ginger than he is. He doesn't care. I asked him if he did not regret a little bit what he'd said. He wouldn't admit it.

'Donald and I were raging – but when we saw the television interview of what he said, we thought: "Is that all he said?" Carrie wouldn't have thought twice about being called a brood mare. It's a term we all use in racing about women within the sport who have had children. But to those outside our world, I suppose it was seen as a term of abuse, a bit like someone being called a cow. In racing, women are used to such terminology.

'Not that long ago, Harvey Smith said to Ginger: "You'll have to get rid of Beryl."

'"Why's that, Harvey?" asked Ginger.

'"Because she's too old to breed – and too savage to keep as a pet!"

'This is the way we are. But I admit I wanted Ginger to apologize – we had huge rows about it. But Ginger wouldn't back down.'

So, I knew from the security man in the car park that I would be in for one heck of a day – but I'd worry about that if and when the time came. Not that I believed for a second that anything would happen. Security at Liverpool is very intense nowadays. Getting into the racecourse is like passing into the departure lounge at an airport, and Beryl was very upset to have a small pair of nail scissors confiscated at the entrance gate on the grounds that they constituted a dangerous weapon. There was no arguing with the policewoman, even though the scissors had been with Beryl over the previous two days.

We'd had a lovely trouble-free run-up with the horse and I had no qualms about the day whatsoever. I'd arrived at Aintree with a large bunch of flowers that my daughter Joanne had got for me to take to Red Rum's grave as usual. By coincidence, Carrie and Richard came in at the same time, and we shared a lift on one of the golf buggies that shuttle between the entrance and the paddock. I asked the driver to pull up near the weighing room, which is twenty yards or so from the paddock. I said to Carrie, 'Come on, follow me.' We went into the winner's enclosure and I presented her with the flowers in front of the television cameras. It was just a bit of fun and Carrie sportingly played along. Then I took the flowers back and walked across the course and put them on Red Rum's grave, where they were meant to be. I had a few quiet words with the old lad.

Afterwards, I went to collect some badges that had been left in the office for me. They are very kind to me at Liverpool and they always give me the badges I request, though I don't think I abuse the privilege. I also get served faster by being allowed in the exit door at the office, avoiding the queues. Must have something to do with age, I suppose.

I love the craic and banter of Grand National day. You bump into all sorts of people you know. One of the first people Sean and I met was Patsy Byrne, an Irishman who is huge in the construction business. That was a bit of luck, giving me the opportunity to remind him that he had bought a horse from us the day before. Yet as it was business that had been done in the owners' and trainers' bar, and at the time he'd been buying champagne like it was going out of fashion, I said that we wouldn't hold him to the sale. Sean had a share in the horse, which, in truth, I'd rescued from him in Ireland when he had declared it surplus to requirements.

But Patsy, good man that he is, said: 'No, I bought a horse and I know how much it was.' He loves the craic as much as the next Irishman, being a successful owner of both horses and greyhounds, and the sale went through on the spot – after a little back and forth on what price had been decided on. I've known worse starts to Grand National day. I felt good, I really did. The job was done, the pressure was off and I'm a bit long in the tooth to fret over too much.

Sean and I walked down the course a little bit and cut in beyond The Chair to come back past the Irish bar. We'd been in there the day before to meet one or two people. I don't think the people who go in there ever bother coming out again! We thought better of making another visit for fear that we might not get out ourselves. Instead, we went to the owners' and trainers' bar, where I had a half of bitter. Then I thought, 'Bugger this, I'm going to look at my horse.'

So I went, as I always do, to see Derek, who manages the stables at Aintree, a real character. I can escape all the hype and palaver there – for a time, anyway. I had a John Smith's with him while we talked. Ted Walsh came in, as did one or two other trainers. Amberleigh House was stabled directly opposite Derek's office in the exact same box Red Rum used to have. Derek has always kept that box bolted until my National horse arrives, as I have always liked the thought of my horse being stabled in the box that had been so kind to us.

When I went across the yard to see Amberleigh House he was standing back in his box, completely relaxed. 'What an old pro you are,' I thought. He was bright, but he didn't have his head over the door or anything like that. He was completely switched off. Lots of horses start sweating and shivering, and get all wound up. But not Amberleigh House. No, he was the ultimate professional.

The BBC had asked me if I would do an interview with Sue Barker for half past one, and of course I agreed. Sue's very nice indeed, and, naturally, she asked me about Carrie. I just tried to keep the wind-up going – and we talked about me giving Carrie the flowers and then taking them back. After that, I was just freewheeling down to the start of the race. Before you know where you are the horses are down at the saddling boxes behind the paddock. I watched Donald and Wizard saddle my little horse, then Sian led him up. The horse looked a picture, and very fit indeed. He had a great bloom on his coat and he was carrying himself with a lot of presence. He was ready for the job. I had no nerves at all.

Once all the runners are in the paddock, in come the jockeys, all together in a file from the weighing room. It's a nervous time for them; they just want to get on the racecourse and away from the crowds. Graham came over to where I stood with Beryl and Donald. Also with us were John Halewood and Judy, who own Amberleigh House. John has had horses on and off with me for twenty-two years – and I introduced him to Judy. John is a friend of mine, but later you'll see why I deliberately say 'on and off'. There were times when what happened between us hurt me deeply and I almost packed the whole game in.

But on this day, as he watched Donald give Graham a leg into the saddle, John said to me: 'Ginger, we can't give this up.' Successful as John is in business, I think the Grand National is one of the highlights of his year. Winning the race with Amberleigh House the previous year had been an ambition come true. And finding a Liverpool horse isn't easy. As Fred Winter, a fantastic man, champion jockey and trainer, said, 'You don't buy good horses, they arrive.'

As the horses went out on to the course, I didn't say anything to Graham other than to wish him good luck. He had talked through the race with Donald, as always – and besides, Graham had ridden the horse over the National fences four times before. I thought we faced two real threats: from Trevor Hemmings's horse, Hedgehunter, and from Clan Royal, owned by J. P. McManus and trained by my old friend Jonjo O'Neill. Jonjo rode my first ever Grand National runner, Glenkiln, and I think the world of him. He'd had a wretched season with the horses in his yard affected by some mysterious virus or some such thing. I thought

Clan Royal could straighten the whole job up by winning the Grand National for him.

Trevor Hemmings, whose empire includes Blackpool Tower, has spent fortunes trying to win the race since he saw his old boss, Fred Pontin, win it with a horse called Specify in 1971. A lot of rich and titled men have thrown around plenty of money without ever having the satisfaction of winning this greatest of all great races. But I felt sure that Trevor's horse Hedgehunter – who fell when leading at the last fence when we came late to win the race twelve months earlier – would be in contention.

But I also thought my little horse was in with a serious shout again. He went out in the betting – at one time he was 10–1 joint favourite – to 20–1. That didn't matter to me. Mick Meagher, who manages Trevor Hemmings's horses, said to me in the paddock, 'Ginger, your horse looks sparkling, I'm going to have a few quid each way on him.' He didn't tell me to back Hedgehunter, though!

I saw the horses go out, then Sean and I cut away. We have this special place where we stand on the stairs to the left of the Queen Mother's Stand. We are directly opposite the large diamond television screen – and we have the privilege of being the only two allowed there. Beryl had gone wherever Beryl goes: I don't know and I don't ask. Donald went down to the start with our horse, but I've no idea where he watched the race from.

They all cantered down to the first fence and then cantered back. I watched them walk around at the start, and I knew that I was looking at forty of the best steeplechasers in the British Isles. It's pretty serious stuff. Magic, really. This all happens right in front of the stands – not in the distance, like at Cheltenham or anywhere else. It's an electric moment.

When the starter called them in, the line was a bit ragged, but that's natural. When the tape flies up, the roar is second to none. Forty horses bowling down to the first fence is something special. This year I couldn't pick my fellow out. It had just been raining, so it was a little murky, I'd suggest. Nothing to do with my age, honest. So I watched the screen and it took me a bit of time to find him. He pitched at the first, I did see that, but from then on he was foot perfect. He was pinging his fences. But he could never get a strike in. The race for us was pretty straightforward. Amberleigh never really got in serious contention. With top weight Grey Abbey withdrawn, we had gone up three further pounds in the weights to 11st 3lb. And with Graham's back protector, Amberleigh was carrying 11st 5lb. I'm not making an excuse, but for a little horse I think the weight did anchor him a bit. And he is getting more and more one-paced as he gets older. I knew before the Canal Turn on the second circuit that we were not going to get in the shake-up. But it didn't matter because he was jumping round nicely, very nicely, and I was really proud of the little horse.

But I wasn't just watching my horse, was I? I had to have a weather eye on Forest Gunner and Carrie. What a ride she gave him. She put the wind up a few people – including me. Coming to the last she was in the leading group that still cradled a dream of winning the National. Regrettably for her, Forest Gunner just didn't get the trip and she finished fifth behind the winner, Hedgehunter, a deserved and sparkling champion. But Carrie still had a day second to none, one that will live with her for the rest of her life. Don't you listen to these people who will tell you how having your first child is the experience to beat them all. Riding such a brilliant Grand National will be far more important to Carrie. At least, that's what I reckon. But what do I know about having kids? I've always left that to Beryl. That's the one thing she's better at than me.

I saw Carrie afterwards – but there was not a lot more I could say to her other than 'Magic!' Richard had a glazed look in his eye. I don't think he thought it had happened. It was just great to see what they had achieved. To some extent, I think I knew how he felt. They are grand, hard-working people, they really are. I could see in the paddock that

Forest Gunner's legs had been heavily bar-fired, in an old-fashioned way, but leaving them hard and clean, enabling him to remain in training. Forest Gunner had come from a modest background – and gone on to be a lovely Liverpool horse and run close to winning a National. It's nice that people like the Fords can take the big guns on – just as I had once, I suppose.

I have a secret to reveal. If Carrie had won I don't think I would have actually bared my arse. That would have been no fun for anyone. But a bet is a bet. So the day before, my family had bought me a big pair of blue Y-fronts to take to Liverpool. And my daughter Joanne had printed a message on the back – 'Carrie Ford Rules'! They were in Sean's pocket all day long and I would have put them on and revealed them happily if required. As it was, I passed them on to Carrie after the race for her to have as a keepsake.

As for my fellow, Amberleigh jumped the last and galloped on like the professional he is. His ears were pricked and Graham was just riding him out hands and heels – perhaps these days the horse needs five miles! He finished tenth of the forty runners and put two other Grand National winners behind him, Bindaree and Monty's Pass. The little horse had done us proud, he really had.

I went down to meet Graham on his return. He said Amberleigh had been in top gear all the way, and that he was galloping as fast at the last as he had been going to the first. He said he couldn't go another half gear quicker. Graham – a nice person and an excellent jockey – then said something I will always treasure. He said that it was a privilege to ride the horse and that he felt very honoured. He tapped his saddle with his whip, indicating that he had been beaten by the weight he'd carried. He's a very astute young man and I should think that's right. Graham gave Amberleigh House a tender pat on the neck and walked away. Then he came back, looked at the little horse again, and gave him another little pat. It was a superb moment.

I wasn't one tiny bit disappointed. I thought my son had done a great job getting him ready. I'd love to have won the National for an historic fifth time, of course I would. Then I would have retired on the spot. I didn't give a great depth of thought to it, but I know that's just what I would have done.

Amberleigh House was turned out into the fields for the spring grass, but once the flies came, he was back doing the same as he has done for the past eleven years. We will aim him at the Becher's Chase in November, then, in discussion with John, we'll see what happens next. We'll play it by ear – but Amberleigh House won't be abused in any way. Come what may, there is a box at my stable that's his for the rest of his days – but then, the bugger will outlast me, so Donald will be left with that responsibility.

OVER THE YEARS I've had some grand success, certainly more than I could have imagined when I was little more than a stable lad who drove taxis – albeit a happy stable lad. I used to get into Liverpool on an old pass and just hope that no one would pull me up to check it. Now I don't have to show anything. Everywhere I go near horses or a racecourse, it's 'Hello, Ginger!' You'd have to have no ego at all to say that wasn't enjoyable.

But in some ways, when you are struggling, though the pleasures are smaller you gain more satisfaction from them. It's not all fun, of course. We've known what it's like to have the bailiffs at the door at our home in Southport. Mind you, they didn't hang about when I had a pickaxe handle in my hand: they left shouting that they'd call the police. I told them to make sure there were at least four of them. I could be a right mouthy young man.

Actually, that was only a minor skirmish, a misunderstanding over the payment of our rates. The real crisis came later, long after Red Rum had retired. It turned out that my partner in the car trade had been fiddling us. We very nearly didn't make it back from that blow, and would have been bankrupt but for the generosity and friendship of one of our owners, Stan Markland, a grand man whom I still miss. His support at that moment was an act of blind faith and true friendship.

To be honest, I wonder today whether, if I had more money and a bigger yard, the job might be too easy . . . You do need to think about things, to duck and dive a little bit. In this sport you meet some lovely people, but you meet some villains, too – which is fine, provided you can tell them apart.

The day after this year's Grand National Beryl and I, along with a couple of good friends, Tony and Elsie Stannard, went to the point-to-point run by the Cheshire Forest Hunt. Donald had two horses running, and I wouldn't have missed it for the world. People had picnics from their car boots, and generally had great craic between the races. The sun shone, and all you could hear around us was gales of laughter as friends came past Tony's car and swapped old stories and a glass or two of champagne or wine. That day represented all that is good and grand about this country of ours – and what Tony Blair's government is trying to kill with his ridiculous ban on hunting. It is my opinion – and my hope – that he won't succeed unless he has room to lock up thousands of innocent people.

Carrie and Richard Ford were there, along with the owner of Forest Gunner, John Gilsenan, a retired local farmer. I congratulated Mr Gilsenan, who kindly asked if Amberleigh House had returned home sound. And he had, a few nicks aside. Mr Gilsenan had bought Forest Gunner rather than splash out on a posh Mercedes after selling his dairy herd. His horse had cost him £4,000 six years ago – and it was lovely to see him have so much pleasure with him.

WITH AGE, IT is easier to get a clearer perspective on life. In the weeks leading up to the Grand National I underwent a course of radiotherapy. Kindly, the hospital near Birkenhead allowed me to be last man in to have the treatment at 5.30 p.m., from Monday to Friday; and for the Aintree meeting, they brought my appointment forward to 8.30 a.m. to allow me to go racing without any inconvenience. I was told I needed six weeks of treatment. The people at the hospital were absolute magic. I have never dropped my kecks for so many attractive girls with no results! They took the mickey out of me, no question.

The treatment was precautionary, as some years ago I had my prostate removed and doctors making a routine check found an irregularity in a blood sample. I didn't ask for the details, but I know it wasn't life-threatening. Actually, I felt I was there under false pretences. There were people around me who were really poorly. What am I – seventy-four? OK, I'm getting to be an old man, but I'm pretty fit and active. I work every day on the gallops; I have almost 200 acres of pastureland that I need to roll, and there are fences that need to be repaired. I can say, hand on heart, that my role in overall charge of the operation has not been in the least bit affected. I truly haven't given my health a thought – the doctors are the experts and you don't argue with them. Whatever I've got, I've got.

A good friend of mine, Emlyn Hughes, who captained Liverpool and England, died earlier this year from a brain tumour. We had some grand times together. I had a great respect for Em, as a sportsman and as a person. He lived well, he wasn't a big drinker, never smoked and was fit throughout his life. He was just a lovely, lovely man, whom I first met when Red Rum was at the top of his game – just like the Liverpool football team. Emlyn would have loved the way Liverpool overcame Juventus, Chelsea and then, most amazing of all, AC Milan in that dramatic European Champions' Cup final.

He also loved his racing and, as a boy from Barrow, he never missed a meeting at Cartmel. You see all these flowery footballers now with X thousand pounds per week wages; most of them couldn't hold a candle to Emlyn. But he never complained that he had lived in the wrong era or anything like that. In fact, I remember him telling me with pride that Liverpool looked after their players and that when he retired he would get £280 per week. I thought, 'Jesus, that's an awful good pension – better than racing.'

When Emlyn was dying, he said to his wife, 'Barb, you play the cards as they are dealt.' That was the measure of the man. I missed his funeral because I had to go to the Doncaster sales, so as not to miss buying three horses that I wanted. I felt bad – I still do; but I thought that of all people, Em, as a sportsman and a lover of racing, would understand.

I've had a great run and I've had a great time. But I wouldn't want to become a doddery, slobbering, incontinent old man. I'd sooner they took me round the corner and shot me. After all, I've had times second to none. I'm not squeaking about anything. And I can assure you there's plenty of life left in this old dog yet! I'm not short of an opinion or two, as the pages of this book will show. And I bet you won't agree with them all. Where would the fun be in life if everyone did?

It has been a grand old journey, but in telling it from start to finish I've often wondered what bugger would want to listen to it all. Is it really worth telling? I'll let you decide for yourselves.

Chapter One

POACHING, PIGEONS
AND PONIES

GROVE STREET, SOUTHPORT, 21 September 1930. That's the where and when of my appearance. I won't go into the how. It was a small back street in town – ten or twelve houses on one side and four or five on the other.

My dad, William, worked for a firm called Marshall & Snelgrove as a dispatch manager, and my mother, Sally, was – well, basically at that time she was just my mother. (Or, I should say, our mother: I had an elder sister called Audrey, born a couple of years earlier.) I was named Donald, but that soon became Don or Donny, and in any case I was known pretty much everywhere as 'Ginger' from as early as I can remember. I had ginger hair, and a fair bit of it – but it was also a nickname I acquired as I was prone to getting involved in pranks like the character Ginger in the 'Just William' stories. Once, for example, with a pal I put some lit fireworks into a dustbin and then we jumped on the lid to see if we could take off like a rocket.

As for the name McCain, I have to be honest and admit that I don't know where the family originates. It could be Ireland, but after three generations the roots are blurred. It's just one of those things that at the time didn't seem important. I do know my mother's family was from Southport; they came from farming stock, I think.

When I was about four or five, we went to live in Liverpool Road in

Birkdale. I had another sister by then, called Sally. We lived in a flat over a fish shop and next door there was a bread shop. Irwins was the corner shop. I suppose it counted as a superstore in those days. After a couple of years we moved again, to 316 Liverpool Road, six doors away from the Crown Hotel. My sister Sally still lives there. It's semi-detached, a good standard of house for working-class people: not over-big, but with a separate bathroom and toilet upstairs. Almost directly opposite the house was Farnborough Road School, which took infants and juniors. All three of us went there. Funnily enough, I was invited back to be guest of honour for an anniversary of the school in 2004. That was rather nice of them, but I couldn't go, as I was already committed to be in Ireland for some horse sales. When your life is horses, these sales are very important. I've had to miss a few things I'd like to have gone to because of them – Em's funeral for one, as I said.

We moved to No. 316 not long before the war started – it'd be around the end of 1937 or the beginning of '38. I enjoyed school, and I did the run-of-the-mill lad type of stuff. My mother did tell a story that one day I was seen outside school offering to take on all-comers in a fight! I don't remember that, but I'm sure it's true. I like to think so, anyway. In junior school there was a competition among the boys to be 'cock-of-the-school', a title given to the kid who could use his fists best. I don't think I was quite ever cock-of-the-school, but I wasn't far off the top of the ratings. I could always look after myself. You'd be in the playground fooling around when, suddenly, someone would shout, 'Fight!' – and a great big mob of lads and girls would gather round two boys having a scrap. They would be rolling over on the floor, wrestling basically. Kicking never came into it. Fighting was cleaner then, somehow.

Teachers didn't make a big thing of it, either. Parents these days worry so much about what their kids do at school. I remember our old headmaster – Mr Bracewell, I think he was called – coming out on frosty mornings and throwing two fire buckets of water (the war was on by now) on to the playground to make slides for us. Imagine that happening these days! All hell would break out.

Not that he was a soft touch. On a couple of occasions, I was lined up outside his office with six or seven other lads waiting nervously to be called in, one at a time – and we were all supposed to be hard men. He used to grip your head between his knees and he held what looked like a two-inch wide leather flap. It seemed pretty long, from memory. He would give you four or five round the arse end, sort of real stingers. You wouldn't look at your friends as you came out of his office; you'd just say 'Phew' and pretend that you hadn't been really hurt. Crying was for girls. But it didn't do anyone any lasting harm, that's a fact. Young lads, young men, get into trouble. That's what you do. Part and parcel of the job, isn't it?

From Farnborough Road I moved on to Birkdale Secondary Modern School, which must have been three-quarters of a mile up the road. The school backed on to the sand hills that rise on the beach, and it was hard against Southport and Ainsdale Golf Club. There was a naval gunnery nearby and you could hear the sound of heavy guns and machine guns. Planes would be towing targets over the sea most of the day and sometimes during the night as well. It was an exciting time, a good time for a lad.

I played for the school football team until I left when I was thirteen and a half. With the war on, nobody sort of bothered very much about whether you were at school or not. The German air force made continuous raids on Liverpool – in the blackout, you could see the glow in the sky over the city – and a number of bombs fell on Southport. Once, when I was staying with an aunt in High Park not too far from our own house, I can recall being blown out of my bed. The next day we were out having great fun looking for shrapnel. That's the way you had to look at things then. Especially as a kid.

About six months after the war started, my dad joined the RAF. Everything was tightening up money-wise. Mum went to work on the night shift at an ammunition factory in Kirkby. Each night at nine o'clock she'd catch the bus from the corner of our road and she wouldn't be back until close on six o'clock the next morning, in time to get myself and my sisters ready for school. I have to laugh when I hear these silly wet bloody women with one or two kids going on about how hard done by they are today. They have no idea, they really don't. Dad's pay from the RAF didn't start coming through for over a month, and that was quite serious for a working-class family.

But we had a grand mother, a really super woman who coped without complaint. As for my dad, he was one of those lovely men that did everything. By all accounts, he was quite a good-looking man (obviously I take after him) and well thought of within his firm, where they called him Mac. Actually, I often wonder about him. There were a lot of very attractive ladies working at Marshall & Snelgrove, and they all thought an awful lot of Mac – I don't know for sure, but it could be that my father flew his kite in one or two camps! But my mother would have straightened him up, if she had thought there was the need. He was a nice man, brought his family up well. I like to think he taught us all manners and showed us how to respect our elders.

Dad was in air traffic control, stationed with an American squadron in Yeovil. Occasionally he came home on leave, but it was too far for him to travel if he had only a forty-eight-hour pass. Besides, the trains were very irregular. I can remember Mum going to spend a week down there with him and meeting her off the train when she came back – which we were keen to do, as Mac always managed to find sweets for us. Even after the war was over, American friends he had made continued to send us parcels of chocolate and other goodies for a long time.

In the midst of the wartime rationing, I learned how to find an alternative source of food. I had a useful little terrier, and I could always get a rabbit or two or bag a pigeon from the bandstand in Southport. I had an uncle who'd taken me shooting before the war, and he gave me my first air gun. A couple of times he took me with him to Wales, in a little Austin Seven, when he went there to shoot, so I was clued up about the country style of life from an early age. I became quite adept at poaching – except we didn't think of it as that. We would go to feed the ducks at Hesketh Park; then, when no one was watching, we'd nick one or two. I used to have ground lines on the beach, too. People fished a lot in the early years of the war, with normal supplies hard to come by. One time I had a 30lb codling off the beach.

We'd take our catch to a local fishmonger, a miserable old bastard. He'd take half a hundredweight of fish and give you about six shillings or five bob, something like that, and sell them for a fat profit. But I could always catch things, and I was really very good with a catapult. On the way to school we would go on to the army range and collect used rounds that made brilliant ammunition. I smashed seven gaslights – they were obviously not working in the blackout – one day. Truthfully speaking, I should have been flogged for it. But nobody caught me – and having done one, I wanted to prove how good a shot I was. I've killed a pheasant in the air with a catapult. We also did some terrible, underhand things like killing water hens as they dived. But as we killed them to eat, it didn't seem a crime.

One night, after Mum had left for the ammunition factory, I headed for the beach to go fishing. Taking a short cut through the sand dunes and the cemetery, it was probably a couple of miles' walk. I always took my dog – but remember it was pitch black. You couldn't see your hand in front of your face, but you didn't think about it. As usual, I came back through the cemetery as it was part of the short cut. My fish were on my back. Suddenly, there was a noise by some gravestones. Well, I dropped my fish and took off. Bloody hell! I had the wind up, no mistake. But as I was running I realized that the fish were worth about five shillings and I couldn't afford to lose that. So I plucked up courage and went back. In the darkness, I found two bikes propped up against a gravestone – and nearby there were two RAF lads snoring their heads off. They must have been in Southport on the pop because there was a Spitfire squadron stationed down the road.

Pigeons played a big part in my life as I was growing up – and I don't mean just shooting and eating them. After the war my dad used to keep his own racing pigeons. The area around Southport was a hotbed for that, and a lot of good birds came out of there. You'd have men who swept the roads, or delivered milk, who owned racing pigeons. Some of them could hardly spell their names, yet they could work out the yardage against the minutes to places in France where their birds had been liberated for races.

At a time when it was uncommon to have a telephone, Mum and Dad had one at home. Around eleven o'clock on a Saturday morning, fifteen to twenty men would sit on the opposite side of the road to our house waiting for news. A call would come through to Dad, and he would write on a board the time when the birds had been freed and the wind speed, and put the board out in front of our house. The men would then disappear to their homes and their lofts and wait for their pigeons. Pigeons are a class unto themselves, pure racing machines. In hard races, when they fly for over fourteen hours, a bird can lose a third of its bodyweight. With the really long-distance races, from cities as far away as Barcelona, the pigeons would take three days to return, having been taken in baskets to Spain by boat and train. If there were no birds home on the day you expected, you'd be up at five o'clock the next morning to wait at the loft. A lot of the older birds got crafty and they would get down before darkness fell, while younger birds would tend to fly themselves into the ground. The old birds would be on the way early the next day. One season we won most of the Channel races. Pigeons are like young men with their tails up: they race to get back to where the hens are housed. We had one old pigeon that lived to over fourteen years. Sadly, he got a bit stiff and arthritic and fell in a bucket of water and drowned. Perhaps he'd also gone a bit senile and thought he was a duck. I hope that doesn't happen to me!

Pigeons are marvellous, marvellous birds and I had a great time with them. I'd have more now, but you have to live with pigeons like you have to live with racehorses. Dedicated. It's a regret that I couldn't cope with horses and pigeons. It's a great way to spend Saturday afternoons, especially as you get older. Bugger the horse racing, I'd go and wait for my birds!

I WAS NINE years old when I was first taken to the Grand National, in the spring of 1940. I went to stay with an aunt in Crosby and we walked along the canal to Aintree. Close to the racecourse the canal was jammed with barges, all with two or three tiers of seats erected on them. The railway embankment that flanked the course was packed with trains full of people having lunch or just partying. There was a constant buzz: tipsters like Prince Monolulu shouting, 'I gotta horse!', escapologists chaining themselves to a fence and then wriggling free. Hucksters worked the five-card trick and pickpockets had a field day. The Grand National was a real occasion, and as there was no television coverage the only way to see the race was to be at Aintree. To a young boy it seemed like the whole world had turned up.

We watched from between the Canal Turn and the Melling Road, and I was mesmerized as the caps of the jockeys flashed past to the thunder of hooves. After the horses had gone, I could see the spruce scattered far and wide and looked at the gaps where the fence had been moments before. The turf looked as though it had been ploughed.

The horses came past a second time, making another almighty roaring noise. Then there was silence . . . until beaten horses started to return in the opposite direction. One horse had three jockeys on its back, two having lost their own horses. Another jockey rode back, leading loose horses on either side of him. It was like a scene after a battle. The winner was a horse called Bogskar, trained and owned by Lord Stalbridge. He was the last until 1946 – the National, like so much else, being brought to a halt by the war, of course.

But it had made a big impression on me – and ended up changing my life in ways I could never have dreamed of.

WARTIME WAS STRANGELY exhilarating for a lad growing up. I shudder when I recall some of the daft pranks we involved ourselves in. To us, the war just added to the sense of excitement and allowed us to get up to all sorts of mischief. My mum bought me a pair of clogs – and my clogs had double irons, not single ones, around the heels and soles. I was very proud of them. And always curious as hell – if not overly smart – I thought I'd see what happened when I deliberately caught the Southport–Liverpool electric line with the heel of my clog. It felt like I got a big breeze up my trouser-legs and I was fired up in the air and bounced off the fence. Daft, but perfectly true.

We used to have a lovely local policeman called Mr Thomas – we wouldn't dare call him anything else. He must have been quite a senior fellow because, obviously, he wasn't in the services. One day he caught six of us carrying a rugby post up the road. We'd pinched it from the local club and planned to mount it in a garden and use it as a flagpole to hoist a flag every time the Allies had some sort of victory. Mr Thomas made us take it back, and a bloody long haul it was. Another time he caught me shooting an air gun in a park. He took me home and I remember my mother saying to him, 'Mr Thomas, next time you catch him misbehaving give him a good hiding. Then you tell me and when he comes home I'll give him another one.' They were only talking about a slight backhander, mind, but it would have taught me a lesson. I think it's ludicrous these days that police officers and teachers are not allowed to discipline children who continually step out of line. Mr Thomas never did give me a good hiding, but I'll tell you that the prospect of it taught me respect. It was a lesson that has stayed with me through life. It's a shame that youngsters today do not seem automatically to treat their elders with respect. Little things do matter. On a bus you stood up for a woman – or a man, come to that –

and if I didn't I'd have got a slap off mother. You just stood up without thinking.

I suppose part of the reason why we got up to so much without thinking of the consequences was that we were all aware that there was nothing permanent in our lives at the time. You saw a telegraph boy going to a house and you knew it was bad news. The telegram would begin: 'His Majesty regrets . . .'.

One memory sticks in my mind to this day. We had gone into the country on our bikes, probably looking for pheasants, and we came across three others on bicycles. One was a naval officer, a young, good-looking man, and with him was a very attractive girl who lived up the road from us, albeit in a far better-quality house. With them was a youngster who I suppose was related to one of them. Sometime later, within weeks of that innocent bicycle ride, I saw her walking down the street and she was crying. Without even knowing I could tell that lad had been killed. It was what happened.

As the war progressed, boys only four or so years older than me were going into the armed forces. My cousin Gerald McCain was one of them. He was sixteen years old when he joined the Marines. My Uncle Tom – Dad's brother – had four daughters and Gerald. Funny the things that stick with you after all these years. He was a big, friendly sort of lad, always grinning, and I remember he had such good teeth. I used to play darts with him and he came to our house before he went away. Gerald was killed two days after D-Day.

Death was around you all the time, so I suppose I never allowed myself to become too soft or sentimental. I am not callous, but I never let things be blown out of proportion. For me at thirteen and a half, and for all the other lads like me, there was too much living to be done.

IT WAS MY grandfather, a man called John Wright, who introduced me to horses. He drove a big, open, horse-drawn float for Southport Provisions, a firm of butchers owned by the Cranshaw brothers, delivering sausages, black puddings, bacon, brawn and butter to little corner shops in the area. Back then, a family could make a living out of a corner shop. One horse was driven out in the morning and another fresh one used in the afternoon.

The town was full of horses, trotting down every street. British Rail had dozens, and the laundries and milkmen all had them. Butchers had those very sharp little ponies in traps and they trotted like mad, just like Hackney-type horses. As a kid, you could put a couple of wheels and a handle on a box and you could go down any street and collect horse manure. You could get sixpence for a truckload for somebody's garden.

Granddad would drive past in his float and he'd stop to let me get up with him.

I was only a little kid, but I was struck by how all these old coachmen always threw a rug over their horses' quarters when they stopped, especially in winter. You see horses at the races and they are left stripped in the cold, often sweating. It's so stupid. You watch an athlete after he or she has competed and the first thing they do is put a tracksuit on. I get after my boys now if they don't cover my horses. It annoys me no end. Those old coachmen used the rugs to keep their horses warm when they were unloading and then, when they moved off, they put the rug over themselves. It was a way of life – but it is also common sense.

Anyway, I remember I'd gone with my granddad one day and he stopped for a bit of lunch, leaving his horse unattended outside as he always did. On this particular day, the horse began to move off on his own. Well, I jumped on the tail end of the float, which was pretty high, and I got hold of the reins and actually stopped the horse. I felt quite brave! I think he gave me a bob for my troubles.

Granddad did suggest that if I helped build a stable he would get me a pony. Dad was still away in the air force and I can recall carrying bricks from a bomb site to make the floor of the stable in the garden. Granddad built it – we even made a manger – but I never got the pony. A bit frustrating, I suppose, but it wasn't a tragedy. Granddad probably just forgot. Perhaps that's who I get my memory from.

I left school to drive the horse-drawn floats, the first time I did anything properly with horses. I was paid a pound a week – it was grand. I remember being surprised that black puddings when they are made are green, not black at all. On the days I came to work when it was freezing so hard that I couldn't feel my hands, I'd head for where the black puddings were laid out in trays, the steam still rising from them. That warmed me quickly enough – and I'll let you into a little secret. If you want to really live on a bitterly cold day, put some coarse salt on a hot black pudding and tuck in. Grand times.

Talking of grandparents I must just tell you of Granddad McCain. Now I never met him, but apparently he once terrorised the local Labour Exchange. In those days when you went to sign on the dole it was expected that you behaved in a very civil manner. It was said you had to stand to attention to get your payout. Well, it seems Granddad McCain had an aggressive streak. He arrived at the Local Exchange with an army sword and ordered the staff outside. Then he proceeded to drill them up and down the street. He was a bit loopy, and I suppose some of it has rubbed off on me. Anyhow, he was whisked off to the local mental institution and never seen again.

MY EARLIEST MEMORY of betting on the horses came immediately after the war had ended, and involved my dad and an uncle. They had been stationed in Egypt when they were demobbed. They might have come out of the services with in the region of forty or fifty quid each – not bad money in those days, but still not much after four years at war. All the local pubs had bookmakers' runners – all totally illegal, of course. To this day I recall them having a spring double: Langton Abbott to win the Lincoln and Lovely Cottage to win the Grand National. Five bob each way for each of them would have been their limit, I reckon. Anyway, unknown to them, the bookmakers' runner decided to stand the bet himself and never placed the money on the horses. And, bugger me, the bet came off.

My dad and uncle were owed getting on for forty quid, a substantial amount to them. When they found out what had happened, I remember my father and uncle chasing this bookie's runner up the street. He was on a bicycle and peddling like mad. If they'd caught him, he'd have been in for a bloody hiding. Eventually, I think he paid them most of the money; a good move for his own welfare, I'd say.

Chapter Two

PRIVATE McCAIN AND
THE MERRY WIDOW

WORKING WITH THE horses at Southport Provisions was satisfying because I loved the animals, but to be honest I still had no idea what I wanted to do in life and I admit I continued with a bit of poaching for a while. The war was still on and meat was rationed, remember. So it was too good a deal for a rascal like me to miss – you might get two shillings for a rabbit, after all. It didn't fuss me too much that I was breaking the law. It was a very different world back then. Like so many lads of my age at the time, I felt no real sense of urgency to plan for a career. I didn't have any ambition beyond the need to ensure that I had a few bob in my pocket.

My next legitimate job was as a milk boy with the Co-op. Every van driver had a boy, and I was with a lovely chap called Stan Bird. He had one leg a bit shorter than the other, so he didn't have to go in the forces. He was a nice man and a good motorcyclist. Stan drove a Bedford van and we used to deliver to boarding houses in Southport, as well as to a couple of hotels. That meant humping crates about, not just a few bottles. When we'd finished, around 1 p.m., we'd go back to Stan's mother's house. Once there, Stan would get out a piece of tubing and siphon petrol from the Bedford into his Ford car – as petrol, like most commodities, was rationed; Stan milked the milk float, you might say. In every other respect, he was as honest as the day is long. It was just that his Bedford van was only doing about eight miles to the gallon — according to his refuelling log, that is.

Thanks to my granddad, horses were already under my skin and so, around this time, I was also bumming some rides on some ponies from a couple of girls in Ainsdale in return for mucking out the stables. In addition, a local butcher called Arty Edwards — a bald-headed fellow and a tremendous character — allowed me to ride some of his horses. Mr Edwards was a bit of a dealer when it came to horses, and he'd be at all the local shows in the summer. We'd go off with these old ponies to try to jump them and some of them would be right dirty buggers you couldn't trust. The only place we could jump them away from the shows was Churchtown Cemetery behind the Hesketh Arms, where he had his stables. We'd put planks of wood or old ladders across the gravestones. There was a mare he had at the time who could really put the brakes on and I remember one time putting her at a jump and all of a sudden she just came to a halt — so fast that she put her feet through a ladder and I flew off. I felt dizzy and sick lying there in the cemetery, then as I began to regain focus the first words that I saw on a gravestone just above my head were not exactly reassuring . . . *Rest in Peace*. It was a bit frustrating, mind you. With Mr Edwards, I'd just get a horse going so that it was jumping nicely instead of leaving a big hole in the first fence and then he would go and sell it. He was always making a deal.

Funny how the decisions you make when you are young — like going out to ride Arty Edwards's horses — can change your life in ways you could never imagine. If I hadn't ridden for Mr Edwards, then I wouldn't have met Jackie Grainger. Jackie, who worked as a lad in a nearby stables, also used to ride for Mr Edwards. He was a little jockey-type fellow, a good horseman and a good stableman. He was also a drinker and a ladies' man, and I admired him no end because that's what I wanted to be like at that moment in my life. And, as it turned out, he was to play a big part in the success of Red Rum.

Much as I liked horses, and I really did, I also liked motorbikes. Stan

Bird lent me forty pounds to buy a flat twin 600 Douglas, a great big bike it was. I kept it in the dining room at home. I couldn't have been more than fifteen, because I wasn't old enough to have a licence – and in any case, there was no such thing in those days as a provisional driver's licence. An old man called Pop Clegg lived next door. He was a stroppy fellow, and perhaps I gave him good reason to be. As soon as Mum went out, I'd fire up the bike in the house. It had an exhaust that made an explosive racket: brrrrooooommmmm, brrrrrooooommmmm. Pop Clegg used to go crackers, and rightly so.

I had a lot of fun out of that bike. I had some friends who also had motorbikes, and some days we'd filch some petrol from somewhere and drive to Wales. Later on, I used to race bikes, but not that Douglas as I probably would have killed myself on it. I sold it to a friend eventually – well, I say 'sold', but he never paid me for it. That was par for the course in those days.

We raced on a road track at an old army rifle range, as well as on grass. The bikes were fuelled with some high-octane dope that smelled like nothing on earth. Brilliant, the racing was. It made your hair stand on end. This kid called Lee was better than most of us: he had raced round the Isle of Man, no less. I had a 350 Norton by then, which I hadn't paid a lot of money for – well I wouldn't. In one race I can remember going up the straight and, to be honest, I wasn't very good and I wasn't very quick. Lee was coming to do me on the outside and – well, I'm fifteen and I'm not going to give way to anybody at that age, am I? I just managed to keep him outside and then all I can remember is hitting the bales of straw at the end of the road. I turned him arse over tip as well. He wasn't very polite when he got up, I can tell you. He was as quick with his tongue as he was with his bike. They were good, good days.

AROUND THAT TIME, in early 1945, I was still wandering through life without a care. Mum at this point was working in the

Circle Bar at the Garrick Theatre in Southport, where some of the big London shows opened, and she recommended me to the management for a job. I was hired to operate the perch lights on the prompt side of the stage, and sat about twelve feet up in the air. This paid twenty-five bob a week, so you can see I was going up in the world.

There were perks, too. When the ballet came to the theatre, the quick-change dressing room was located underneath my position. I'd be working my lamps and the girls would be changing, not realizing that one or two stagehands had their eyes glued to a crack in the boards. These boards were black and dusty, so the unsuspecting stagehands would return to their posts with a streak of carbon down their faces – a right giveaway. We were all just lads on the lookout for a little light relief. A friend of mine was prompt for the theatre, and for a laugh during one performance he blew up a Durex like a balloon. But no one thought it funny when the Durex drifted on to the stage during the play. He got the sack.

I was still working at the theatre when the war came to an end. On VE Day all the lights went on over town and when I came out of the Garrick, Lord Street was jammed with masses and masses of people. Lord Street is roughly a mile long, lined with Victorian buildings, shops and trees. I'm told it's considered one of the most attractive streets in Britain, and it was certainly an impressive sight that night, with people clambering on roofs to get a good view of the celebrations. Grand indeed – and a long time coming.

AND SO LIFE flowed along until just before my eighteenth birthday, when I received my call-up papers for National Service. I had to go to Liverpool for my medical and I was scared to death in case I wasn't eligible. I'd always thought of myself as a fit man and I would have been mortified if I'd been declared otherwise. Some boys were ducking and diving, trying to get out of doing their National Service. I never could understand that. Anyway, there were about a dozen of us lined up in the doctor's room and he came along and, one by one, grabbed our balls and told us to cough. Thankfully, I was A1.

After all the preliminaries had been taken care of, I was told to report to Aldershot. My dad came to the station to put me on the train. It was not until years afterwards, when I put my own son Donald on the train south to spend two weeks with the Territorial Army, that I realized what a significant moment that must have been for my father. It's a funny feeling. My dad had done his bit for King and country, and now he was sending his son away to do his duty.

For us boys, there were three options: the armed forces, the merchant navy or the mines. Those who volunteered to go down the mines were called the Bevin boys, I remember – after Ernest Bevin, the National Service minister. I shuddered at the thought of that; I'd have hated the mines. Being so close to Liverpool, many opted for the merchant navy, but for me it had to be the RAF, like my father. At least, that's what I requested. But in the perverse selection process it seems they tore up your first two choices and then sent you to your bloody third one. Of course, you did as you were told and thought no more about it. Aldershot? That'll do for me, sir.

After a few weeks of basic training, I was posted to the Sixth Training Battalion, Yeovil; coincidentally, the same town in Somerset where my dad had been stationed with the RAF. I was more than happy to be taught to drive an army truck. By the time my group were getting close to our passing-out parade, we'd been in the army almost ten weeks, and the changes in all of us were visible. We walked differently, we carried ourselves differently. We didn't have our hands in our pockets. We were clean – and a lot of lads weren't the cleanest people in the world when they first arrived! It was all down to discipline; and at the end of the day getting a good bollocking never hurt anyone. All in all I'd say the army made a lot of boys into men, proper men. As for me, I was driving a three-ton truck from Yeovil along the south coast in a convoy in the middle of summer;

it was beautiful. I mean, you wouldn't have swapped places with the King.

Having passed out, I was posted to 12 Company, Chester. Here's a bizarre story I remember. I was in the Company Sergeant Major's office with a number of other soldiers when the CSM came in and said: 'I want two big men – *you* and *you*.' He was looking at another soldier I hardly knew – and me. He told us to draw forty-eight hours' of rations before returning to his office. When we came back at the appointed time, there was a corporal waiting for us. The three of us were instructed to jump into a fifteen-hundredweight truck and given orders to drive to a nearby detention centre to collect a detainee. This turned out to be an impressionable young soldier. I was quite surprised at what I saw at the detention centre. If a prisoner carried a broom, he carried it like a rifle. Everything was done at the double. We picked up this little Scotsman, who had deserted in Germany two years previously. The civvy police at home had picked him up and it was our duty to take him back to Germany to face a manslaughter charge.

We got on the train at Chester to go to London, where we had to take the Underground from Euston to Liverpool Street Station. We had implicit instructions to handcuff our prisoner; the CSM warned us that if he gave us the slip, he didn't want to see either of us back at barracks. The message was very clear: we lost him at our peril. Even so, we felt sorry for him and we didn't want to walk on to the Underground handcuffed to the little bugger. We'd already heard other passengers whispering to one another about how it was a shame to see a little man being so roughly treated, so out of sympathy we took off the cuffs. We didn't think there was much of a risk as we were confident we could outrun him if he did try to make a break for it.

At Liverpool Street, we caught the boat train to Harwich. There were lots of troops on the move and some red caps – military police – spotted us and gave us a dressing down for having taken the cuffs off. Right bolshie bastards, they were. On the train, we had a private compartment, and when we discovered there was a Naafi coach for the troops we bought our prisoner some cigarettes and chocolate. I remember when we arrived at Harwich seeing lines and lines of military hardware, like motor torpedo boats, all being prepared for the crossing to the Hook of Holland. It was a show of force.

We made it to Germany without mishap. It was bitterly cold, with nearly a foot of snow on the ground. Our destination was an army camp located in a small forest. There were military policemen waiting to greet us in one of the huts in the camp. In the middle of this otherwise cold room was a cast-iron stove that glowed red-hot at the top. The little Scotsman was unceremoniously stripped to the bone – the MPs even checked his backside to see if he was hiding anything there. After their search, the officer in charge signed for 'one body'.

I'd been in the army no more than five months and I was stunned. The form required those taking custody of the Scotsman to confirm if he was dead or alive, striking out whichever word wasn't applicable. It seemed to me that if they had had to sign for a dead body nobody would have been that bothered. Funny thing was, it put the wind up me. Was everyone that disposable? The episode left an impression on me that I never forgot as I made my way through later life. What I'm saying, I suppose, is that the army stripped life of much of its feeling, and while that hardened me I can't say I much cared for that aspect of military service.

But I still had a fantastic experience and wouldn't have missed a day of it. After I came back to England I was on the telephone one day when the Sergeant came in and asked, 'Anyone ride a motorbike?' In a flash, I responded: 'I can, Sarge.' Outside, he threw me a crash helmet and told me to get on a bike. Shortly afterwards, we were weaving in and out of the side streets of Chester. The upshot was I had just become Company Dispatch Rider. Chester was North Western Command HQ, a garrison town full of soldiers and transport, and being Company DR was an absolute star job. There were only two DRs in the company and me and my mate had super competition bikes. We had an arrangement with the local bookmaker, running the bets from the camp, and another deal with the local photographer to collect and deliver rolls of film. We would get a couple of bob for this job and a couple of bob for that. We also ran errands for the company sergeants. I loved what I was doing and almost signed on to stay in the army – if only to stop one of my mates getting his hands on my bike! Luckily, I figured eventually that that probably wasn't a good enough reason to sign on again.

If I have one regret about my National Service, it is that the closest I got to being placed overseas was being put on a posting to Korea. The Korean War had just begun, but negotiations were going on and the draft was cancelled before I could be sent. I've often wondered what it would have been like to have served in a combat zone. Surely there is no other experience to compare with that.

In those days, after you were demobbed you had to do four years in the Territorial Army. I never thought of that as a hardship. In fact, going to TA camp proved to be a cracking fortnight's entertainment. The firm you were working for paid you, and you drew money from the army as well. Basically, it was a fortnight of drinking and fornicating. What's to complain about?

After leaving the regular army in 1950 I came back to Southport. It was the middle of summer, and all my friends were at the beach or round the municipal swimming pool getting sunburned. We all had our demob leave, and that was a pass to have a good time. Then the trick was to sign on, and if you played your cards right you'd swing drawing the dole for a month or six weeks.

Except I didn't get a chance to do that. In fact, I never drew a penny, as the buggers at the labour exchange found me a job inside three days. I worked in the dispatch department of a wallet company, packing one bloody wallet after another. I was told that if I looked after the job it would be mine for life. I could think of nothing worse. I stuck it out for three weeks, until I heard that Frank Speakman needed someone to work at his stables in Tarporley, Cheshire. I went to Cheshire the very night I heard about the job, and never did get round to handing in my notice at the wallet company. I guess if they read this they'll know I'm not coming back now.

Mr Speakman had kept a few horses at Southport and I had already ridden out for him; I also knew his head lad Jeff Langhorn quite well. So I got the job, and began to work with the horses for three pounds a week and my keep. Dick Francis and Tim Molony used to ride for the stables, and I thought this was all absolutely marvellous. I looked after three horses in Mr Speakman's yard and picked up the racing side of things from senior lads. When I was twenty-one, I had a rise of ten shillings a week as I rode schooling. I was as happy as I had ever been. But my weight was to beat me. I was 11st 7lb going on 12st, big and getting bigger.

After a time I moved a short distance down the road to Hulgrave Hall, an establishment belonging to a woman called Mrs Chambers, who kept some top-class hunters and point-to-pointers. Mrs Chambers was a tough old lady who rode side-saddle in point-to-point races and hunted three times a week. Her stud groom was old Jack Cook, then over seventy, who had been with the Duke of Westminster. Cookey always claimed that he trained Tipperary Tim to win the Grand National in 1928, as the licensed trainer, Joseph Dodd, was ill. Cookey also used to say an Irishman will do twice the work of an Englishman, but only half as well! That's certainly not been my experience, but old Cookey wasn't too enamoured of the Irish for some reason.

It was all going pretty well until, rather abruptly, my time with Mrs Chambers had to come to an end when the German housemaid Carole became a bit too attached to me. She was a good-looking woman, already twice married and something of a merry widow. Her German husband had been killed, and then she'd married an American who was also killed. I think she fancied an English variety next – and I was fairly sure I was being lined up for the job. I wasn't having any of that. With the heat on, I did a runner: borrowed a tall ladies' bike from the yard, left it at the local pub and caught a bus home to Southport.

Chapter Three

CONFESSIONS OF A
TAXI DRIVER

I'D LEARNED TO drive in the army, so on returning home I went to work for a private car hire company called Goulders. Their office was opposite Birkdale Station and they ran between eight and ten cars. We would sit in a line outside the station and wait for businessmen to come home from Liverpool or Manchester. There were plenty of expensive properties in the area and these regular customers would be good for a tip of sixpence, sometimes even a shilling.

Goulders worked on a rate of ninepence a mile, but we tried to make the odds favour us drivers a little better. We used to disconnect the milometer to make it seem we had done fewer miles than we really had, but charge the customers the full amount, of course. You handed over your money at the end of each day based on the mileage that had been recorded. No one made a fortune from this little scam, but a few bob here and there were always welcome. It was just part of the circle of life, wasn't it? At the end of each night you'd be broke after having had a few drinks; then, by lunchtime the next day, you had five or six bob in your pocket again.

We had some good customers, and not just those who lived in the big houses. The hotel trade was important to us. For instance, the Palace Hotel in Southport used Goulders' cars for their guests. One Tuesday I answered a call from the hotel and arrived to find Frank Sinatra and his agent waiting. Sinatra was a pretty big star at the time – but here he was, doing a short season at Blackpool. I was no great fan of his: I've never bothered that much about music, and I could take or leave him as a singer. I always thought Bing Crosby was better. Anyway, Sinatra climbed in the car and asked me to take him to where he could buy a hairbrush. As it was half-day closing in Southport this wasn't as simple as it sounds. I drove all over town looking for a chemist's shop that was open. Sinatra didn't appeal to me. I thought him an insignificant little man. How conceited of him to worry about his hair that much, I thought. It wasn't as if he had that much of it, anyway. Later, I drove him back and forth from Southport to Blackpool for his show. Do you know, he never gave me so much as a penny tip? He may have become one of the greatest singers of all time – he sold millions and millions of records – but as a person Sinatra didn't impress me one little bit. I can honestly say I met much nicer people mucking out horses.

One or two other celebrities rode in my car – isn't that what all taxi drivers boast? – and I remember driving Norman Wisdom and Margaret Rutherford when they were at the top of their careers as entertainers. I collected Ms Rutherford from Liverpool, where she was on stage at the Empire. Outside the theatre there was a group of lads, real scallies you'd call them. They were well pickled and getting irate with one another. I watched with the hairs on the back of my neck standing on end as this tiny little old lady went up to sort them out. She did the trick. The lads quietened down and drifted off. Nice woman.

I actually had a taste of showbiz myself while I was driving for Goulders. I was invited to be an extra in a film being shot on Southport Beach. The film was called *Forbidden Cargo* – not a box-office smash by any means – and I was given a part as one of the Customs and Excise Officers patrolling the coastline. One of the stars was Jack Warner, better known as PC George Dixon from the popular television series *Dixon of Dock Green*. As a customs man, I was part of a team that had to nab him as he tried to come ashore with whatever it was he was smuggling. Here's the good bit: as an extra I got three pounds a day, over and above my wages, and I had access to a super mobile canteen. I wanted filming to last for ever.

IN REALITY, I was just doing whatever I fancied – but there was always something there, nagging away at the back of my mind; something that I knew I wanted to be doing. I may have been driving taxis for a living, but I had not lost my love of horses. So my ears were always half-open, listening for opportunities, and one day I heard something. When I had been working at Frank Speakman's stables in Cheshire, one of the horses I looked after was called Scottish Humour. He had been placed in races on the flat and over hurdles, but now I heard from people at the stables that he had 'got a leg', which is a catch-all phrase for an injury. He was also 'tubed', meaning he'd had breathing problems that had been dealt with by an operation that requires a horse to breathe through a tube inserted in his windpipe. I called Mr Speakman and agreed to pay him twenty-five pounds for the horse, and the deal was to include a sweat rug, a headcollar – and his tube.

I rented a box for Scottish Humour in Westbourne Road, Birkdale, and looked after him for months, living in the hope that he might one day be able to race again. As I had a horse, it made sense to me to apply for a permit to train. Imagine my delight when I received a letter from the offices of the National Hunt Committee with, inside, a trainer's permit made out in the name of Donald McCain of 316 Liverpool Road, Birkdale, Southport, Lancs. It was dated 3 February 1953.

It was no more than a toehold in the old game – a permit, as opposed to a full trainer's licence, only qualifies you to train horses for yourself and your family – but it was a start. Scottish Humour ran in some 'flapping' races, unofficial meetings mostly run on tracks on the outside of football fields. Jackie Grainger rode the horse, and we had some success – probably too much, because one day a bunch of miners took exception to us winning at a 'flapping' track beyond Manchester and we had to load the horse into the box and disappear down the road in a rush! We'd had a good few bob on our horse too, but we didn't think it wise to stay around to wait for the payout.

DAY AFTER DAY I sat in line in my car outside Birkdale Station, waiting for the trains from the big cities to pull into town. It turns out I caught the eye of a young girl named Beryl Harris. At the time she worked for an insurance company in Liverpool. She was a good-looking girl, but she was only eighteen – a lot younger than me, a proper man about town!

In my spare hours I was riding and fiddling about with horses at a riding school just outside Southport owned by Kath Walsh. An aunt of Beryl had suggested she take riding lessons, so we came into contact at the school. Beryl admits she had a crush on me from the start. I'd pop into the stables before and after work, and one day Beryl was with a friend in a house in Westcliffe Road when she responded to a dare to come out and say hello to me. I had no idea who she was, but as bright as a lark she said, 'Hello, Ginger.'

Beryl worked for nothing at the stables because she loved being around the horses, just as much as I did. She recalls that one day we passed on the stairs leading to Kath Walsh's flat and I stopped to give her a kiss on the cheek. Does that sound like me? Encouraged that she might be interested, not long after that I asked Beryl to go to the pictures. Beryl likes to remind me that the date did not begin well. I'll let her tell you:

'I came out of my house in Seabank Road to see Ginger walking away. He was wearing a suit with a big iron mark on one of the elbows. I wondered what on earth I was thinking about going out with him for. When I caught up with him, he said that he didn't think I was coming and that he was going to go out with the barmaid at a local pub as she had, and I quote, a "big arse". What a charmer.'

Clearly, I was a natural romantic. But somehow I managed it; Beryl took a shine to me. I boxed at the time in a gym above the Bold Hotel in town – I was quite handy and fought at 12st 10lb; those cock-of-the-school fights must have paid off – and Beryl used to wait outside for me after I had trained. I asked her to come to a boxing show in Liverpool once, but her mother forbade her to go as she said that only prostitutes went to fights. So Beryl suggested that instead I take her to some of my old haunts at Tarporley. She was becoming totally hooked on horses. Jackie Grainger came with us and we caught up with a few of my old pals. It is fair to say we had a few scoops during the evening; quite a few, if truth be told.

It was late by the time we returned. It seems I'd caused quite a drama in the Harris household. Again, Beryl is the best one to recount the story:

'When I arrived home I found that my mother had the police out looking for me. I will always remember a policewoman taking me into the hall to ask: "Have you done anything to be ashamed of?" I wondered what she meant. In the meantime, my mum had gone to look for me at Jackie's little place. She saw a car parked outside and when she opened the door Ginger fell out. My mum called him a drunken fool – then came back to tell the police that they would find a drunken driver if they hurried. The police left our house destined to book Ginger – but on their way they were diverted to attend reports of an explosion in Ainsdale. It turns out someone had tried to bypass their gas meter and blown up two houses, so Ginger had a lucky let-off. Another time, Ginger made me sit on the front of his old army Jeep so that I could keep my hand over the air intake on the carburettor as we drove along the A49. I must have been soft in the head – or in love.'

Beryl came from a modestly comfortable family – in comparison to me, anyway – and admits they were a cautious family, careful with money. They had a house just off the promenade in Southport and they certainly didn't approve when I began taking their daughter out. I can't say I blamed them. All they saw was a taxi driver who lived for the day and the craic. I might have a pound in my pocket today and be skint tomorrow. I was not the kind of man they had in mind for Beryl.

I recall Beryl's father asking me what my intentions were towards his daughter. Well, I'm a very honest person. So I told him I wanted to go to bed with her! Perhaps it wasn't exactly what he wanted to hear, but he couldn't accuse me of being devious. Anyway, he said he wanted to have words with my father. What did he hope that would achieve? I was a grown man; what was my father going to say to me?

Beryl says that when she heard her father was on the way to my house, she jumped on her bike to try to stop him. She rode furiously for about three miles from her house to mine to catch up with her dad in our garden. I didn't see this go on, but Beryl says her dad said to her: 'I don't know why you want to go out with him. You've got a nice house, you've got a television set, you've got all you could possibly wish for, so why do you want to go out with him?' I could see his point.

There were an awful lot of very attractive girls in Southport – and I used to go down quite well with them, even if I say so myself. But Beryl intended marrying me, and she says that the objections of her parents drove her into my arms more than anything else. Beryl is a strong-minded woman and hard to argue against, as I am reminded almost every day. At any event, her father came into our house to see my dad. Actually, my dad could never fall out with anyone even if he tried, and he had a nice way of putting things. I think he said in a polite way that he thought his son was good enough to go out with any girl.

I wasn't fussed by the indifference of Beryl's parents. I wasn't going out with them, was I? Gradually, Beryl wore me down and we started to see each other. Not that I complained. As I say, she was a very attractive girl. She also shared my enthusiasm for horses. Beryl rode out at the stables at first light and then went back again in the evenings, when I was often around. In fact, she spent all her free hours involving herself with horses. I remember once she took a mare I was training, called Kara

Valley, down to a stud in Newmarket. If you sent the horse by train a groom travelled on a free return ticket. Even so, it cost twenty pounds from Southport and as I look back I cannot think how we could possibly have afforded that. Still, that's what we did, and when Beryl came back she was full of what she had seen at Newmarket.

Almost as soon as she got off the train at Birkdale, she suggested: 'Let's go to Newmarket together.' We weren't even engaged – but I do know I gave the idea serious thought. It was tempting. Newmarket was the heart of Thoroughbred racing and had a unique aura to us, as horse lovers. Sometimes I still wonder how we would have fared. Beryl would have been more than capable of getting a job as a secretary in a racing yard. I'd have probably ended up driving a box, or working my way up to head lad. Who knows, in time I might have become good enough to take over from Sir Michael Stoute.

It's funny how you get challenged, and your life is shaped and defined by how you meet those challenges. It was, truthfully, just too big a step to take at the time. But we were at the point in our lives when challenges began to present themselves at regular intervals.

Beryl was by now itching for us to get engaged. At nineteen she had changed jobs and was now working in the secretarial pool at the Borough Architect's Office. A lot of the girls around her in the office were getting engaged, and she wanted to be one of them. For a bloke like me, this seemed like a bad idea. But Beryl persisted, so I tried another tack. I told her that I would get engaged on the condition that we wouldn't get married for two years. I was twenty-eight at the time – and two years seemed like a lifetime away. Thankfully, Beryl agreed.

So we were engaged – on Grand National day in 1959. I suppose I was under starter's orders, but no more than that. Naturally enough, we went to Aintree to watch the race. People like us had just started to have enough money to start going out to eat at night, and so we had arranged to go on with a couple of friends to a pub in the country after spending the day at Aintree. For two pounds ten a head you could have a pretty decent meal and a few drinks. I was confident I could pay for the evening by backing the winner of the National.

The big race never disappoints – how can it, with continuous tales of bravery and skill from man and horse? – but my plans began to fall apart as I watched Oxo come home first, ridden by Michael Scudamore, whose son Peter never won the race despite sustained success that brought him the jockey's championship eight times. Of course Peter Scudamore is not the first good horseman – nor will he be the last – to have been denied success in the Grand National. I can't remember the name of the horse I backed, but I can remember it was not in the frame.

I might have been close to skint, but I was not downhearted. I was enraptured by the day, by the race, by the emotion of the occasion, by the sheer scale of the Grand National. One day, I thought, as I watched those who had supported Oxo begin to celebrate in the grand tradition of Liverpool, I just might find myself with a horse to run round here. A man's allowed to dream, isn't he?

As luck would have it, I found a winner in the last. A man called David Rosenfield, an owner I used to drive to race meetings, or just take around town, had a horse running and I liked his chances. I had two pounds on the nose and the horse, My Tips I think they called him, came home at 100–8. So I had enough to pay for our engagement night out after all.

But life was to take another twist when Goulders shut down. I didn't have that many options open, so I thought: why not start my own taxi business – or private-hire firm, call it what you will. Kath Walsh from the riding school agreed to be my partner and with the cash flow from the merger, we got a couple of cars and got cracking. I had good connections and soon I was regularly employed driving hotel staff. One of the hotels I drove for was the Palace, where I was well known through Goulders. I'd take the waitresses, waiters and bar staff home after they finished, past midnight. I'd pile as many as I could fit into my car, and run a 'shuttle bus' round town. We wouldn't get half a mile without being pulled over today. Invariably, I'd get a stack of tips – not amounting to a fortune, but more than that miserable bugger Sinatra gave me. And at six-thirty the next morning, I'd round up those members of staff who had to be back to serve breakfast or clean the rooms. It was a good system and kept us in business.

Another valued client of mine was Mrs Botterio, who had a smaller hotel in Southport. I used to get three pounds ten a day to drive her in her own car, a Rover. One day she wanted to go to Scotland with her daughter, grandson and granddaughter. The trip was supposed to last a week to ten days. We ended up going as far north as Thurso, and I was away for three weeks. Beryl thought I was never coming home. Mrs Botterio was a lovely woman, but her daughter was a little strange and married a scruffy chef. Often I took the granddaughter to Linaker Street School and then collected her in the evening. I cannot remember Mrs Botterio's daughter's name, but I will never forget taking her one particular afternoon to pick up her girl from school. I had the door open for them to get into the car as usual. As they approached, the woman threw her daughter into the back seat and shouted at me in panic : 'Drive off . . . drive off!'

I couldn't drive until she had shut the door – and there was some fellow trying to climb in after them. The mother was screaming and shouting and there were kids pouring out of the school. I grabbed hold of this fellow and hauled him away. Kids were shouting as kids do, 'Fight, fight!' The man was still trying to get at my two passengers, so I banged his head up and down on the bonnet a couple of times and flopped him on to the pavement. Then I got in the car and drove off. Three days later, I heard he was involved in the death of the little girl – his daughter – in the Palace Hotel. I've often thought about that. I just didn't bang his head bloody hard enough.

I KNEW I had found the right girl for me when I saw Beryl washing down the legs of a horse we had with a hosepipe. She was sitting on the kerb wearing an old duffel coat. My mum later told Beryl that I had looked at this scene and said to her: 'Oh, I suppose I'll have to marry her!'

On 25 March 1961 Beryl and I were married at St John's Church, Birkdale. It was Grand National day, of course; and of course, after the reception, we went to Aintree, where we saw Fred Rimell win the race for the second time with Nicolaus Silver. Old Fred went on to train a total of four National winners, a record that he held alone until 2004.

Our wedding reception was held at the Palace Hotel, which was actually very plush. Ol' Blue Eyes stayed there, after all. Beryl organized the whole thing. Her mum and dad said they wouldn't come – and, looking back, I wouldn't have been too happy if my daughter wanted to take on someone like me. As it turned out, her mother did arrive on the day, and I am sure that made Beryl feel happier. Beryl's dad was a quiet, unassuming man in, I reckon, a house dominated by women (I seem to remember Beryl's aunt also lived with them) – though Beryl says that this is an unfair assumption on my part. He was very deaf, she says, but to her he was a decent man; a war veteran, but a man who liked the quiet life. The bottom line is that we never did become friends and I could take or leave him. In the end, I did get on very well with my mother-in-law, once she realized I wasn't a fly-by-night, but by this time the old man had died. As for Beryl and me – well, to this day we've never had a cross word!

We had thirty guests at the wedding and the hotel put on a right show for us. The bill turned up a couple of years ago in a box of old photographs . . . the whole lot cost forty-eight pounds, including all the drinks. I couldn't believe it. The hotel didn't charge us for the room and the waitresses worked for nothing. What a lovely gesture.

We spent our honeymoon by first going racing in Nottingham, and then going on to stay at the White Hart in Newmarket – so we did manage to get there together in the end. I remember the manageress not believing that we had just got married, as each morning we were out on the gallops before first light and back before breakfast ended.

Two things stick in my mind. There was this small stableman sitting on a big horse near the gallops. As he waited for horses to come and go, we got talking to him. He turned out to be Norman Bertie, who had trained Pinza to win his Derby in Coronation year, 1953. Beryl and I were struck by just how neatly the hedges were kept around the various stud centres; Norman said that you can judge a man by the way he trims his hedge. The other memory was of seeing Captain Cecil Boyd-Rochfort, who had trained for the Queen. He was a big, big man, and red in the face. He watched a string of horses walk past, then said something to one of his staff. He was an old-fashioned horseman, tall and lean – a vanished breed. We heard the other man, probably his head lad, tell him, 'Sir, you told me to send them home' – and then Boyd-Rochfort exploded in front of our eyes. Instantly, I thought him to be an ignorant man. Nobody should have to be spoken to in the manner he spoke to his lad. But as a place, Newmarket was magical.

BERYL AND I were hooked on horses – simple as that. And now, for better or worse, we were married. We were earning about five pounds a week when we went to live in two rooms, one up, one down, in a house in Churchtown, which was on the wrong side of Southport for me. I never quite took to it. Half of that – two pounds ten shillings (£2.50 in today's money) – went on rent. So we were struggling, no question: but we were training a horse.

Our friend Albert Wake, a great character, a huntsman and a man who loved a deal, had paid thirty pounds in Ireland for a big, heavy-headed old horse called Home Chief. Albert had a very grand house backing on to Rotten Row, one of the most desirable areas of Southport. But he could not resist buying and selling. One morning his wife woke up to see most of their furniture being carted away as Albert had sold it to dinner guests the night before without thinking of mentioning it to her. Albert would stop someone in the street and ask them if they'd like to sell the dog they had with them. Albert was one of a kind.

In reality, Home Chief was a bull of a horse, but I volunteered to train him for Albert. We kept him in a stable just round the corner and agreed that if he won anything in point-to-point races we would share the prize money. I was delighted to have a horse to play with at no expense. Home Chief ran well in a couple of point-to-point races and we entered him for the John Peel Cup at Manchester, a hunter-chase worth £500. Now that was a fair bit of money, and we were excited. Unfortunately, on the day my amateur jockey failed to turn up. We were looking around for another rider when this chap called Don Charlesworth said that he would ride him. As we didn't have an alternative, we agreed. Well, Home Chief just put his head down from the start and took off with Don. After three miles, he still couldn't pull him up. Now Don was a nice person, but I wasn't to know that he hadn't had a proper race ride before in his life. Old Home Chief had the better of him and loved every minute – and, with Don holding on for dear life, they finished third, which won us forty or fifty pounds. Albert gave me half, which was great. Poor Don was so exhausted that when they came in he had sweat running off his very, very red nose and couldn't even loosen off the girth. That tickled me, actually.

Anyway, Don was now the official jockey for Home Chief. We went to Cartmel for a Bank Holiday Saturday meeting, and as we didn't have a lot of brass Beryl and I went in the trailer. Home Chief jumped off with Don and, just like before, the old horse was in charge from the beginning. At the water jump opposite the stands, Don came tearing up the inside of Larry Major and Stan Mellor, two very hard professional jockeys. They stuffed dear old Don rotten. They put him straight through the wings of the fence. He went up in the air and did a somersault. Actually, it was a better game in those days when you could do things like that. Young or inexperienced jockeys had to learn not to take liberties with the pros, and going up on the inner was something that men like Mellor did not take kindly to. It was sort of an unwritten law that top professionals wouldn't allow amateurs to get away with that sort of move.

I admit Don was not my first concern. He'd only landed on his head, after all. But Home Chief had taken off and so I went running after him. I was with my friend Jeff Langhorn, who had been head lad at Frank Speakman's yard during my time in Cheshire. The horse was a bit too nifty for us, so eventually we decided we'd better check on Don. I will always remember the grass – it was that brilliant spring green colour. And Don was there with his head to one side and his nose was redder than ever. Jeff suddenly shouted: 'Oh, shit, look at his leg!' Dear, oh dear: he'd broken his thighbone, and it looked pretty nasty – but just then, my horse came flying past, so I took off after him again. Anyhow, as they loaded Don into the ambulance, he told his wife: 'Tell Ginger and Albert to run the horse again on Monday and back it for me.' And off he went to Lancaster hospital.

We thought poor old Don might be on to something. I had to come home as I had work to do on Sunday – I was still driving a taxi – so we left Beryl with the horse near Cartmel. As the racecourse stables were full, Beryl found a stable for him at a small farm down the road. If I remember rightly, I had to borrow money to pay for my petrol back on the Monday. I'd said to Beryl to turn out the horse in one of the small fields at the farm for half an hour or so on Sunday and that would be fine. By the time I returned, Beryl had been 'strapping' Home Chief – attending to his coat – and said she'd found some little thorns stuck into him. As there had been none of the usual bedding around, Beryl was given some bales of brown bracken to lay across the stable floor. This turned out to be lethal.

In actual fact, it wasn't the thorns in the bedding that was making Home Chief look so sharp when I saw him! Beryl had been helped in 'strapping' the horse by the head lad from Dennis Yeoman's stable, who had found himself in the same predicament as us after the

Saturday's racing. As they were talking together, the lad suggested that Beryl should put two measures of Hague's tonic into Home Chief's water bucket – which she duly did. And now, Home Chief was standing there with his eyes popping out of his head. We were stuck for a jockey, of course; so I found a lad to ride him, but after all these years it's hardly surprising to admit I don't recall his name. I had four quid to my name – and, unknown to Beryl, that included the week's rent. But I thought: to hell with it! and put the lot on Home Chief at 20–1. He won by twenty lengths – I mean, he found form he'd never had before. I wonder how?

Some months later, Don Charlesworth decided he was taking out a trainer's permit. Albert sold him Home Chief and the horse lived on Hague's tonic. So when I am asked if I have ever doped a horse, the answer is categorically: No. But Beryl has! Of course, she had no idea what she was giving the horse.

We lived in different times then. There was no dope testing control as there is today, and I knew of trainers who used a mixture that was designed to help stop horses from bleeding. It did that, for sure; but a side effect of this concoction, called Macdonald's Styptic, was to make horses run considerably faster. It seems a lot of trainers knew how it worked. As a means of stopping the bleeding, of course.

SOON BERYL AND I had to deal with another change of circumstance. Kath Walsh told us she wanted out of the taxi business. We were adrift. I took what business I could rescue, but the best bit of luck at the time was that Jeff Langhorn decided to come into partnership with me. Jeff, who had been with me in the stables at Cheshire, now owned a little grocer's shop. Together, we bought three vehicles on hire purchase, got them on the road and called ourselves Cutler's Cars, named after a racehorse we'd looked after.

Beryl and I needed somewhere new to live, and we discovered there was a little property for sale not too far away. It had been a brewery with a shop attached to it but had been turned into a two-car showroom, and there was some accommodation over the top. Across the road was a Chinese chip shop, the paper shop was two doors away, and slap bang between the two was the off-licence. Down the road you had two pubs on your doorstep, and the railway line was no more than seventy-five yards away. Everything you needed was on hand.

I think the price they wanted for it was £2,500. We didn't have that sort of money, but we did have £1,800 as Beryl had been saving her wages. On advice of the agents Ball-Percival, we made an appointment with the manager of a branch of the National Westminster bank in Manchester. He agreed to give us the necessary loan and we bought the place in Upper Aughton Road, Southport. One day television stations from across the world would film at these premises, but we could never have imagined that as we moved in.

Once we'd got the private car hire business going, I began to look at selling some old cars as well, on the suggestion of a good friend, Alan Dawson. We were working all hours God sent, seven days a week. Alan, who was in the motor trade in a biggish way in the Manchester area, sorted us out with some old bangers to put in the showroom on sale or return. We dared not stop running the private hire cars, though, as that was the sheet anchor that had to pay the bills.

I didn't like to turn down jobs. If there was a profit to be made, I would consider all requests, however bizarre. And they certainly could be. Some of the loveliest of the big old houses in Southport were in Westbourne Road. The houses had been homes to mill owners, timber merchants, exporters – all people with a lot of money. Those houses would have had two or three maids each in their time. It was claimed to be possibly the wealthiest parish in England. I had customers in Westbourne Road who regularly wished to be driven to the station at 9 a.m. and collected on their return from Liverpool or Manchester at 5.30 p.m. So I was up and down that road a lot.

There was one gentleman I always used to see walking to the station, roughly a mile and a half away. He was aged between forty and fifty, wore a bowler hat and carried an umbrella. He preferred to walk in the mornings for exercise, though sometimes he took a taxi in the evening. On this particular day, I was in my car as usual and he was walking down Westbourne Road when a full-grown lion appeared from the front garden of one of the houses. It sounds crazy, but it is perfectly true. This gentleman must have been pretty fit (all that morning walking?), because he shinned up a bus stop in the road rather sharpish, leaving only his bowler behind. Fortunately, as he had only his umbrella as protection, the lion took no notice of him. Someone called Southport police station to report the lion's presence, only to be told by a duty copper that they did not have the facilities to handle a lion! Apparently it wasn't that common an occurrence . . .

In actual fact, I knew the man who owned the lion. He had started Southport Zoo and was an eccentric, some might say a bit of a head-banger. I knew him because he had given me a little filly called Karen Rud. He used to keep the filly in a stable in his garden, and Jackie Grainger and I went to see him before we took on the horse. At the time Jackie worked at the slaughterhouse, so he was not squeamish. We were shown in and were standing in the big open hallway when this bloody great lion appears. I beat Grainger in the race to take cover behind a big easy chair in the corner of the hall. Whether it's true or not, Grainger says the lion sniffed him and licked his hand. He swears he thought he was going to lose his arm at the elbow. I don't blame him – I remember seeing scratches and gouges on the oak doors in the house. Even supposedly tame lions can be ferocious, I guess.

Some time after the escapade in Westbourne Road, the owner of the lion rang me up to ask if I had got a van. I hadn't. He asked me if I could find a suitable vehicle for a job. A couple of times in the past, I'd taken him and various animals to Granada Television studios. Now he wanted the lion taken to London.

I could see a profit in the journey if I could only get the right vehicle.

I went to see a character named Jimmy, who'd been in prison during the war for black-marketing. If anyone would have a cheap van, it was Jimmy. He asked what I wanted to transport. I told him and he never blinked. He didn't have a van, but he did have, he said, just what I needed. And he pointed to a Vauxhall 25, a big old beast with leather seats. I gave him twenty-five quid for it on the spot, which, as I was being paid forty pounds, gave me the chance to make a couple of days' wages on the job.

Back at the house, the owner of the lion loaded him into the rear of the car, where it straight away lay down on the back seat. The owner joined me in the front. I wasn't bothered to begin with, but I soon became conscious of what was behind me: whenever I looked in the rear-view mirror, all I could see was this great big lion's head. There were no motorways, remember. We were driving south on the A49, and the journey took hours through the night. I thought to myself, 'This is bloody idiotic.' Each time I heard or felt the lion move in the back of the car, I don't mind admitting that the hairs on the back of my neck stood on end. The chap who owned the animal had absolute confidence in him, but I confess it was a confidence that was hard to share. But I must say that he and the lion did seem to be the best of chums.

We made it safely to London and I drove home the next day – alone. I think it worked out that after all my expenses I had got the Vauxhall for nothing. Not a bad return for a couple of days' work. Stupid? Maybe, but when you were young, you did these things to earn a living – and have a great story to tell down the pub.

Chapter Four

SAN LORENZO

Beryl: 'If that horse comes, I go.'
Ginger: 'All right, get your bags packed. He's on the boat.'

I KNEW I had gone up in the world when I started to drive a Rolls-Royce. Of course, it wasn't mine, but that didn't matter.

The car belonged to David Rosenfield, who had an Austin Rover car agency in Manchester. David used to stay in the main suite at the Palace Hotel, and we met as I was there on a regular basis to collect guests. He had racehorses so, inevitably, we would talk about racing, and one day he asked if I fancied going to the races with him. That's how I came to be driving his black-and-white Rolls.

David was a generous man and he would often invite me to have a meal with him and his wife when we were at the course together. He had horses in training with Willie Stephenson and Eric Cousins, and we had some fun together. He was not the least bit snobbish. He would come round to our little showroom in Upper Aughton Road – 'McCain's Car Sales', the sign read – and park his Rolls beside our old beat-up cars. We lived in the flat above the showroom and, in time, I thought Beryl made it a super little home. She disagreed, saying that we had second-hand furniture because I spent any money we ever had on horses. I think Beryl feels that she has been fighting an uphill battle in that department for our entire lives together. She has always considered putting together a beautiful home more important than I ever have.

Anyhow, David would come round for a drink and to talk about horses. We went together to the reopening of the horse sales at Doncaster, brought back to life by Ken Oliver and Willie Stephenson. Both men were good trainers: Willie trained a Derby and a Grand National winner, Arctic Prince and Oxo, while Ken trained some of the highest-class chasers in the country. One Christmas, I recall, he won eleven races over two days. The opening was quite an impressive affair, with fresh salmon and a grand buffet. As an owner with deep pockets, David was one of the star turns. Time can make a liar of a man, so I am not sure if it was on this visit or a subsequent one, but anyhow I bought a foal at the sales. Don't ask me how much I paid because I cannot remember, but it's safe to assume it wasn't that much, as I didn't have a lot of money lying around. When we brought the foal home, there was nowhere much for him to go – so we put him in the little wash-house at the bottom of the yard behind the showroom, surrounded by the second-hand cars I had out the back. After a few days we found proper stabling for him down the road. I'd like to say he went on to become a good racehorse – but he didn't!

The foal wasn't the only oddity to be lodged in the back yard. My best man Raymond Johnson, sadly now dead, refurbished theatres, and he had a huge crane-like machine with a platform that could be raised into the air in sections. It looked like a diving board. I let him park it in our yard, where it towered above the roof. When we'd had a few drinks we'd have a competition to see who was brave enough to climb to the top.

There was always something going on. In those days you could sell a car for eighty pounds, put sixty quid through the finance company and make more money on the commission from the HP than you would on the profit from selling the car. I had now begun a partnership with a friend, Peter Cundy. We were young and we were cocky. Oh, it was a buzz. And without getting carried away we were making a nice few quid, and finding some interesting ways to spend it. It makes me sound like

Arthur Daley, I know, but somehow we managed to find a source of whisky straight from the Western Highlands. A pound a bottle we paid – and it was great stuff. We bought three cases and there was always a bottle in the desk in the office of the showroom. But you know what they say: if something seems to be too good to be true, it usually is. One day we read in the paper that a chap had been arrested for making whisky in his garage. This was the stuff we'd been buying. Later we noticed that varnish had been taken off the desk – spillage from the whisky glasses had left burn marks! God knows what it was doing to our insides. But we weren't too bothered, to be honest. It still tasted good. My dad wasn't very well at the time, and I gave him a bottle. He used to have a large nip every night and he went on to last for ages. I swear to this day that the biggest contributing factor to his recovery was that whisky.

Life was never dull. One night Beryl and I heard a noise and looked out the window to discover a guy sitting cross-legged on the bonnet of one of our cars playing a guitar. We had something like sixteen or eighteen cars strung across the paved area in front of the showroom beneath our flat, and while they were not worth fortunes they were not meant for drunks to sit on. I shouted out the window and got a mouthful back. So I ran down and took off after the guy in my pyjamas. I was a bit quick-tempered then (I've mellowed a lot now – honest, just ask Beryl). I caught up with him and threw him over a garden wall, and then chucked his bloody guitar over after him. To be fair, he wasn't doing that much wrong, but he never came back to serenade us again.

At night, I left the cars unlocked on the pavement in front of the showroom with the keys in the ignition. You just never thought about them being stolen. But one of my friends – Phil Tinkler, a small, dark, good-looking chap who had an eye for the ladies – knew a good thing when he saw it. He'd been on a big night out and realized he couldn't get home. That was the morning I came down to discover one of my cars was missing. I needn't have worried. Later that day, Phil brought back the car and explained that he had just borrowed it in the night. I really liked him – he'd been on the professional staff at Manchester United and he was a big mate of Nobby Stiles, as they'd joined the club together. But while Phil never made it, of course Nobby became a household name. Who will forget his toothless dance across Wembley after England won the World Cup in 1966?

Actually, I picked up Nobby in the car one day when Manchester United were staying at the Palace Hotel. He was with Bobby Charlton and Denis Law, and they were going for a round of golf at Hillside Golf Club. When we arrived at the club, the footballers, huge stars at the time, were told that because of the weather, temporary greens were in use. They decided not to play. Bobby suggested that they go back and do some training; but I'll always remember that Denis, a wild young Scotsman with blond hair, tried to persuade them to go to a pub instead. Bobby won the day, I seem to recall.

DRIVING, AND WHEELING-and-dealing second-hand cars, paid the bills, but my obsession with horses remained. Perhaps you make your own luck in life, or perhaps you just get lucky; but one day I noticed that an old horse I once rode out when I was at Kath Walsh's riding school had been pulled up in a race in Ireland. I bet the old lad's broken down, I thought. San Lorenzo had been a top-class chaser in his day, with trainers Neville Crump and George Owen, and had won the Lancashire Hurdle at Liverpool. I used to ride him on the beach at Southport and wade out into the sea on him. If I remember correctly, he was owned by Major Ainscough, a corn merchant in Southport. In time, the old horse succumbed to wear and tear and he was sent back to Ireland to be with Aubrey Brabazon, a respected trainer.

When I saw that he had been pulled up, I rang his owner to ask him what he intended to do with the horse. He told me San Lorenzo had broken down, and that he had given instructions to have him put down. I asked him if he would give me the horse instead, and he said that he would with pleasure, but that I had better call Mr Brabazon immediately.

So I did – only to learn that the old horse was not headed for the knacker's yard at all. Mr Brabazon, it seemed, thought too much of him. We talked for a while, and he agreed to put the horse on a boat across the Irish Sea.

Having made the arrangements to have San Lorenzo sent over from Ireland, I happened to spot Beryl as I drove into town. I can still see her to this day. She looked very elegant in high-heeled shoes. I couldn't wait to tell her the news, so I dropped the car window and said: 'You'll never guess . . .'

Beryl, being Beryl, instinctively knew what I was about to tell her. 'You've got a horse, haven't you?' she said.

'I have. They gave me San Lorenzo.'

'If that horse comes, I go.'

'All right, get your bags packed. He's on the boat.'

End of subject. You see, Beryl worried that we couldn't afford the horse, and there was a stony silence between us for some days. Still, the old horse arrived, and that's what mattered. I rang Jack Cook from Mrs Chambers' stud and we discussed what I might do to try to get San Lorenzo right. They'd lock you up today, but we decided to give him a blister. You clip the leg that's troubling the horse, then rub a red mercury blister into the leg. It cauterizes the tissues; then you apply a bandage and leave it on for six weeks. The bandage tightens as the leg swells. In my ignorance, I think I may have tied the bandage tighter than I should have. When I took it off six weeks later, San Lorenzo was climbing the wall in his box for about thirty-six hours. Anyhow, when the old horse had calmed down I started to ride him out, steady at first as there was no rush.

BY NOW I felt the time had come for me to apply for a public trainer's licence, allowing me to train horses for other people as well as my own. I had several other horses around, basically given to me by friends to look after. We had the use of some farmland at the back of a council estate as a makeshift training gallop, and I also cantered horses along the beach – though it was a good couple of miles away. We were learning how to use the sand then, not really appreciating that the beach was the best natural all-weather gallop you could think of.

In response to my application for a trainer's licence, the Jockey Club informed me that they would be sending an inspector to meet me. We tried to get everything shipshape and looking better than it really was in preparation for the big day. On the morning of the appointment, I'd even been out shooting and killed a brace of pheasants. I had them hung for when the inspector arrived, a big fellow who had been in the police force. He asked me how far it was to where I trained and I told him it was six furlongs, when it was really closer to two and a half miles. I showed him our natural gallop on the sands at Southport – except I couldn't show him much at all, as there was a really dense fog and he couldn't see more than thirty yards in front of him. Still, he didn't seem that concerned.

Back at the stables, he wanted to know where my other gallops were, so I took him over to the farmland, not much more than half a mile away, only to find myself staring in horror at the field we used, which had been ploughed up. I thought that had blown any chance I had of being granted a licence. But back at the stables again, the inspector continued to be pleasant; I made sure he had a drink – and probably insisted that he take the brace of pheasants I'd shot that morning. All the same, I must have looked troubled, because as he left I remember he said that he would do his best for me. And he must have done – because soon afterwards I was issued with a trainer's licence.

Today the old yard at Southport would never have passed an inspection, but had it been declined at the time there would never have been a Red Rum story. We small trainers all had to start somewhere, didn't we? But it's fair to say that not too many have started with stables behind a car showroom . . .

After months of nursing him back to health, I finally felt that San

Lorenzo was ready to return to the racecourse. I aimed him at a race at Cheltenham, and there was an obvious choice of jockey – Stan Mellor, who had been stable jockey for George Owen and had ridden San Lorenzo to win a number of races. Only trouble was, by this time Stan was champion jockey. But I booked him anyway – cocky bastard that I was. It was autumn and the ground was fast and, truthfully, I should never have dreamed of running a horse just recovered from a leg injury. But we did anyway, and in a chase to boot. Stan pulled the horse up, as he was just not in contention; but afterwards, he came back and said, 'He'll win you a race.' And that was it: gone. A champion jockey doesn't have time to waste with a taxi driver from Southport.

So we ticked away at the job until the time seemed right to pick another race for San Lorenzo. This was at Liverpool, on 2 January 1965. Now, one of our regular customers was a gypsy fortune-teller called Suzy, who drank in the Blundell Arms not far from us. She told fortunes in the Burton Arcade by day and sat on a stool at the bar by night. About nine o'clock in the evening the phone would ring at home, and Suzy would be on the other end asking to be picked up and taken back to her little council flat, where she lived on her own. I think the fare was one shilling and sixpence, but Suzy, a nice old woman, nearly always gave me a couple of shillings.

I picked her up as usual the night before San Lorenzo was running, and Suzy told me, in that knowing way of clairvoyants, 'Ginger, the horse will win for you tomorrow.' I winked at the publican Jack Owens, a lovely man who never charged me rent for the stable he let me use at the back of the pub, and smiled: 'Jack, if the horse wins tomorrow, Suzy can have as much as she wants to drink for as long as she likes, down to me.'

San Lorenzo was entered in a selling chase. As usual I hadn't got a lot of brass, and so I tried to get an amateur to ride him to save me the expense of hiring a professional jockey. But I couldn't find one, and while I was wondering what to do, a pro called Robin Langley asked if he could have the ride; he used to ride for George Owen, he said, and he thought that the horse would run well. Well, I told him he'd better take the ride. That decision cost me seven quid in the jockey's fee, and then I had to find another three pounds to enter the horse in the race. Problem was, I only had a fiver to my name. Luckily, at that time you could pay both your entry fee and jockey's fee at the scales, so I borrowed a fiver from a friend in the Blundell Arms and we were ready for the off.

So we go to Liverpool – and the horse bloody wins! Twelve years after I received my trainer's permit, I had my first winner: a fourteen-year-old broken-down horse called San Lorenzo had won the Burscough Selling Handicap Steeplechase over two miles and eighty yards. I was over the moon.

As I said, this race was a 'seller', which meant that the winning horse was put up for sale in the ring afterwards. In those days, the owner of the second horse in the race was entitled to a share of the price the winning horse made above the reserve. So it paid the owner of the second to run the price up if he thought you wanted the horse back. Before San Lorenzo went under the hammer, a man called Colin Wiston tapped me on the shoulder and asked for fifty pounds not to bid. I'd won about a hundred and sixty pounds in prize money, and now straight away I was having to shell a load of it out! But at least there were no other bids, and so we brought San Lorenzo home in the trailer to Southport. I put my horse away in his stable behind the Blundell Arms, then, as I walked in, I remembered my promise. 'Where's Suzy? I asked Jack. He replied: 'Ginger, she fell off the bar stool half an hour ago.' Apparently, Suzy had been drinking gin and tonics at my expense until she keeled over. And if Suzy's prediction wasn't strange enough, what do you make of this? The horse San Lorenzo beat that day was owned by a certain Arthur Mitchell – and thirty-one years later our daughter Joanne married his son!

A fortnight later we ran San Lorenzo again at Haydock Park in another selling chase, where he was beaten a head in a driving finish with a horse called Miserable Monk that belonged to the Barclays in Scotland. And of course, by now I'm an expert on selling chases, aren't I? So I touched Sandy Barclay on the shoulder and suggested he should give me fifty pounds not to bid against him. He said he wasn't sure about that, and then offered me a 'pony'. Now, I have always got my animals mixed up in punters' slang. Which is worth more: a 'monkey' or a 'pony'? I didn't know. I worked on the principle that as a pony is bigger than a monkey, that must represent a larger amount. So I told him I'd accept his 'pony' not to bid – and felt rather silly when he handed me five fivers. I'd never again forget that a 'pony' is twenty-five quid and a 'monkey' five hundred.

Next stop for San Lorenzo was Windsor, where I asked Dave Dick to ride him. Dave was a God-like figure to me, a very special jockey. With Dave in the saddle and a bit of form, our old horse was made favourite, which seemed to justify the decision to travel so far from home. I was wearing a tailor-made thornproof tweed suit that set me back twenty pounds. I called it my San Lorenzo suit, and I wore it for ever until Beryl burned it.

Out on the course, Dave suddenly pulled up the old horse in mid-race. I feared the worst and went straight to see him in the weighing room. Some of the other jockeys there were beginning to wind Dave up for my benefit, light-heartedly accusing him of stopping the favourite. But Dave confirmed what I had suspected: San Lorenzo had broken down again, and there wasn't going to be a way back for him a second time.

I wasn't going to risk the old horse finishing up in the knacker's yard – not after all he'd done for me. I finished up giving him to a good friend of mine, John Irving. John was a senior sales manager for a big car firm in Southport, and he did me a fair few turns selling me some good cheap cars. He liked to have a horse around the place and San Lorenzo lived for another five or six years. God bless the old boy. He was my first winner and, as I relive his part in the earliest stage of my career, when I was struggling to make any kind of mark, I can't help but smile. I often wonder whether everything that was to come would have happened if it hadn't been for him. He gave me the confidence that maybe – just maybe – I could crack this training lark. I am glad he ended his days being well looked after.

Chapter Five

BABY TALK?

BERYL WAS NEVER pregnant. Well, at least, we weren't allowed to *say* she was pregnant.

She really didn't want kids, as she felt motherhood would interfere with her action-woman lifestyle. It would mean she'd have to stop riding horses, and that wasn't on the cards. It would also mean she couldn't go on racing bloody quick little cars like the Mini Cooper she ran. So when Beryl did become pregnant, no one dared discuss it. She was in denial and just carried on as normal. I think she was five months gone before she saw a doctor. To be fair, not too many people realized she was pregnant, as she was a very fit girl and the bump just didn't show.

At six months gone, Beryl was still riding out for trainer Mick James, an ex-jockey. One morning she came home soaked to the bone. The story took some dragging out of her. Apparently, this big horse of James's had run away with her and flopped her upside down in a ditch. But did this slow Beryl down? Not a bit. Even at this late stage of her pregnancy, she couldn't see a reason to stop racing cars. And that Cooper she drove was *quick*. She was going to compete in some sand-racing competition on the beach, and some of our friends shared my fear that this was not a good idea. 'I don't think you should, Conk,' I ventured. (I call Beryl 'Conk' – and still do to this day – because I think she has a slightly big nose. Well, she used to fancy herself – and with good enough reason – so I needed to put her in her place. You've got to try sometimes, haven't you? Not an easy task when it comes to Beryl, mind you.)

Anyhow, Beryl insisted that she was fine to carry on. The motor-racing crew weren't my type of people, but I went the back way to the sand hills to watch Beryl's heat without her knowing. It was a Sunday, I think. And there she was in this Cooper, legging it round at full belt. All four wheels were off the ground on some of the bumps, and she was sliding sideways round the bends. Walking back, suddenly it struck me as being very funny. I thought: this poor little baby's not even born yet and it's already been upside down in a ditch and flung round in a racing car. Oh dear, oh dear!

The big day – or I should say night – arrived after we had been out for a meal. We'd gone to bed early, when Beryl said, 'I think we ought to go to the hospital.' Her waters had broken. She was pregnant now, all right.

I told her – listen to this – that there was no need to be alarmed until the pains came every two or three minutes. How I had suddenly qualified as an expert I don't know. Beryl persevered for a little while, then said, 'Let's go now!' She's always made the important decisions, no question. Beryl had a bed booked in a Catholic maternity hospital in Crosby around sixteen miles away. We aren't Catholics, but it had a good reputation.

Now, we had a fleet of cars outside the showroom, probably between fourteen and sixteen at that time, and all right, most of them had seen better days, but you would have thought one of them would have got the job done. But it suddenly dawned on me that not one of them had any petrol in it. Or at least, no amount worth talking about. It was a fail-safe security ploy of mine. If a car should be pinched, the thieves wouldn't get far if there wasn't any petrol in the tank. That was all well and good normally, but this wasn't normal. This was an emergency – and one growing by the minute, as I searched for a car that registered any sign above the empty mark on the fuel gauge. No luck – so I chose a Morris Minor 1000 that I hoped might have a splash in it, but I admit we set off on a prayer and fresh air in the tank.

As cars passed us I thought of all those lucky sods having a good night out while we were hoping we had enough fuel to get us to the maternity hospital. Beryl was extremely calm in the circumstances, but I kept noting where there was a farm or a barn that we could use if the Morris Minor came to a spluttering halt.

Thankfully, the car kept going and we made it to the nursing home at Crosby. I made sure Beryl was in good hands – and then walked back to the car and drove off. It wasn't quite closing time yet, so I stopped at the first pub and had a large Scotch. I didn't care if I drove or walked home now. I'd got Beryl where she needed to be and I wouldn't have to get involved. Later, Beryl explained how she had been left alone in a darkened room and told to take gulps of gas and air as she felt she needed to. She admitted that she had been frightened.

Blissfully unaware of all that, I slept like a baby. The next morning I was wakened by a telephone call from my mother. She told me I should ring the hospital. Beryl, she said, had had a baby girl. That was our Joanne – born at 6.15 a.m. on 19 March 1967, weighing in at 5lb 15oz. When I came to the hospital, Beryl apologized to me that she hadn't given birth to a little boy. 'Stupid, wasn't I,' she says now.

OUR LIVES DIDN'T change dramatically, it must be said. Joanne couldn't have been more than six weeks old when we took her to a point-to-point meeting in her carry-cot in the back of a Mini van. Beryl's not a drinking lady, mind; but I got rotten, stinking drunk on whisky with a group of friends. Poor old Beryl and Joanne were stuck in the back of the van waiting for me to rejoin them. Very naughty I was. Beryl may not have wanted to be pregnant, but I have to say she is a very good mother. What was I like as a father? I think I was busy. It wasn't up to me to change nappies; that's women's work. I was out making a living for us.

We struggled on, with the cars subsidizing anything I was doing with horses. Some weeks you sold three or four cars; at weekends you might deal a few more than that. You weren't taking big lumps out of them, but there was a profit and a lot of it was in cash. And somehow that tended to disappear! Second-hand car salesmen like me had, to a point, taken over from the old horse traders. It's the same line of business, if you think about it: transport. You get honest and dishonest men in all walks of life. Speaking personally, I never went back on a deal that I shook hands on. I've taken a few good hidings as a consequence – but you have to bite the bullet. You can't win all the time. But to have a day pass without a deal of some kind is a bad day, no question about that.

At the beginning, I could never stretch to buying a horse at Doncaster bloodstock sales for more than £200 – and then I had to duck and dive to find the money. Those circumstances changed, though, when Ken Oliver became a friend. As I have mentioned, Ken ran the sales with Willie Stephenson and he was a great drinking man and a lovely person. He pestered me to buy horses, but I told him I didn't have the kind of money that was needed. Ken reckoned he had the answer to that by giving me two thousand pounds' worth of credit on the spot. Only a drink and a half later, it had gone up to ten thousand pounds. It was like offering booze to an alcoholic. The deal got even better when he went on to suggest that it would be a condition of the loan that I didn't have to pay him back until I'd found an owner for any horse that I had bought.

I didn't use my credit line to a great extent – I'm not that stupid – but there were times when you were on to a hiding to nothing with Ken as auctioneer. At one particular sale, I had made a bid of six hundred pounds and I think we were going up in units of twenty. Someone bid against me and Ken turned in my direction, with a very red face that made him look like Mr Pickwick, and intimated that I should keep the auction alive. Now, I don't like to let people know I am bidding, so I shook my head as discreetly as I could to let Ken know I wasn't interested in going any higher. Ken blindly ignored me and signalled that I had raised the stakes. Somebody came back and Ken suggested to me, 'You'll go again, sir.' No, I said. But he knocked the horse down to me anyway

– and it wasn't worth thirty bob! I never did any good with it at all. Still, that was Ken; I wouldn't knock him for it – and the horse might have turned out to be a cracker. That's the fun of it. You can never know for sure.

Ken was a star in my book, and he was very kind to me. Doncaster Bloodstock Sales as a whole have been good to me – but then, I have been good to them as well. Mind you, occasionally I abused the credit I was given. I might 'forget' to pay my account (more likely, I couldn't afford to pay them). I'd then get a letter from managing director Harry Beeby politely reminding me that I owed them money. Of course, whenever that happened I would try to get a cheque in the post to them as soon as I could.

I do love sales. At that time I'd be going to two or three motor-car sales a week, and I just enjoyed the craic of being around people who liked to wheel and deal. To my mind the ideal way of spending holiday time would be to go the Punchestown sales in Ireland in April, the Doncaster May sales and the November sale at Newmarket. I'm not interested at all in going abroad. I just like to watch horses being sold, and that pleasure becomes all the better if you've got an owner who's given you a few quid to spend.

But if I had my way I'd do away with bloodstock agents. Often they act on behalf of trainers who aren't bold enough to bid for themselves. A trainer will tell you soon enough when he has bought a good horse, but he won't tell you when he's bought a bad 'un. If a football club manager buys a bad player, we can all see he has made a mistake, sometimes a very costly one at that. By using a bloodstock agent, a trainer has an excuse should a horse turn out to be unsuccessful. The agents themselves can't lose, working on a commission of around 5 per cent. They think they are smart; but I was a car dealer and I can read the buggers like a book – or the large majority of them, at least. They think it's amusing, and profitable, to bid against one another. It's an ego trip. But they forget that they are in business to do their best for their clients.

I'd also say they buy a sight more bad horses than good ones. So I'm not that enthusiastic about them; but then, I also blame some trainers for not making their own judgements and putting their money where their mouths are.

There are a few agents I'd trust – John O'Byrne from Ireland is someone whose word and judgement I value – but there are some I wouldn't trust to tell me the date. In the motor trade we have *Glass's Guide*, which is a regularly updated magazine that publishes a reliable and respected valuation for any car subject to its age and condition. There is no *Glass's* for horses. You have to rely on bloodline and an eye for a horse. And I suggest that if you confiscated the sales catalogue from most of these bloodstock agents, they would be lost. Yet most of them could bullshit for England.

As for me, I was at the sales still looking for that one good horse, without the resources to have much chance of succeeding in the quest. But you can always afford a horse if you are not wasting your money elsewhere. The car business was ticking over, and I was not afraid of hard graft. I'd have got a job as a coalman or carried bricks if the need had arisen.

IN RACING, HOPE springs eternal; with owners as well as trainers. However bad the horse is, an owner will always believe that somewhere down the line it will do something. As a trainer, you can tell a man his wife is having an affair and he will laugh. But you tell him his horse is useless, and he will take it off you and send it to someone else. Never insult a man's horse, no matter what.

Part and parcel of that respect for an owner's horse is making sure it is turned out properly – above all when it goes racing. The racecourse is your shop window. I don't wish to sound pretentious, but I think it's disgusting the way some trainers present their horses. Even if your horse is no good, you can at least make him look good. There is no excuse for a horse not being tidy, not looking the part, neat and plaited.

Too many come to the races looking like hairy dogs. I firmly believe that when they appear in public they should look as though they have been attended to and prepared like the athletes they are. However, sometimes you can pay a bit of a high price for your principles – as I did one day at Chepstow. We had this nice little horse called Secret Affair, who had won a race or two as a two-year-old, but had then gone wrong for reasons we never quite got to the bottom of. We decided to take him to Chepstow with another horse whose name I don't recall. With us was Derek Critchley, a nice lad who lived on the estate near where we trained the horses and had a few rides for us (and played golf pretty well, I seem to remember). When we led the horses out for morning exercise at the racecourse, Derek had Secret Affair and I had the other horse. Like I said, I think it is a trainer's responsibility to turn his horses out as well as he possibly can, and both ours had sheets on them. It was a breezy morning, and in the gusty wind the sheet on Secret Affair blew up. As I attempted to replace it, the sharp little horse whipped round and kicked me in the mouth. Next moment I am on the ground spitting out teeth. When security staff arrived, they called for an ambulance and I was whizzed off to the hospital in town.

For reasons I didn't understand, a nurse ordered me into a bath. I grumbled – or mumbled, more likely – as I couldn't see how this was going to help fix my teeth. But as I always tend to do what I'm told (I'm sure Beryl would agree), I climbed in – and I wasn't very enamoured to find the water wasn't especially warm. I still had two or three teeth hanging by a thread, so I pulled them out as I sat in the lukewarm water. It turned out eight teeth on the top of one side of my mouth had been shifted by the force of the blow. It was decided I needed to be anaesthetized.

When I awoke, I was in cloud-cuckoo-land in a ward with men who were much worse off than me. In the meantime, Beryl had arrived at the racecourse; when she couldn't find me she spoke to the stable manager, who told her about my accident, but also told her she had nothing to worry about. He advised her to run the horses as planned and then go to the hospital to visit me. So I don't think she was prepared for the sight that greeted her when she came to see me. She later admitted that the sight of me banged about had made her feel sick. To add insult to injury, Secret Affair's reins had broken as he passed the grandstands on the first circuit, putting an end to his race, and the other horse had fallen. Great.

The doctors wanted to keep me in the hospital for observation, but I was keen to leave. Next morning I called home and asked for someone to pick me up. When I told the ward sister I was leaving, she said that the hospital would not be responsible for me if I did. Anyway, Beryl arranged for one of our lads, George White, to drive down to collect me, and he told the nursing staff that we were running a good horse at Haydock Park that afternoon and that they should put a few quid on him. I can remember one nurse muttering darkly about what they were going to do to me if the horse didn't win. On the way home, I had to ask for the car to stop two or three times to let me be sick. Anyhow, my horse finished second at 20–1, so the nurses won a few bob with their each-way bets.

BERYL'S NEXT TRIP to hospital was to give birth to our second child. Again, we hadn't been able to talk about her pregnancy, but just a little over three years after Joanne was born Beryl had a date fixed to go into hospital to have our second child induced. I dropped her off at St Catherine's in Southport.

I'll always remember that as Beryl was going in I met another chap, a bit younger than me, entering with his very fat wife. He asked me all enthusiastically: 'Are you staying to watch?' Bloody hell, cock, no thanks, I thought. What a repulsive sight that would be. No, I wouldn't be staying. Beryl recalls watching the Trooping of the Colour on television – then being whisked away to give birth. Our son appeared at 3.15 p.m. and he weighed 7lb 15oz. (I only know this because Beryl told me as I was writing.)

I took the call to tell me that Beryl had given birth to a boy from a friend called Sandra Fish. I immediately disappeared for a jar or two in the Blundell Arms, then with my partner Peter I was popping champagne corks over the road from the balcony of our car showroom. A few other friends were nicely oiled with us – but I had the good sense to remember that before I went to see Beryl I had to buy her some flowers. I'd taken other new fathers into the hospital in my taxi and I'd seen them all going in with bouquets, so I knew the form. Actually, I was still outside the hospital when I heard a window open. I looked across the path and Beryl waved at me. She looked like she'd been on holiday. She was absolutely stunning, bright as a button, and she was laughing her head off at me.

Inside I found Beryl sharing a room with another woman, an ex-nurse from Ireland. I asked which baby was ours. I took one look and I said, 'Christ, Conk, it's ugly. And why on earth have you called it Baby Maxie? Where did you get a silly name like that.' The lady in the other bed began to laugh hysterically. 'Don't worry, Ginger, that one's mine,' she said. She was a lovely, big Irish girl with a great sense of humour. Our son, born on 13 June 1970, had a no-nonsense name: Donald.

SO NOW WE had our two kids and the business was starting to go better. We were getting a few bob in the back pocket, and Beryl was getting accustomed to the fact that we had the odd horse or two.

It wasn't all plain sailing, though – like women, horses can be unpredictable at times. One morning when there was ice on the ground Beryl was riding our only decent horse, called Implicate – he never turned out much good, to be honest, but he was decent for us then – when a pheasant took off in front of her as she came back over the Mosses, the lanes across the farm that we used. The flurry startled Beryl's horse – and she was buried. Worse, she was clipped in the face by the horse's foot after she landed. As she sat on the ground holding her face I took off after the horse.

When I brought him back, Beryl was back at the stable but still in some distress. She had found a cloth and dipped it in icy water and pressed it against her face. She said that she felt unwell, and walked groggily to her car to set out for a local hospital. Of course, I felt I had to stay and look after the horses, as we only had a boy helping us. It was not until several hours later that I received a call to tell me that Beryl had fractured her cheekbone in the fall. When I walked in the ward I felt pangs of guilt as I could see how sad Beryl looked behind a big black eye.

She was discharged to allow the swelling to subside but readmitted a few days later for an operation at Broad Green hospital in Liverpool. Beryl's a good lass, you know. Through all these years with me she's had her ups and downs, and this was definitely a down – although, thankfully, she was not in a fit state to let me know about it. The good news I could tell her, though, was that the horse had returned home sound. Look, you get your values and stick to them, don't you?

Yes, by the turn of the decade things were in decent shape, even allowing for the odd nasty accident. But it was all about to change – suddenly, and for ever.

Chapter Six

THE GUV'NOR

ONE OF MY most pleasant jobs was to drive a lovely old man called Noel Le Mare to a dinner dance at the Prince of Wales Hotel on Saturday evenings. Mr Le Mare – or the Guv'nor, as I called him – was a man of substance as well as style. He had a lovely, lovely house in Waterloo Road. He also had a chauffeur, but on Saturdays he liked me to drive him. I'd pick him up at eight o'clock and take him into the hotel; and on the dot of midnight, I would return to take him home.

The fare was three or four shillings in each direction, but the Guv'nor always gave me a pound tip. That was good money. But there was another reason I enjoyed driving him. At the end of most evenings, he would invite me into his house. I'd be finished for the night, so I was glad to join him for a Scotch or two. The Guv'nor was a super raconteur – and he had the same passion for horses as me.

He had some stories to tell. He'd begun his working life at the turn of the century as a fourteen-year-old boy on trawlers that fished in the waters close to Iceland. He said that it was so cold that when he took off his waterproof clothing in the galley the trousers would literally stand up on their own: they were frozen stiff. Then he had to put them back on when it was his turn to be on watch again. Those trawler crews, the Guv'nor said, consisted of seriously hard men. After some time on trawlers, he became a merchant seaman; he had always harboured an ambition to become an engineer, and the merchant navy gave him an opportunity to serve an apprenticeship.

It was by sheer chance that he became hooked on the Grand National. In 1906 he was a junior fitter and working in port at home when a more senior seaman asked him to go into town to find out what had won the big race. The young Noel had not paid the slightest attention to the Grand National until then, but he was instantly smitten by the magic of the race. He told me that what first impressed him was that when he reached the Town Hall he saw an American handing out gold sovereigns, his generosity having been sparked by backing that year's winner, Ascetic's Silver. The Guv'nor says the next day he read about the race and discovered the gambling excitement it generated, and learned that it was the longest race and the hardest race in the world. He told himself right then, 'I'd love to win the National.'

The Guv'nor also told me that as a young man he had two other ambitions, besides winning the National: he planned to marry a beautiful woman and to become a millionaire. That was three rather special ambitions, if you ask me – even if they seemed fanciful given his impoverished circumstances at the time.

In the First World War he was twice on ships that were sunk by Germans. I think the first time he was in an open boat for two days before being rescued. Then he endured the ordeal all over again. But the Guv'nor's love affair with the sea never weakened, and after the war ended he continued to sail all over the world. In New Orleans he visited a house full of, shall we say, a lot of bright and not so virtuous women. They pinched his chief engineer's hat – and he had to pay to get it back. He always made it sound like a grand life.

I do remember that the Guv'nor – who had a super mind – was an atheist. But nevertheless the local parson used to visit him nearly every month. They would debate the existence of God with arguments that were light years beyond my comprehension. I used to sit and listen and drink Scotch.

One by one, the Guv'nor began to make his dreams come true. He did find his beautiful woman; but as she wouldn't marry a sailor, he came ashore to start a new life. She worked with British Insulated Calendar Cables (BICC), and she put her husband's name forward for a job. He was employed by them for a couple of years, but the Guv'nor was not a man to settle for a mundane existence. He craved adventure, and as his life at sea was over he had to look for it elsewhere. His life changed for ever when he agreed at a meeting in a teahouse in Manchester to form a construction company with three friends. He needed to borrow most of the £250 he had to find as his quarter-share in the capital they invested in the venture. Basically, they hired labourers to dig trenches for other contractors who were laying cables.

From this humble beginning, Mr Le Mare developed a big civil engineering company, Norwest. At one point, I think they employed in the region of 6,000 people. But the Guv'nor told me how, in the early days, as they were expanding, his wife would be driven around in her chauffeured Daimler to pay the labourers in cash on the roadside. Later, he dealt with government contracts on a vast scale, but things did not necessarily always run smoothly. During the Second World War his company built some offshore platforms for gun placements, I believe. They had great trouble getting paid in full by the government. So the Guv'nor went down to the offending ministry in London and argued his position in a room full of top brass and boffins – and he won the day. I looked upon him as a very, very astute old gentleman. He was also a generous man, and, with other prominent Liverpool businessmen like Robert McAlpine, a giant of the construction trade, he made contributions to good causes without people knowing.

He was always immaculately dressed, a tall, slim man with a pianist's hands. He chain-smoked, although he only smoked half a cigarette before he stubbed it out, and he drank a cocktail that would have killed an elephant, it was that potent. I tried it just the once and vowed never to allow it to pass my lips again. I think it is fair to say, too, that Mr Le Mare remained a great admirer of the ladies. I heard one story involving the

Guv'nor that amuses me to this day. At a dinner function at the Royal Birkdale Golf Club (of which he was a past president), it seems that he flirted with an attractive waitress serving his table. His wife took exception and turned her soup bowl over the Guv'nor's head before sweeping out of the room. The old man would accept that as par for the course, if you like. He was a star – and I will be eternally grateful to him for giving me the opportunity he did. He was what I would call the first proper owner to give me a chance.

He was also the man who gave me the money to buy Red Rum to train for him.

Our first business dealings together were far from smooth. I'd bought a horse called Cambuslang at Doncaster, and Beryl was so mad she didn't speak to me on the journey home. Around this time Eric Cousins had endeavoured to help me out by sending me a horse named Bardolino to train. One Saturday evening back at Mr Le Mare's house, I persuaded him to buy them both. They were cheap, perhaps a couple of hundred pounds. They also proved to be next to useless. Cambuslang had a heart complaint and, after running badly at Liverpool, was given away. Bardolino, having come a commendable second in a handicap, then broke down and had to be destroyed. It wasn't that I had deliberately lumbered the Guv'nor with bad horses. They were the best that I had – and I so wanted to gain his confidence. If we could be successful with these horses, I reasoned, he would allow me to buy some more to run in his name. Instead the whole episode backfired. It was a worst-case scenario – and I admit that I thought I had no chance of training for Mr Le Mare again.

His first Grand National runner was a horse called Ruby Glen, who had been sold to the Guv'nor by trainer George Owen. Ruby Glen won them a lot of races – but not the National. In general, Mr Le Mare did not have that much good fortune with his horses. For his eightieth birthday in 1967, his family paid 7,000 guineas in Ireland for a horse named Busty Hill. Well, what do you a buy a man who has everything? I suppose they hoped this might turn out to be a Liverpool horse, as I believe it had won a novice chase at Cheltenham. Sadly, Busty Hill broke down. The Guv'nor didn't have much better luck with Furore II, who cost £6,000. He was to break down as well.

As for me, well, I was still thumbing the Doncaster sales catalogues. All I wanted – ever wanted, really – was a horse that could go to Liverpool and just run in the National. I wouldn't have cared if it had turned arse over tip at the first, so long as I had a horse that had gone to Liverpool. In reality, what we had at home were three or four broken-down old nags. So picture my face when I discovered that a horse qualified for the Grand National was coming up at the Doncaster sales. His name was Glenkiln, and I reckoned he could be bought for around £1,000. I told the Guv'nor my news, trying to whet his appetite for another modest plunge, and got his agreement.

As an unbroken four-year-old, I think Glenkiln originally cost £7,000, but Beryl had heard he had become Ken Oliver's hack. They called Glenkiln 'that dear horse', and they didn't mean dear to your heart; they meant dear to your pocket! He'd won a few races for one of Ken's better owners, then disappointed. He was a bright bay, tall and good-looking. But his big attraction for me was the fact that he had fulfilled the conditions to run in the National – which were, at the time, so far as I recall, to have won a race to the value of £1,500 (which he had done), or to have won a race over three miles, or to have been placed around Liverpool.

There was a whisper, though, that the horse had a suspect leg. I carefully inspected him in his box at Doncaster before he came into the ring. He definitely had a leg that was stuffy, by which I mean a little fleshy, but this can be brought on by body heat. When I looked at him again in the outside parade ring thirty minutes later he was perfect. Armed with the Guv'nor's chequebook, I was determined to bid for him. Glenkiln was knocked down to me for 1,000 guineas. I was delighted and apprehensive at the same time. What if I had made a grave mistake? Mr Le Mare would not be idiotic enough to give me another chance.

Back in our yard at Southport, Glenkiln was shown into the best box. After all, he was the most expensive horse we'd ever had, so he was given top billing. We had begun with just four boxes, after converting two stall stables and an outhouse that had been used as a bottling room when the premises belonged to a brewery. In the middle of the narrow, cobbled yard there was an elm tree where sparrows used to collect. By the time Glenkiln came to us we had probably expanded to having six or seven horses in the yard. The boxes were small, but the horses were happy and, if I say so myself, it was a very contented yard. Glenkiln provided the tonic we needed. At last, here was a horse to give us real hope and show the Guv'nor that maybe I had some potential as a trainer after all.

But then I made a complete cock-up. I was so concerned about the paperwork for our entry in the 1972 Grand National that in my haste to get the form off in good time I made a desperate mistake. I thought I was completing a form declaring Glenkiln to run, but I had in fact withdrawn our horse from the race. It said on the form 'Declaration to Run', but it was actually declaring forfeit. When I found out what I had stupidly done, I was devastated – and I didn't know how or what I was going to tell the Guv'nor. He was eighty-five; how many more horses could he expect to own with the right credentials to race in the National? Through sheer inexperience, I had cost him his dream. And mine, for that matter. I just didn't know how I was going to break the news – but Beryl insisted that I went to see him straight away. When I arrived at his home, I just spluttered out what I had done and tried to tell him how sorry I was. And do you know what? He was more sorry for me than himself. He could have fired me on the spot – but he stood by me. He just said to me, 'Pour yourself a drink, Ginger. Worse things happen at sea.' And he should know.

The Guv'nor really was a gentleman. We ran Glenkiln in the Topham

Just William or Just Ginger?

Even then I had difficulty keeping my gob shut.

Private McCain on the left with a fast car at the ready in case the Merry Widow appears.

Previous page: Keeping a watchful eye on Red Rum at Southport beach.

FIRSTS

An innocent-looking Beryl and owner Albert Wake with Home Chief – the first winner we were involved with. Don't ask Beryl what she put in the water.

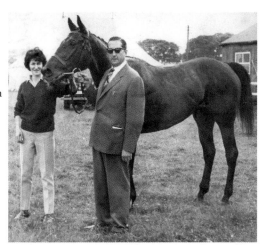

San Lorenzo out in front. Our first ever official winner when I held the licence.

Glenkiln, our first really good horse. Although I did manage to withdraw him from the National.

Beryl gets her man – 25th March 1961.

Proud Dad. Joanne on Gambol – bought from Sir Bobby Charlton no less.

Not the most traditional location for a stable yard. On the way to Joanne's christening. I hope Beryl isn't indicating how many cars we sold that day.

BEGINNINGS

Mared, Red Rum's mother.

The man who gave us our chance: Mr Le Mare, the Guv'nor, with Red Rum.

What lay behind the car showroom. Beryl, Red Rum and myself
at our stables in Southport.

On the way to the beach for the morning session. Red Rum leading the way.

The old horse gives our Donald an affectionate rub.

Sometimes we let anyone ride the old horse.

Our good friend Richard Pitman on Red Rum at Aintree.

And me on my old friend, spending time together after he retired.

at Aintree instead of the National, and he produced a tidy sort of race to finish seventh.

MR LE MARE told me we'd look around for another horse for Liverpool, and that was the best news I could hear. When the catalogue for the sales at Doncaster in August 1972 arrived I went through the listed horses with care and attention. And then I saw just what I was looking for. A well-known owner called Mrs Lurline Brotherton, whose Freebooter had won the 1950 Grand National, had placed in the sale a horse I had seen dead-heat over five furlongs at Liverpool as a two-year-old. The catalogue details made no mention of the fact that the horse was now qualified for the National, but by checking the value of the races he had won I worked out that he was eligible for Aintree.

His name? Red Rum.

Chapter Seven

GREEN LIGHT FOR RED

RED RUM WAS born in Ireland in 1965, when I was battling hard to stand still, or so it seemed. His dam was called Mared and, by all accounts, she was mad. His sire was a grey stallion, Quorum, who came second in the Two Thousand Guineas behind Crepello and who won races over distances from five furlongs to a mile.

Red Rum was bred to be a sprinter, no question.

When he went to the sales as a yearling, he was bought by Tim Molony for 400 guineas, half his reserve price. Tim, an Irishman, was training in Leicestershire at the time. He had been an exceptional rider in his day, winning the National Hunt jockeys' championship five times and, remarkably, the Champion Hurdle at Cheltenham four years in succession. Three of those victories were in partnership with a horse called Sir Ken, owned by textile merchant Maurice Kingsley. Tim had bought Red Rum for Kingsley, who, they say, was a hard-headed beggar.

After Tim had had Red Rum home for a while, he took the decision to geld him. Now, Molony was a bit of a god to a man like me – one of the old-fashioned jockeys, very special. Years later, we were having a Scotch at some racecourse or other when, in a dry voice, he said: 'Ginger, I was champion jockey five times, but the only thing I'm known for is being the bastard that castrated Red Rum.' Thinking of that conversation still makes me smile.

As I said, I watched Red Rum's first-ever race, a five-furlong selling sprint at Liverpool. Hard ridden by Paul Cook, the colt ran a cracking race and caught a filly named Curlicue on the line – well, Cook swears that he headed Curlicue, though the judges called a dead heat. I recall thinking that Red Rum was an attractive bay. Afterwards, Molony bought in Red Rum in the sales ring, an indication of what the stable thought of him. I am not going to claim I followed Red Rum's career from that moment, but I do know that he raced often and that he had a succession of jockeys. Everyone who could hit a horse, from Lester Piggott downwards, hit Red Rum. Lester rode him twice, at Liverpool and Pontefract. Years afterwards, he declared: 'Red Rum must have been a freak – he was bred to go less than a mile.'

When Red Rum won another seller, this time at Doncaster, Molony bought him back in for a second time – only this time, when he told Maurice Kingsley what he had done, Kingsley refused to repay his trainer, arguing that Molony had paid too much for him. I believe Red Rum had been knocked down for 1,400 guineas or thereabouts.

Without an owner, Molony was left with Red Rum on his hands wondering how he would raise the money to pay for him. Then, the story goes, Kingsley rang the next day and said that he would take the horse after all. This must have seemed like great news to Tim – until the reality came home to him. What Kingsley had actually done was find a new owner for Red Rum; he was selling him on to Mrs Brotherton. That Kingsley seems to have been a real dodge-pot.

Tim was sick to lose Red Rum, but he was powerless to prevent Mrs Brotherton's trainer, Bobby Renton, from taking him back to his yard just outside Ripon in Yorkshire. Renton was an old-time horseman, very stiff in the saddle and very proper out of it. He had a huge house and a butler. He had trained Freebooter to win the National for Mrs Brotherton back in 1950, and was well over seventy when he rode his own last race. Renton trained Red Rum to win some races – including, crucially, some over hurdles.

But, the story goes, as a four-year-old Red Rum started to become intermittently lame and inconsistent. That's as may be, but around this time an Irishman called Tommy Stack had gone to Renton's yard to ride for him as an amateur jockey. Stack's earliest memories of Red Rum were recorded for posterity in a BBC documentary film made years after the old horse became a star. His judgement was not entirely complimentary, as he reported: 'He was always on his toes, jogging around the place. He was not the nicest horse to be riding out every day.'

One day Renton asked Stack to school Red Rum over fences at home, as he had a mind to run him in a novice chase. The horse would have been a five-year-old by then, I reckon. Stack says Red Rum blundered over the first fence, then at the second, which was an open ditch, dug his heels in and refused to jump at all. Stack turned him back and came at the fence a second time. Again, the horse stubbornly refused. The trainer told Stack to call it quits – for the day. 'He runs at Newcastle tomorrow,' said Renton. 'And you ride him.' Stacky thought to himself, 'Thanks very much, that's magic.' But he wouldn't dare refuse, so off they went to Newcastle – and Red Rum never put a foot wrong in a two-mile novice chase among a good-quality field. He finished third – and for many millions of people, not least me, that race proved to be a key point, because from then on Red Rum's life was over fences. After Renton retired, Stacky took over the trainer's licence. He hoped to train and ride, but, understandably, found he had too much on his plate, so he gave up his trainer's licence to concentrate on riding again. Into his place as trainer stepped Anthony Gillam, a gentlemanly sort of lad who'd had some rides as an amateur.

In April 1971, Martin Blackshaw rode Red Rum in the Scottish Grand National at Ayr. Apparently, Blackshaw was told to kick on from the bottom bend, but the instructions got confused and he kicked on from the top bend, way too far out. Even so, Red Rum ran a blinder to finish fifth.

This was the form that stuck in my mind when I was going through the catalogue for the Doncaster sales in the summer of 1972. I had tried to find out as much as I could about the horse, but there is only so much you are told – and I didn't know that Red Rum had consistently shown a touch of lameness after his races. Stack, an intelligent, likeable man, who would one day play an even bigger part in Red Rum's triumphant tale, was riding for a good friend of mine, Stan Wareing, and Stan suggested I ring Tommy and ask him about the horse. Tommy said the horse was an all right sort, but a bit 'footy'. Coming from an Irishman, that could cover a hundred things! Obviously, he was unable to go into great detail, as his first loyalty had to be to his own stable.

I also spoke with Blackshaw to get his opinion of Red Rum, and he said, yes, he's a grand young horse. It was then that he told me about how he had misunderstood the instructions he had been given in the Scottish National. 'I got a real bollocking when I came back,' said Martin. All in all, I felt reassured by what I had been told. He obviously stayed. Anyway, I would back my own judgement.

Now, people have since claimed that they knew Red Rum was qualified to race in the Grand National, but I am willing to dispute that. I don't think anyone but me had done his or her homework to the extent of realizing that, as Red Rum had won a three-mile chase at Catterick worth £1,500, he was qualified for Liverpool.

Excited, I had to let the Guv'nor know my discovery. When I went into his lovely lounge, he was sitting in his chair by the fire as always. He had a glass in his hand, and soon I had one as well.

'Guv'nor, there's a horse coming up for sale at Doncaster that might be good enough to run at Liverpool and he *is* qualified.'

He asked the horse's name, and I told him. Sharp as a tack, he asked: 'Do you realize what that spells backwards?'

I didn't – it's as much as I can do to spell my own name.

'Murder!'

He liked that, and he asked me what he thought the horse would fetch. Truth to tell, I wasn't sure. I guessed that he might attract bids of £4,000 or thereabouts. Of course, this was hugely more than I'd ever spent on a horse. In fact, before that I'd never even been given above

1,000 guineas, and that happened to be from the Guv'nor when I bought Glenkiln for him. At least Glenkiln had won a race by this time, even if it was only at Cartmel.

Mr Le Mare reached for a pen and began writing. When he had finished, he handed over the piece of paper to me. I read it slowly: 'I hereby authorize Ginger McCain to go to the sum of up to seven thousand guineas for the horse Red Rum.' His signature was scrawled underneath.

I had another couple of large Scotches on that, didn't I? I came out of the house jumping and kicking, damn near doing somersaults. I couldn't get home quickly enough to tell Beryl. She remarked how coincidental it was that the name of Red Rum's dam – Mared – sounded and looked similar to the Guv'nor's own name, Le Mare. We both hoped it might prove to be a good omen.

A few days later, I headed off for Doncaster sales, a journey of about 110 miles from Southport. I went to see the horse and he looked an absolute picture as he stood in his box. He was good-looking; I'd describe him as a big, quality Flat horse, not one of these raw-boned chasers. I thought he looked good enough to run in the Derby, I really did. I didn't hang around his box for long, though. The last thing you want is for someone to notice that you are interested in a particular horse.

In the ring it was busy, and I took up my usual pitch in the balcony. When Red Rum was led in he did look tremendous, yet I recollect that the bidding still opened as low as 1,000 guineas. Harry Beeby was the auctioneer, and a good one. He had dark curly hair and a lovely manner – and, unlike Ken Oliver, he didn't invent phantom bids from you either! I got in at round about 3,000 guineas. I'm a motor-car trader, so I know the ropes, don't I? Basically, the art is not to let anyone else see you are bidding. They want to know whom they are taking on and are keen to see if the horse is just being run up to the reserve placed on it. By being as discreet as possible I had more chance of keeping my identity a secret. I'd just nod my head a fraction, or raise an eyebrow. Once the auctioneer knows you are involved, he'll watch you.

Anyway, a new bidder came in at 4,000 guineas. I had no intention of being beaten now, but I didn't have too much of a margin to work with. I think the bid had been driven up to 4,600 guineas when I decided to use a ploy that is common at motor auctions. I wanted this horse more than any other I'd ever bid for. I knew what had to be done. I had to be cool, though my heart was pumping, and I had to make an incisive move. I was outwardly calm when Harry Beeby next looked in my direction. 'S-I-X,' I mouthed. Old Harry looked bemused. I saw him raise his eyebrows, questioning what I wanted.

So I raised one hand and a finger from the other one. In one jump, I had raised the bidding to 6,000 guineas. Did anyone have the nerve to come with me? Nobody came back. Next minute, Harry's hammer is down, bang! I was thrilled – but also scared to death. This was suddenly the big league. Out of the sales ring went Red Rum – and I rushed after him.

It was a beautiful sunny day; I can remember it like yesterday. As I looked at Red Rum, now back in his box, young Tony Gillam came towards me. 'Are you the buyer?' he asked. I told him I was.

'What do you intend to do with him?' he asked.

'I thought we might go to Liverpool,' I replied.

'Not a bad idea,' said Gillam. He was a lovely young fellow, and told me what he knew about Red Rum. It was clear he was sickened to lose the horse.

And that was it – oh, except that I bought another horse that day for another owner. I paid 940 guineas for The Tunku, and he went into the horsebox with Red Rum for the drive back to Southport

A few hours later, we pulled up outside the car showroom, dropped the ramp and led Red Rum into his new home. Of course, he was given pride of place, in the first stable on the right-hand side of the little cobbled yard. We could keep an eye on him from the back windows of our flat. How could we have possibly known then that this lovely bay horse would change our lives for ever?

I DON'T THINK there was another trainer in the country then who used a beach as their gallops. I had little option as our yard was in the middle of town and most of the surrounding countryside was used for arable farming. There were no meadows as such. One or two others, like Fred Clarke and Frank Speakman, had trained racehorses in Southport in a small way before me. When I worked for Frank, he had permission to gallop his horses on the grass at a nearby aerodrome, but even then he could only take his horses when there were no planes flying. That seemed pretty sensible.

In the beginning, we never prepared the beach. It was trial and error, really. There were times when the sand was absolutely brilliant the moment we arrived, but other days it was a mess. You see, the council used to tip much of its rubbish into the sea, and a lot of it used to be washed up on the shore. But the beach was the beach to us: mile after mile of sand for the horses. You could do a steady canter in a straight line for four or five miles if you wanted.

We broke a few horses down on the beach, but every trainer has a horse break down now and then – by which I mean a horse sustains an injury in training; sometimes it just sets them back, but on other times it signals the end of their career. Anyway, the vast majority of the horses I had were bad-legged from the time I had them. Trainers today get lovely material, and most of them wouldn't know the first thing about a bad-legged horse. They rely totally on a vet. Actually, there's not a lot a vet can tell you. If a horse has got a 'leg', he's got a 'leg'. What do you give a horse like that? Time, that's all.

Before do-gooders interfered, you could 'fire' a horse's bad leg. There were two forms of firing: pin-firing was done with a red-hot needle, while bar-firing was done with a poker striping the leg or shin. It had the effect of cauterizing the leg and tightened things up, causing a flow of blood to the area. It did a beautiful job. But a few years ago it was banned in this country – not by horse vets, but by budgie vets and cat vets. And what happened then? There were boatloads of horses sent to Ireland to be fired. A few older vets in this country continued the practice, too, defying the authorities to lock them up. I'm not talking about Mickey Mouse vets, I'm talking about good, experienced men.

Nowadays, you get told that the only cure for a leg injury is to rest a horse for twelve months. Old-style vets didn't have the anaesthetics or painkillers available today. So they would rub a blister in. The horse would be climbing up the wall and he would have the sweat running off him for two days. These men were hard – you could say brutal on occasions – but they knew how to cure horses far better then, and kept them on the road. If that sounds like I am advocating cruelty to horses, I am not. I am saying that sometimes it is necessary to be tough for the horse's ultimate benefit. It is just a matter of being practical.

Look at prints or photos of old chasers. They were either heavily bandaged or had hard-fired legs and goodness knows what – tall, gaunt horses that withstood a hell of a lot. I have always run my horses big – too big some might say, carrying too much condition. I'd love to have them looking leaner and a lot harder, but if I get them looking like that I start to think I'm not doing the job properly. So most of my horses run tending to look a bit on the big side – it's as simple as that.

Occasionally, another trainer came to Southport to use the beach. Colin Crossley, who trained on the Wirral, called me one day to ask how far we could take the horses. 'How far do you want?' I replied. I assured him that he could get two and a half miles without any problem. He brought three horses over. One was a tough, hard chestnut called Scoria who was entered in the Tote Cesarewitch Handicap at Newmarket. He jumped one of his other two horses in with Scoria and they went a mile, maybe slightly further. When that horse, who'd won two or three races, had tired, he slipped his other horse in alongside Scoria. Old Scoria put his head down and galloped and galloped. Later, at home, I told Beryl that I had seen Colin Crossley's horse leave his Cesarewitch on the beach as I thought he'd done too much. I was sure of it; but Scoria went down to Newmarket and won. Shows what I know – or knew at that stage. I would come to learn that horses are like athletes: some need hard work while others need more sensitive handling.

The beach and the sea had another critical advantage as far as I was concerned. If you had a bad-legged horse, you took him in the sea. We always worked the horses away from home on the principle that if a horse is travelling away from his stable he will not pull as hard as he will when he is coming back. At the end of the work, if the tide was anywhere near striking distance, the girths would be loosened off and the horses would walk back in the sea for a mile, or sometimes a mile and half. I always thought it was very good for them – salt water is bursting with minerals.

I never forgot as a boy seeing the shrimpers working the beach. These men used high-wheeled, horse-drawn carts, and they would trawl a net either side of the cart, with their animals often chest-deep in the water. These shrimpers were miserable men and deeply religious, and never missed church on Sundays. They bought horses that were probably destined for the knacker's yard, right old cripples when they began working on the beach. Yet after they had been in the sea for a couple of hours, twice a day, they became transformed animals. Within no time, these broken-down horses would start to come off the beach and strike out along the promenade with a breezy step. It was an image that never left me. Their recuperation could only have been caused by their trips into the sea. They were pushing and working against the water, but without any stress on their joints or feet.

I tell you this about the beach, sea water and old nags making miraculous recoveries for a good reason. Because the morning after we brought Red Rum home, I got a nasty shock.

Chapter Eight

BEACH BOYS

I'D GONE AHEAD to the beach to prepare the gallop, as by now we understood more about the job. I towed a harrow behind an old pickup truck or a Land Rover to smooth the sand. If the sand was particularly hard, we'd place old bits of old driftwood on top of the harrow to provide the weight needed to make the spikes bite.

Anxiously, I waited for Red Rum to appear. Robin Greenway, our vet's son, was staying with us and I'd asked him to ride our new horse from the yard. Robin had won a race on Glenkiln a couple of months earlier, so I was content for him to ride our prized newcomer down the streets that led to the beach. At last, after struggling for all those years, I had got my good horse. I had eyes only for Red Rum on this morning, and I was excited and tense in equal measure as he came into view.

He came on to the sand, and Robin asked him to trot. But wait . . . what had I seen? The horse was favouring a leg – Red Rum was lame. Oh shit, I thought. I've gone and spent all my only good owner's money on a bloody lame duck; or, more precisely, a lame racehorse.

Quickly, I pulled my thoughts together. I remembered those shrimpers with their crippled horses and I shouted to Robin, 'Put him in the sea!' Red Rum had never even seen the sea before, but he didn't blink an eyelid as he walked knee-deep into the water. He stayed in the sea for around an hour. When he came out he was as sound as a pound. To this day, I can't properly explain what really happened. But those shrimpers had cured many a horse by taking them in the sea, and the trick had worked wonders for Red Rum. He never took another lame step until the day before he should have run in his last Grand National in 1978.

The picture gained a little clarity when I delved into his history. I discovered that at some stage Red Rum had been diagnosed with pedalostitis, a debilitating bone disease that usually signals the end of a racehorse's career. All manner of things had been tried to get him sound, I found out. For instance, Red had been given a total blood transfusion in Yorkshire. But nothing had put him right until we walked him into the sea that first morning.

Red Rum's good fortune – and mine, come to that – was that our other great asset, besides the recuperative powers of the salt water in the Irish Sea, was a blacksmith called Bob Marshall. Bob wasn't a fancy man. He lived on a local council estate and he had been around for an age. He'd shod my first horse from Frank Speakman, Scottish Humour. He charged a pound for a set of shoes – that's 25p per foot. I priced a blacksmith a few months ago and it was sixty pounds. Now, I begrudge paying thirty quid for a set of bloody shoes for myself, never mind twice that for a horse. I thought it shattering.

Bob was great. Bob was his own man, an old-fashioned blacksmith in the days when they were more like veterinarians. They did both jobs. Bob had been a smith since the streets of Southport were over-run with horses. Like a mechanic with a car today, it was a blacksmith's role to keep a horse on the road. From the moment we first saw that Red Rum had his problems, Bob took care of him. No other person ever shod him. He wouldn't let anyone else touch his feet. Neither would I.

So I put the fact that the horse stayed sound down to the brilliant blacksmith we had. Later on, Bob's son Robin, who followed in his footsteps, talked his father into entering the British championship for blacksmiths – and Bob won, which was no surprise to me. When he was older, Robin emigrated to Canada and became a kind of professor of the blacksmith's art, lecturing at shows all over North America. When Bob retired, he went out to join his son. Robin persuaded him to start shoeing again and Bob won the world championship at the Calgary Stampede. That was the quality of the blacksmith that he was.

On occasions, I'd go and find him of an evening in the Railway Tavern at Ainsdale to tell him what horses needed his attention the next morning. 'Don't let me down,' I'd say.

'I'll be there, Don, don't worry about it,' Bob would reply.

I'd get up at half-past six and there'd be no sign of him. I'd be hopping mad. Eventually, I'd track him down and Bob would ask: 'Have you looked at the horses?' He'd been in at four o'clock. This must have happened three or four times. Lovely, lovely man. I owe a lot to Bob Marshall.

Around the time we acquired Red Rum, I was struck by the fact that world champion boxer Sugar Ray Robinson had taken his own hairdresser with him wherever he went. I thought, well, if Sugar Ray had a personal hairdresser, Red Rum can have his own blacksmith. So, when Red Rum went racing, Bob went with him. I'm sure he would have done it for nothing, but I gave him a fiver a day anyway. Even though he had put on Red's racing plates the night before, I wanted him there in case anything went wrong. Quite simply, racing plates are light alloy shoes as opposed to heavy solid metal ones, and they are designed to improve a horse's speed. Think of it like this: when Henry Cooper did his roadwork in training, he would go on his early morning run wearing army boots; then, when he put on lightweight boots to box, he felt the benefit from having strengthened muscles in his calves, while carrying less weight on his feet. He was lighter and faster in his movement. It's the same principle at work with horses – with an additional safety advantage: racing plates lessen the chance of a horse hurting himself badly should he strike into himself when galloping or landing over a fence.

So, with Bob looking after his feet it was our job to get Red Rum ready to return to the racecourse. When we came out of the yard, we turned left into Upper Aughton Road and crossed the railway line. We used to come down the middle of the road – and basically Red Rum would go where he wanted. He was a right old showman. He'd go sideways up the road, jumping, plunging and kicking like he was carrying a gunslinger coming into town in a Western. People would step back to get out of his way, moving to the other side of the road to stand under the canopies above the little parade of shops. Then, once we'd turned the corner, he'd drop his head and walk off like a good old Christian. But although the old horse was a showman, he never, ever acted the fool. If the ground was slippery, he would never do anything silly. That was the kind of pro he was.

When we got nearer the beach, we would go along a path between Royal Birkdale and Hillside golf clubs that went straight through to Ainsdale. We'd work the horses on the beach, then come back through the sand hills. Some of the hills were really steep, and they had the effect of making the horses think all the time. They used to sit down on their backsides and slide down them, but they loved it. Some of the bolder ones would take off and jump six, maybe eight feet. They would glide though the air and then land on the soft sand and skid. The boys enjoyed it – but it wasn't for the faint-hearted. You had to sit right back in the saddle, and let them have a long rein. It was all good fun, and meant things were never monotonous – and the horses were getting themselves fit, because they were using muscles that they would never use on flat ground. It was as nice a way of training horses as any I can think of, and they always had a good footing. We had enough horses by now to have to take them out in two lots, the first horses pulling out around 8 a.m. Beryl rode out, too.

From the start, Red Rum loved the sea. He'd damn near have breakers knocking him over, but he loved it. Most of them did once they got used to it. An occasional horse might panic, especially if a breaker or two rattled his ribs, but for the majority it proved to be a great preparation. I think it helped them mentally as much as physically. You could have a horse a little bit sore at the end of a gallop, put him in the sea and walk him back and he'd come out of the tide sound. I don't mean that he would stay sound, but it had been good enough to get him sound until he came out of the sea. Then, what you would do is jump off and lead him home and hope that the treatment you gave him at the stables would complete his recovery. Unquestionably, we found the sea to have a pretty good healing power. It wasn't a cure-all, it would be daft to suggest it was. But it certainly helped.

The Guv'nor liked to be kept up with the news of Red Rum, but he never interfered. He left me to my own devices, rarely if ever coming to watch Red work on the beach. Mr Le Mare was content for me to make all the decisions.

WE CARRIED ON training Red Rum in this fashion, all the time planning when we might race him next. We had a bit of a quandary, as from the enquiries that we'd made we had been told the horse wanted soft ground. But I decided not to wait and entered him for a three-mile chase at Carlisle when the ground was still firm from the good autumn weather. I rang Tommy Stack and asked him if he would ride Red Rum on 30 September 1972. He said he would, but reinforced the message that he thought the ground would be a bit quick for him. On the big day – well, we were all nervous as to how our very expensive, good horse was going to run – I met Tommy in the paddock, and clearly, from what he said, he wasn't expecting a great deal. I told him he might be surprised. There were four runners – and Red Rum won by twenty lengths on the bridle, running well within himself.

Eleven days later he won with Ron Barry in the saddle at Wetherby, and a fortnight after that Tommy was back on board at Newcastle. Tommy cut lumps off him that day. He looked beat, but he battled back, head down, running for the line, to get up on the post. I remember Tommy coming in and asking me to get the sheet on Red Rum in double-quick time before anyone could get too close a look at him.

'I've been a bit hard on him,' he said. Now, that was a very fair statement. Red Rum was striped on both sides of his flanks – he wasn't just a sergeant, he was a top sergeant. These days jockeys would get locked up if they took their stick to a horse like they did then – but that's how it was. An old boss of mine didn't think his horse had been given a ride if he didn't come back with stripes on.

Red Rum had beautiful skin, but it was thin and he marked very easily, no question. Yet I was conscious of the towsing he'd had so I nipped over to the stables to see how he was. I didn't know what I would find – and I was a bit worried. At Newcastle racecourse, there is a square grass yard in front of the stables, and when I got there I saw a horse with all four feet off the floor having a right jump and kick. The boy hanging on to him had his eyes popping out of his head. It was Red Rum. He'd just run three miles over fences and been slapped on both sides, and had lumps like a bunch of grapes down one shoulder, yet here he was doing somersaults as bold as you like. That was the courage of the horse; that was his vitality. He was a tough, tough horse.

Tommy Stack rode us another winner at Haydock Park, then Brian Fletcher was in the saddle when Red Rum won yet again at Ayr. In a little over six weeks, he had won five races on the trot. Fletcher would become associated with Red Rum's success in the Grand National, but he could be a bit hard on the horses he rode.

The jockeys these days are powder-puff men as opposed to the old ones. They ride with padded whips – and I am not saying that is wrong. Their behaviour is more closely scrutinized on the racecourse, and that is no bad thing either. But to be fair, if a thin-skinned horse is sweating I could leave fine marks on him with just a slap of my hand. Stewards don't take this into consideration.

Today, we listen to all these self-anointed experts who say that if a horse won't run for one slap, he won't run for five. What nonsense they talk. Fred Archer used to cut horses to pieces when he rode 2,748 winners in the later years of the nineteenth century – and if he was hitting them for nothing there has to have been an awful lot of bad jockeys over the centuries that didn't know what the devil they were doing. I don't accept that is true. It has to be an effective way of encouraging a horse to dig deeper within himself.

A racehorse is a very hard-trained athlete. You don't put a footballer into a match without him being prepared to be tackled. You don't put a boxer a ring without him being prepared to get punched. The same applies to rugby players and cricketers. In sport, you've got to expect to take knocks. Now, I'm not advocating thrashing horses, not for one minute. But a few backhanders in the right place never did any harm – or did very, very few horses any harm. Anyway, this modern-day whip controversy, with jockeys finding themselves in the dock with the stewards for over-use of their stick, came to the foreground of the sport because some lads who know no better go on flogging a beaten horse. And when I say beaten, I mean they are still knocking spots off them when they are half a furlong behind.

Another factor is the annoying trend nowadays of jockeys riding with short leathers. In the old days jockeys rode longer of the leg. As a young man, I can recall standing at about the furlong marker to watch the horses come past. The whips would be pinging off the horses, making the sound like a stick being pulled along a piece of corrugated iron, especially in a Flat race. And the jockeys were kicking their horses out with their legs. These jockeys today can't kick a horse out with their legs because they're perched up on the back. So they bang their arses down on the saddle and try to bump them forward – and many of them wouldn't know how to use a stick properly. I am not a great believer in this modern style. To me, it kills much of the horsemanship. I know things never look the same when you're getting old and grumpy, but this is a hard sport. Jockeys are hard men riding hard horses.

When it comes to a schooling session at home, and you find yourself dealing with a dirty horse, there is only one way you are going to cure him. You've got to get after him. By a dirty horse, I mean one that is likely to come round and kick you or something like that. Or else it might be a complete ignorant fool. In either instance, you've got to teach them manners. For most of them, it's no good patting them on the neck and being nice. With some, you have to get stuck into them and let them know who's boss. These days it is politically incorrect to talk about 'breaking in' a horse – you have to say 'handling' instead. But at the end of the day, you are breaking a horse and that's all there is to it. If the right people are doing the job, the job gets done with a minimum of pain and effort.

Some hard, hard men down the years hit Red Rum. There was no harder man than Lester Piggott on the Flat, and there were no harder men that Paddy Broderick, Josh Gifford or Brian Fletcher in the jumping game. In all, twenty-four different jockeys rode him. He was not discouraged by the experience, and nor did the old horse go sour or become what I call a thief and try to take short cuts. He was always gay and bright and just glad to be with people.

Red Rum was a May foal, and because all Thoroughbreds are given the same birthday of 1 January, that put him as much as five months behind some of his contemporaries. He was bred, as I said, to be a Flat horse, and a cheap one at that: the type that are basically worn out by the time they're three-year-olds. I suppose that was considered his destiny. But through good luck or good fortune, or perhaps a bit of both, Red Rum proved himself born to be a chaser.

After he had won those five races in a row, all three- or three-and-a-half-mile chases, he went up from 10st to 12st plus in the handicap in the north of England. And we were starting to become better known, I suppose. As everything had happened so quickly, I suggested to Mr Le Mare that we should put him on ice and bring him back in the spring. The Guv'nor was always very good in accepting advice. 'You think so, Ginger, then you do it,' he said. So we eased him off, and just let him paddle around the sea and hack through the sand hills.

*

NOBODY HAD ALL-WEATHER gallops at that time, but I don't think we quite appreciated what we had on the beach. I was a bit brainwashed by a shrewd, old trainer called Fred Clarke, whom I'd known for years and who was convinced that we would struggle until we had a grass gallop. He stayed with us from time to time in the early days and was a sort of assistant to me. I always enjoyed having a talk with him. He had trained at Southport before the war and was hooked on horses, even though he had made a successful living in business. He was a top-class stableman, with old-fashioned virtues. He stayed in the next-door flat at the yard with the boys, who, left to their own untidy ways, had the place looking like a tip. But when Fred was there, the place was immaculate. Fred knew, too, about the benefits of giving horses supplements and salts, that kind of thing. He even knew how to give them a bit of assistance, as it were – something to make them go a shade quicker – which he used to do before the war. Of course, there wasn't the dope testing then.

Early on when Fred was around, we had very, very moderate horses. He always warned me that I'd never do any good until I got a grass gallop. I had an old four-horse transporter, a Dodge I think it was, and I do remember it only did eight miles to the gallon. We'd take the horses up to Parbold Hill and nip into the park to work them until we got caught. It was a full morning's job. Sadly, Fred died before we started winning.

Looking back now, I don't think we made as good a job with the beach gallop as we possibly should have done. We were always under pressure for a few quid for this and a few quid for that, always struggling. So I never really threw the boat out and said, 'Right, I'm going to have a tractor.' In fact, I did have one briefly. But if you had a loose horse, you could wind the tractor up as fast as possible and never get your horse. I got rid of it sharpish. Besides, with a Land Rover or pickup I could measure the gallop on the trip counter and the speedometer. I have never used a stop-watch in my life – I've left that to those American trainers. With Red Rum, as with the others, I'd drop off about twenty yards behind him in my Land Rover as he cantered along the beach. You never drove upsides with the horses because they would start taking the vehicle on.

The way that Southport beach shelves, the tide is always nearer to the shore at Ainsdale than it is at Birkdale. If it was early spring or autumn, when you had nice quiet tides, you'd have the horses in the water at chest-height and they would stay in the sea for ten or fifteen minutes. But in the winter there would be big breakers. I'll never forget one episode involving a horse named Prehistoric that belonged to the Guv'nor's son, Dennis. Like his name suggests, Prehistoric was a big, ugly horse, with enormous ears, and he was being ridden by a lad called Alfie. Well, they must have stepped down a shelf in the sand and when a big wave hit them, horse and rider vanished under the water. Moments later, the horse rose out of the sea like a monster, his ears flattened and water streaming off him. There was no sign of Alfie. Eventually, he turned up on the edge of a breaker about fifteen yards away. It was very funny.

The story of Prehistoric is one worthy of a larger audience, actually. Dennis Le Mare had asked us to find him a horse for Cheltenham, not Liverpool, as Red Rum was already on the scene for his father. We shopped around a bit – and decided to go for this horse named Prehistoric, trained in Ireland by Edward O'Grady. So we went over to Ireland with Ron Barry – and it was on this trip, incidentally, that I first came across John Magnier, whose Coolmore Stud is now one of the most prestigious breeding establishments in the world. My first impression of Magnier was that he was a big man who drove a Mercedes – I felt he was headed somewhere even then.

Prehistoric had won his 'bumper' – a race on the flat for potential hurdlers and chasers, to get them used to being on a racecourse – and was being talked up as likely to become one of the best novice chasers in Ireland. But they wanted rather a lot of money for him. Eventually a deal was struck around the swimming pool at the Europa Hotel in Killarney, at two o'clock in the morning after a few drinks. I agreed to pay £10,000 for the horse, with the proviso that Tommy Stack would ride him.

As it happened, our vet Ted Greenway, a decent jockey in his day, was in Ireland at the time, so I asked him to inspect the horse, which is customary before you complete a purchase. Ted rode Prehistoric and said that he could not fault him – yet nevertheless he didn't like the horse. Fair enough, I thought. Young Mr Le Mare wanted to know if he should insure his new acquisition. I told him that the decision was down to him, but I did tell him that the Guv'nor never insured his horses. He decided to follow his father's example – even though £10,000 was a vast sum of money at that time.

After we'd got him over we took Prehistoric to race at Haydock, and he was backed down to 7–4 favourite. It must have been all Irish money; it certainly hadn't come from the stable, as we weren't gamblers. From the start, Stack jumped Prehistoric into a commanding lead. Big and strong, the horse pulled away, eight or ten lengths clear at least. But as he came to the second last – it was a misty day – it looked like the horse was coming to the end of his tether; and bang, he turns arse over tip. I've as good as said to the owner, don't insure him, and here's the horse seemingly dead as a kipper. Great trainer I am. Anyhow, to my relief the horse struggled to his feet.

But the upshot is, Stacky no longer wants to ride Prehistoric. So when we took him to Doncaster, the horse's new jockey was a lad who looked like a choirboy called Jonjo O'Neill. He was a healthy-looking little lad, with the rosiest cheeks you'll ever see, and Ron Barry spoke very highly of him. But in the race, after they came past the stand, I watched Jonjo take out the first obstacle down the back of the course and come out of the hurdle ten lengths behind everything else.

Well, now I'm angrily jumping up and down in the stand. This was a very expensive horse – don't forget we had given only 6,000 guineas for Red Rum – and I was not best pleased with what was happening. I suspected that some older voices in the weighing room had put it in Jonjo's head that Prehistoric was a difficult ride. Eventually, the horse finished fourth and I thought Jonjo had let us down.

So when Jonjo came in, I got stuck into him. As I was tearing him off a strip, calling him all the names under the sun, he tried to speak. But I was in no mood to listen. At the end of my rant, I yelled at him, 'Go on, bugger off!' I was still on the steps of the weighing room when another jockey, Gerry Griffin, came to Jonjo's defence, telling me that I had no reason to be calling Jonjo names for the way he had ridden. In fact, said Griffin, Jonjo had been no less than brilliant on the horse.

What had happened, I learned, was that at that first fence down the back straight Prehistoric had landed with his head touching the ground, ending up with both reins on one side and leaving Jonjo without any steering. After a struggle, he had managed to scoop the reins back, but only after he had got to the top of the hill. Then he had put Prehistoric back in the race and astonishingly got him running on again to finish fourth. It had been an absolutely brilliant piece of horsemanship – and he came back to get a right old bollocking from me. He'd been trying to tell me what had happened to him, but he couldn't get a word in edgeways as I cursed him uphill and down dale. I apologized, naturally. And we have had many a laugh over that introduction to our relationship.

For me, Jonjo O'Neill is an absolute star of our game and a lovely man, too. As a jockey he was second to none as far as I'm concerned – and that takes into account the incredible record of Tony McCoy. Jonjo was more fragile than McCoy. He broke bones more easily. But he was such a competitive little lad he couldn't help himself. He had to throw his horse into the fence or into the hurdle, no matter what. It was that strength of character, that remarkable spirit, that no doubt proved vital when Jonjo was diagnosed with cancer in later years. He was determined to win the hardest fight of all – and he did.

We actually gave Jonjo his debut ride in the Grand National on Glenkiln; yes, the same Glenkiln that I had mistakenly withdrawn from a previous National. In October 1972 I took the horse to the BP Grand National trial over two miles six furlongs at Liverpool, where Gordon Richards had the short-priced favourite. Jimmy Bourke rode our horse and he was a good man round Liverpool. Before the race, Fred Clarke suggested to Beryl, 'I don't know why Ginger has entered him as he hasn't got a cat in hell's chance of winning.' Glenkiln was never headed in the race – and qualified himself for the 1973 Grand National and forever after.

If Glenkiln had done that beforehand, as I'd intended, we would never have bought Red Rum – that's a fact. Strange how things work out for a purpose in life, isn't it?

Chapter Nine

GRAND NATIONAL

I SAID WHEN Red Rum started to become a good horse that I wouldn't sit on him until he retired. If truth were known, I didn't want to insult him. A lad called Billy Ellison had him to start with while Jackie Grainger was my head lad. Jackie was a good bit older than me, of course, but we had become friends. I had met Grainger when I was a kid show-jumping and he had just been demobbed. He was a good horseman and a cracking stableman, even if he was a bit of a gypsy. He was positive in his outlook, and a hard-headed man: he'd give the lads a clip round the ears or get stuck into them, taking them into a box and giving them a bit of a shaking. He was that sort of fellow. When he'd had a drink or two his eyes used to pop out of his head. He was a bit of an actor, too. But I had admiration and respect for him, and that admiration lasted until he fell foul of me.

Ellison, too, went the wrong way in the end, but at the outset he was an asset, along with Grainger. Ellison was not that good-looking a lad, in fact he was a squat little bugger who couldn't see properly. Yet he could pull the birds out of the trees. He knew how to feed the horses and he was one of the two best lads I ever had at strapping a horse.

When you strap a horse it is like giving him a massage: slap slap, slap, slap. Racing lads today wouldn't know what you were talking about if you asked them to strap a horse out. Now, when I was growing up in stables you went to do your horse up at night and took your jacket off and rolled up your sleeves and got to work. You started with a sponge, and then you used your body brush and stable rubber or hay wisp. And that's when you started slapping your horse. You began at the back of his head and worked down. The muscles contracted and tightened. By the time you finished you would be sweating and tingling, even in the middle of winter. Then you knew you'd done your horse properly. But that's gone out of the window completely. Boys in good yards never did more than three horses; in the top yards they would only do two. Nowadays, boys (and girls, of course) are doing three, four and five horses. And there is not the time. To this day I still insist on my better horses being strapped out. For instance, Sian has always strapped Amberleigh House and that seems to have worked out OK, hasn't it?

Ellison on Red Rum and Grainger on Glenkiln would work upsides on the beach as we trained the two horses to run in the 1973 Grand National. In reality, we used Glenkiln as a yardstick for Red. He was a good horse in his own right, but he wasn't as a tough as Red Rum, who was a bit of a destroyer when it came to work companions. He jumped off and never liked to be headed. He may have been largely one-paced, but he was in charge. I remember seeing Billy just sat there with legs out front locked against him. And that did the old horse's ego all the good in the world, he really loved that sort of thing. The lad might think he was in charge, but Red Rum knew he was the boss.

With both Tommy Stack and Ron Barry unavailable, and remembering that Brian Fletcher had given Red Rum a good ride at Ayr to win his fifth successive race, I decided to ask Fletcher to partner the horse in the National. We took Red Rum to Carlisle at the end of January, then a week later we went to Haydock, returning to the same track at the beginning of March. He finished third, second and third; and there was no doubt that people had taken notice of him.

With one month to go to the Grand National, Red Rum and his companion Glenkiln knuckled down to their work on the beach at Southport beside the rhythm of the sea. On the eve of the biggest race of my life – never mind the horses'! – I asked my good friend Stan Wareing to come and watch them gallop on the sand. I didn't know it then, but this was the start of what would become a ritual for us on the eve of the great race. Stan had a big pig farm at Halsall on the road from Southport to Aintree. He shared my love for life and a bit of craic, and I valued his opinion.

As usual, Billy rode Red Rum, with Jackie on Glenkiln. We had already become celebrities of a kind, and there was also a television crew filming on the beach. The horses worked over one and a half miles – but something nagged at me inside and told me to send them back again. So they galloped at full speed over another four furlongs. Was it reckless? Was it a calculated gamble? I couldn't give you a truthful answer. I was responding to a gut instinct. I just felt that I needed to see them do some more work to be confident that I'd done my job and was sending them to the big race as fit as they could possibly be. Others might have felt that demanding a second gallop could have been over-working them so close to the National. It is not something you can legislate for – you have to react to what you've seen. I decided I wanted them to have another run. All I can tell you is that at evening stables the horses were as sound as I could hope.

The next morning – 31 March 1973 – Beryl plaited Red's mane in his box. At around 10.30 a.m. I watched my two horses being led up the ramp of our old horsebox to begin their journey to Aintree, some sixteen miles away. Grainger and Ellison went with the horses, proud as Punch. This was a day I had dared not dream about, really. I certainly hadn't aspired to winning the National; that was much too grand for me. I was still a second-hand-car dealer who kept some racehorses in a cobbled yard behind a showroom on a busy road in Southport. But I did take the job seriously, and I did believe I was sending two rather fit horses to be competitive in the greatest steeplechase in the world. I travelled in hope, but not much more than that. One thing was for sure, however. I was going to enjoy myself.

Beryl and I had been invited to Stan and Carol Wareing's home, as they had arranged a Grand National party. We were among friends – and the shampoo flowed like water. Stan was a great champagne man. I told them that I believed in that old adage: win or lose, we'll have the booze. It was not about being cavalier or anything of the kind. Simply put, there was nothing more we could do; Grainger and Ellison were competent with the horses and the work had been done. Stan and Carol were perfect hosts – and the morning's few scoops relaxed us nicely.

Stan insisted that Beryl and I should travel to the racecourse in his Rolls-Royce. A red ribbon had been tied round the Silver Lady on the bonnet for good luck. In all, six of us squeezed into the car and we set off with the others in convoy. It's such a long time ago now, I am not going to pretend I can remember exactly how I felt. But I do know I was a happy man – and I wasn't the least apprehensive. I was pretty confident we were going to run a good race. I'm not a nervous type, and from the earliest days when Red Rum was turning into a good horse I told Beryl: 'We are going to enjoy him. We're going to get the press and others climbing on our backs, but they're just doing jobs like we all do jobs, so we'll be nice, and we'll be helpful provided it doesn't interfere with the horse. Let's try to do it right.' And that's what I think – hope – we did. Mostly, I found the press and television people good to work with.

At Aintree, I went to the stables to check the horses were settled. Those stables reek of history, and as I approached Red Rum in Box 46, virtually opposite the stable manager's office, I certainly didn't imagine that on this very day the horse was about to begin carving out his own place in that history.

We reconvened with our friends for another glass or two at the bar, and there was a real buzz about the place. These were the days before corporate hospitality boxes were introduced, but Mr Le Mare had a private table in the upstairs dining room in the Queen Mother Stand, where he also had seats reserved for his company guests. There was a touch of Edwardian antiquity about the arrangements. I went to pay my respects to the Guv'nor and to let him know that everything was all right.

Actually, at the time, it is worth pointing out, the Guv'nor thought Glenkiln had a better chance in the race than Red Rum. That is why Jonjo O'Neill was wearing his first colours of maroon shirt and cap, both decorated with a yellow diamond. They were the colours of his company Norwest. Brian Fletcher could be distinguished as he wore a plain yellow cap. And do you know, those now-famous colours Red Rum carried were never registered in his lifetime? It was years later that a diligent clerk of the course at Carlisle said to me: 'Mr McCain, those are incorrect colours. The cap should be maroon with a yellow star.' But as it was Red Rum – by then a national treasure – he never said another word, bless him. After the old lad had died, Beryl picked up on it, not me. I'm far too thick! She said that if we didn't act someone else would register the colours and history could be rewritten. So she went ahead and sorted out the registration details – and now Beryl McCain has Red Rum's colours.

Of course, Beryl had a new outfit for the Grand National. I will say with some pride that my wife always looks very smart indeed. She has style and a bit of poise. The only dose of bad luck she ever had was marrying me – well, that goes without saying. And I am always proud to take her anywhere. I wouldn't tell her that, but I am. As for me, I think in those days I had a brown sheepskin coat with a big collar. In recent years, you might have seen me at the races in my trilby, but back in '73 I probably didn't have a hat on as I used to have a decent head of hair then! In all honesty, though, I didn't care what anyone was wearing. All that was important to me at that moment was the horses.

Liverpool is entirely a law unto itself. You get some old horses, staying chasers long in the tooth, who go to Liverpool and become revitalized as they have to think their way into every fence – and think their way out, too. They're not just bowling along on autopilot to meet standard fences and jumping them like they've been doing all their lives. Then you get others who will go there, take on four or five of the fences and spit the dummy. The fences used to stand up straight like walls, not bellied out as they are now to make a horse stand off and bend his back. That's grand – but Liverpool has to represent the toughest challenge to horse and rider, and the uniqueness of the Grand National has to be protected. No other fences in the world are built like the ones on the National course at Aintree. The timber comes up absolutely straight and it's as thick as my wrist. Okay, they place spruce in the top six or eight inches, but if a horse gets below that, then that's it. The fences turn them over. And that's how it should be. The Grand National is supposed to be a challenge like none other. That's why I talk about horses with the 'Aintree Factor'. Red Rum most definitely had it. He went on to become a very different horse on park courses. But take him to Liverpool and he loved it. He forgot that he was racing.

The buzz on the racecourse on National day is phenomenal. From this first visit, I got into the habit of bringing Red Rum out of his box early. I thought he would be motivated by the atmosphere, that it would get him on his toes, so I liked us to be in the first three or four horses in the paddock. I saddled him with Grainger. We were a good team. He always used to say, 'Pass me the girth . . . check.' All you heard out of Jackie was check . . . check . . . check. But the job was done right. He had the old horseman's trick of blowing his breath out the entire time – to soothe the horses, they used to say. Of course, that too has gone by the board these days.

When the jockeys finally arrived in the ring, the Guv'nor was waiting for Fletcher and O'Neill. He said to them just what he always said to his jockeys: 'Good luck and come back safely.' But Mr Le Mare was conscious that this was the last Grand National to be run while Aintree was still in the ownership of Mirabel Topham, an actress of some repute in her younger days, before the course fell into the hands of property developer Bill Davies. The Guv'nor liked Mrs Topham and the traditions she stood for at Liverpool. He wanted to win the race – and didn't mind who knew it.

I didn't see the point in giving Fletcher any instructions. He'd won the Grand National on Red Alligator five years earlier. He knew far more about what to expect and what to do than I did. He was the jockey – and, as the old expression goes, what's the point in keeping a dog and barking yourself? I can't remember what he told me his plan was now, but it was along the lines that he would settle Red Rum, then move up on the second circuit. He was a very good jockey, or he had been. In a way, I think, at this point in his career he was trying to make a comeback, having slipped down the ladder after sustaining a bad head injury in a fall. Part of the problem was that, perhaps because he came from County Durham and had a thick accent, Fletcher wasn't a great communicator. He didn't manage to sell himself well.

After watching Red Rum and Glenkiln leave the paddock, I went to find a vantage point from which to watch the race. There is a place reserved for owners and trainers at the top of the County Stand. To get there you are required to walk up an old and narrow winding staircase. The press use the same stairs to get to their viewing point just behind where we were entitled to stand. Yet the reality is that if you leave it until after your horse has left for the parade, the owners' and trainers' stand is jammed before you can get there. Typically, it was full of people who have no right to be there. I managed to find myself a spot, though.

The Grand National is raced over 4 miles 856 yards, and features thirty fences with evocative names like The Chair, Becher's Brook, the Canal Turn, Valentine's. And then there is the Foinavon fence: the smallest obstacle on the course, named after the 100–1 outsider who won the 1967 Grand National by sidestepping the carnage that accounted for all the horses ahead of him as they fell or refused in the pile-up at this previously innocuous obstacle.

That spring of 1973, thirty-eight horses went to the start line to compete for a first prize of £25,486. Red Rum was sent off joint 9–1 favourite with a big Australian horse called Crisp who carried top weight of 12st and who was being ridden by Richard Pitman. Crisp had been sent from Australia to Fred Winter's yard at Lambourn to be trained for the race. When he arrived I seem to remember he had a woolly coat as he had been out of season at home. He looked a bull of a horse. The ground was firm, as Red Rum liked – but so did Crisp.

Once the starter released the tape restraining the horses, it was like a cavalry charge to the first fence; it always is, and it probably always will be. I followed the race through my binoculars – this was, of course, many years before the advent of big diamond screens. Imagine my sense of pride when I saw Red Rum and Glenkiln upsides in the air together as they cleared Becher's for the first time. After Becher's, though, it was Crisp who took up the race at a right gallop.

Pitman just stretched the field out behind him. Crisp was magnificent in the way he was jumping from fence to fence. He made nothing of those big, big obstacles. But I couldn't help thinking he was jumping just a shade too high; and the higher you get, the more energy you are using. Red Rum just slipped over his fences, like the old pro he was, and he was always making ground: half a length, sometimes a length, at each one.

We lost Glenkiln at The Chair, almost in front of us. He took a kick from another horse flying over his head, but still – now minus Jonjo – went to jump the next, the water jump. The horse was in cuckoo land, clearly concussed. When I looked up to follow the race, Crisp must have been more than thirty lengths in front. But Red Rum was second – and there was still the best part of two and a half miles to race. It was bloody great! Here was my horse going out in the country for the second time . . . with a serious chance. I had waited a long time just to see a horse of mine run in the National. I honestly, honestly wasn't thinking of winning, but we were competitive. We were running a big race, and the thought occurred as Crisp bowled along jumping Becher's for the second time that we might be second. And what bad luck it was that we should meet Crisp on a day like this, because without Crisp we'd have a serious chance of winning. I can't remember another horse being so far in front at this stage of the Grand National as Crisp was that afternoon.

Fletcher was hard on horses, as I said. After the Canal Turn, I saw him pick his stick up and give Red Rum a good slap. Then another one. Old Red's head was down as he plugged away, creeping, creeping up, pulling back a length or so at every fence. That's what I was telling myself. I was aware that it was probably just wishful thinking, but it was like the story of the tortoise and the hare being re-enacted in front of our eyes.

Still, I refused to allow myself to believe that Red Rum would get on terms with Crisp – and yet, Fletcher was making ground. We were second, on our own – behind Red Rum was a seriously good horse called Spanish Steps, belonging to the Courage family, the brewers. At the Canal Turn, I think Red Rum was around seven seconds behind Crisp. The rest were racing for the minor placings.

From the Melling Road, all I could hear were people excitedly shouting, 'Crisp, Crisp, Crisp.' As a reflex, I suppose, I yelled: 'What about Red Rum?' I couldn't truthfully describe what I was feeling – it's too long in the past. But, oh, I was lit up all right. Fletcher was getting stuck into my old horse. Only a game horse would respond to that kind of treatment, because Fletcher didn't seem to realize where he hit them. Lots of times he used to hit them well forward of the saddle, right in the soft part of the belly. I had words with him more than once over that. Some horses would curl up and call it a day.

But not Red Rum. I could see Crisp's lead shrinking . . . then shrinking some more. Perhaps the fact that he was carrying 23lb more than my horse was beginning to tell. Listen to the inimitable race-calling of Peter O'Sullevan, commentating for the BBC, in the closing stages:

'At the second last . . . Crisp is over and clear of Red Rum who's jumping it a long way back. In third place is Spanish Steps then Hurricane Rock and Rouge Autumn and L'Escargot. But coming to the final fence in the National now . . . and it's Crisp still going in great style with twelve stone on his back. He jumps it well. Red

Rum is about fifteen lengths behind him as he jumps it. Dick Pitman coming to the Elbow now in the National. He's got two hundred and fifty yards to run. But Crisp is just wandering off the true line now. He's beginning to lose concentration. He's been out there on his own for so long. And Red Rum is making ground on him. Still, as they come to the line, it's a furlong to run now, two hundred yards for Crisp, and Red Rum is still closing on him, and Crisp is getting very tired, and Red Rum is pounding after him and Red Rum is the one who finishes the strongest. He's going to get up! Red Rum is going to win the National. At the line Red Rum has just snatched it from Crisp. And Red Rum is the winner . . .! And Crisp is second and L'Escargot is just coming up to be third.'

That's precisely how it was. At the Elbow, Crisp went left, then he went right. He looked drunk – he didn't know where he was going. Meanwhile, Red Rum had his head down, still galloping on, game as a pebble. Crisp was utterly exhausted, run to a standstill. Yet to be fair, Richard Pitman told me later, 'I was even more tired than the horse.' I had great admiration for Richard and the way he accepted what had happened. He would never get that close to winning the Grand National again, but he is a first-class sportsman, and a good friend. We had won our National by what, two lengths and going away! And Red Rum had broken the course record by twenty seconds.

I floated down the stairs from the top of the stand, taking them three or four at a time. I shot off through the archway to see my horse. I arrived to meet him coming back towards the winner's enclosure, escorted by two mounted policemen – and a few thousand other people, it seemed. One minute I was at Red Rum's head – the next I was being passed by his backside as I was swept aside on the human tidal wave. I wasn't brought up to throw my weight about so I tended to get pushed around.

Anyhow, I followed Red Rum into the winner's enclosure – hallowed ground as far as I was concerned. And the Guv'nor arrived, smiling broadly. At eighty-six, finally, he had realized the third ambition of his extraordinary life. He had his Grand National winner – and I had trained the horse for him. There's only one word to describe that: magic.

I remember David Coleman, the BBC's leading sports broadcaster before Des Lynam or Sue Barker came along, saying, 'They tell me, Mr Le Mare, you spent over a quarter of a million pounds trying to win the Grand National.' The Guv'nor, a very cool old gentleman, thought hard before replying. Then he said that when you had bought horses and kept them in training, the amount involved to experience a moment like this was 'chicken feed'. In a way, he put Coleman in his place, as I thought what he had said to Mr Le Mare was quite rude.

Then Richard Pitman came in. He wasn't the prettiest sight, with what hair he had plastered to his head, no front teeth and sweat pouring from him. Richard made light of the pain he must have been feeling. He said he was glad for Mr Le Mare, who had been trying to win the race for so many years. That was generous, I always thought.

I was interviewed as well; that goes without saying. Please don't expect me to recall what I had to say. I'll put it to you this way: I didn't feel sick! It's a cliché, I know; but quite simply we were over the moon. Couldn't really believe what had just taken place.

With Billy and Jackie to take the horses home, we returned in the Rolls to Stan's house, Holly Farm, where we picked up three cases of champagne to take back to our place in Upper Aughton Road. When we arrived, we found it surrounded by a mass of people, something like five hundred of them. Then I recall my Bedford TK horsebox with its timber body coming into sight with the headlights on and the horn beeping. Grainger was at the wheel, grinning from ear to ear. Great, it really was. I told Ellison to walk Red Rum up the road while we quietly led Glenkiln down the ramp and back into his box in the yard. He looked like he'd been in the wars and, of course, he was given a feed and monitored to ensure he had suffered no lasting damage. We got the champagne opened and our house just became overrun with people.

Mr Le Mare wanted us to join him at the Prince of Wales for a party.

After all, it wasn't every day a Southport horse won the Grand National, was it? The hotel reserved an awful lot of tables for Mr Le Mare and the rest of his guests. Champagne and wine never stopped coming round – and I think I may just have got drunk. At about two o'clock we came back to our little place and had a few more drinks. I did eventually get to bed – I never have trouble sleeping. What a special, special day it had been. All I had ever hoped it would be.

And the celebrations were nowhere near done yet. I was up early the next morning, and the yard soon started to fill with people who had come to see Red Rum. We went to the nearest pub, the one we called 'The Upsteps'. I received a huge ovation when I walked into the already crowded bar. I called out, 'Drinks all round twice!'

Let me tell you, I could get accustomed to winning the Grand National.

Chapter Ten

PLAY IT AGAIN, RED

LIFE WAS PRETTY good. The Guv'nor had generously doubled the percentages of the winnings that came to me, to Brian Fletcher and to the four lads in the yard, where we had a total of eight horses. I must have come out with around £7,000.

I suppose the realization that I had trained the winner of the Grand National took a bit of getting used to, but there was still plenty of graft to be done, so no one was allowed to rest on their laurels. Except Red Rum, that is. He was given the summer off.

When he came back into school we tried to work him over hurdles at the schooling ground we used at Stan Wareing's place. The theory runs that after a horse has jumped the big fences at Aintree it is likely that he will lose time in the air over smaller obstacles, and we wanted to avoid this. So we arranged for Red to school over hurdles with three other horses of ours. They came to the first three in a line and jumped together. At the next hurdle, Red Rum refused. It was as though he thought to himself, 'This is not for me, old son!' I never asked him to school over jumps again.

We decided to give him his first race that season at Perth in Scotland towards the end of September. Now, to take a horse that had won the last Grand National to Perth was a compliment to them, I suppose, but we were looking to ease Red Rum back in with a comparatively simple race.

I met up with Alan Percival, who lived near Morecambe and had a horse running that he trained under a permit. His son Victor used to have the odd ride for us. At Perth the stables are some way from the racecourse, and as soon as Alan got out of the car several other trainers buttonholed him. I stayed in the car, wondering what on earth was going on. When he got back in, I asked curiously, 'Alan, what's the score?'

He looked stunned. He had the favourite – Wigan Park, I think the horse was called – in a conditional jockeys' seller that same day, and the trainers were looking to 'hook' a couple of the serious contenders. In other words, they were trying to fix the race. There was only a small field, six runners I think. Even so, the trainers couldn't get hold of one owner. So they decided his horse was the one that would win. Alan went along with them.

It was a set-up job. It went on in the north a bit in those days, no question. There was a certain little clique within the game – jockeys included – and on occasions they, shall we say, organized things to their benefit.

Alan said that if we wanted to have a bet the money had to be placed off the course. 'Can you arrange that?' he asked. A good friend of mine called Tony Stannard, a successful club owner, then restaurateur, was at the racecourse with his wife, Elsie. He owned racehorses and he was a big gambler – I'd say, a good gambler. I asked Tony if he could get a bet on off the course. I told him what horse I fancied, and he asked me how much I wanted to bet. 'Two hundred pounds,' I said. I'd never had £200 or anything near that on a horse in my life. Tony knew me well enough. 'Are you serious?' he demanded. I told him that I was, so Tony went to place the bet with a bookmaker in London. When he came back, I asked him if the money was on.

'Yes,' said Tony. 'Two hundred for you and one thousand for me.' From memory, we were looking at odds on the horse of 8–1. Anyhow, the horses went down to the start for that race, but I couldn't watch it as Red Rum was due to run in the next and I had to go to saddle him. I strained to listen to the commentary over the racecourse public address.

This horse of ours had gone straight to the front – and the others let him go maybe twenty-five lengths away from them. Then, as I put on Red Rum's girth, I heard the commentator say that the leader had made a bad mistake. I thought to myself what a bloody fool I was. I'd blown two hundred quid . . . and I felt really stupid as I listened to the commentator describing the other horses catching the leader. But, then, all of a sudden, our horse is drawing clear again; and he won – just as he was supposed to do.

It's not an incident I'm proud to relate. I tell the story to show that sometimes even the most honest of men can be seduced by the possibility of making a few bob. As for the general integrity of racing, I am very confident that the sport is run honestly. I rarely gamble, and I have no knowledge of the world of big-time punting. Yet it would be a naïve man who did not suppose that the occasional coup is sprung on the race-course. After all, wherever money is involved – on a racecourse, in the City or in the boardroom – there is the temptation for corruption to take place. Yet I must stress that I have never run a horse in a fixed race, nor have I ever been asked to be party to a fix.

On this afternoon at Perth, Fletcher was riding Red Rum in a three-mile chase with a field of just five runners. Of course, my horse was top weight with 12st 4lb. Gordon Richards had a horse called Proud Stone in the race, belonging to one of his good owners, I think. Proud Stone had been heavily backed to odds-on favourite. Anyway, Red Rum and Proud Stone, who was being ridden by Ron Barry, jump the last together. Our old horse motors on and wins by a length and a half going away.

And that was that; or so I thought. But, no: this horse of Gordon's had been gambled on. And next minute there's a stewards' inquiry. I wasn't too bothered, as in my view there was no reason to take the race from Red Rum. Yet that's exactly what they did. The race was awarded to Proud Stone on the grounds that Red Rum had squeezed Barry's horse before the last, over the last and on the run to the line.

I couldn't believe this, and said as much when Barry came out of the stewards' room. Ron said, 'Ginger, Brian beat himself in there.' Fletcher apparently took a verbal cut at the stewards for daring to inquire about a horse that had won the Grand National. It wasn't the most diplomatic of defences – though I am probably not the best qualified person in the world to give a lecture on diplomacy.

I was disappointed to have lost the race, but I had much else to be delighted about. As I said, quite often when a horse has won the National, he completely loses form. He starts jumping fences bigger, and wasting time and effort. Red Rum had proved he was all right.

As Red Rum was running at Carlisle just three days later, I left him at Perth with Grainger. At Carlisle, he won by twenty lengths running away. And there was an amusing postscript to the incident at Perth. The next summer, Ron Barry was getting married – and I found the perfect present for him from Beryl and me. We'd been sent a photograph of Ron jumping the last at Perth with more than a yard of daylight between his horse and Red Rum, so we blew up the picture and had it framed. We captioned the photograph 'Squeeze me' – and had a good laugh as we wrapped Ron's wedding gift!

Red Rum won his next two races, at Ayr and Newcastle, and then I decided to take on Crisp again, at Doncaster, this time at level weights. This was not my finest decision. It was a shade ambitious – a bit of stupidity on my part, to be honest. The Doncaster Pattern Chase over three miles and two furlongs ended up being a duel, at the end of which Red Rum was beaten by eight lengths. But I refused to be downhearted – after all, Red Rum was being targeted for the Grand National again and that presented an entirely different set of circumstances from those that prevailed at Doncaster.

On a rare visit south, Red Rum finished second to Red Candle in the Hennessy Cognac Gold Cup at Newbury in his final race of 1973. He was then eased down, not racing again until late February at Catterick, where he won. Once more I opted for the Greenall Whitley Handicap at Haydock as his final prep race one month before the National. I wasn't too optimistic here: I feared the heavy going, as well as the 12st 7lb Red had to carry. In the event, Fletcher was knocked out of the saddle by another horse driven into the backside of Red Rum at the first. Red then continued to jump the fences alone – and came to no harm. At the end of the race, Beryl eventually cordoned him off and caught him after he had shown no inclination to stop.

We now had a month to prime him on the gallop on the beach, and were hoping for some dry weather to improve the ground. Fortunately, the weather was perfect. The days ticked down towards the great race. Sometimes, I was hopeful we were on track. Sometimes, I wasn't sure. The BBC asked to come and film Red Rum, and we had no problem with that. This time we had three horses in the National: Red; Glenkiln, with Reg Crank in the saddle; and The Tunku, the horse I'd bought at Doncaster sales on the same day as Red Rum. Richard Evans was to ride our rank outsider.

Red Rum had been given 12st in the handicap, and when the weights were announced the press were on to me, fully expecting me to let rip, I suppose. Initially, I did feel that piling on the weight from 10st 5lb to 12st was a harsh penalty – but then I came round to the opinion that it was a backhanded compliment. If the handicapper says you've got the best horse, so be it. You work away at the job and get your horse fit enough to carry the weight he's been given. Red was a very fit horse that year. He'd kept improving, and he was on an upward curve. That might sound silly, given that the horse was now nine. But he had carried big weights and let no one down.

On the morning before the race, Stan Wareing came to the beach to watch the work, just as he had twelve months earlier. Stan had two good racehorses of his own and I considered him to be an expert. I looked to him for advice, and also I just liked talking horses with him. Deliberately, he never came to see Red Rum work for six weeks before the National. Then he would run his eye over him twenty-four hours before the big day – and I valued his judgement. This morning he looked at him and declared the old horse to be spot on. When Red was at his sharpest, Stan and I had only to nod to one another to show that we liked what we had seen.

Red Rum had something of an eagle about him, you know. He might be walking along the beach when something would catch his eye, and he'd stop to look hard at what captured his attention. We'd let him stand and stare, clearly lost in his own thoughts. He would move on when he was satisfied that he had seen enough.

By now, we were keen to follow as much of the same routine as we could – but we did make one significant change. We hosted an eve of National party at our flat. Over the years, this party earned quite a reputation. I think we did it with a bit of style, but the credit for that belongs to Beryl and one or two others. Half the Liverpool football team, including my pal Emlyn Hughes, turned up. It was always a bit of a squeeze, but we managed to accommodate between forty and fifty guests.

Next morning, Beryl plaited Red Rum's mane as before; and then, as before, once the horses had set out for Aintree, we drove to Stan and Carol's home to sample their champagne again. They were superb hosts. 'We dare not break the mould,' said Carol. So a few bottles were cracked, and we piled into the Rolls with the same passenger list as the previous year: Beryl and me, Stan and Carol, their daughter Gillian and her friend Joanne. I am not naturally superstitious – but I wasn't tempting providence. We lorded it to Liverpool with ribbons tied to the bonnet and waved to those who recognized us.

At the racecourse, I could tell Red Rum was very well in himself and looked set fair in the sunshine. He was a spring horse, and he loved the sun on his back. If you were riding him out on a wet day he'd be growling at you. If I had a regret, it was that I might have had Glenkiln fitter than I did. The fact that we used him as a work companion for Red Rum all the time probably took that bit of edge off him, which was rather sad from his point of view.

In the countdown to the National, I had a pleasurable couple of hours wandering around Aintree, as I had done twelve months earlier. Of course, there was more notice taken of me this year. People wanted to know how my horse was, and if he could win again. I tried to keep a lid on expectation. All I could tell them was that, with a little luck, he was sure to run a big race. Actually, Red Rum drifted gently in the betting, falling out to third favourite as money came for Scout – with Tommy Stack up – and L'Escargot. But I never bothered myself with the market.

Again, like the previous year, I saddled Red Rum with Grainger. Again, Brian Fletcher had licence to ride his own race. He said his plan was to hunt round the first circuit before putting Red Rum into the race as they headed into the country for the second time. I had no quarrel with that – if you have a horse that makes half a length or more with his jumping, that's a fair old bit of ground over thirty fences. The Guv'nor gave Brian the usual cheery send-off. With Stan, I went to the same spot at the summit of the County Stand and drew out my binoculars awaiting the start. I felt calm. Honestly, I did.

Brian plotted the race as he wanted and began to get Red Rum into the race as the field came to The Chair in front of the grandstands. It is not a moment to get too excitable, as there are a good two and a half miles still to be negotiated from this point, and the big fences like Becher's, the Canal Turn and Valentine's have still to be jumped again, as well as some daunting open ditches. Yet there was a thunderous roar from the crowd as the horses passed us in a blaze of colour and noise.

At Becher's on the second circuit, Fletcher had Red Rum in front. Later, Brian said that he had to take up the race as my horse could not be held up any longer. I saw Red Rum get in close to one of his fences and pitch on landing. I think Brian tried to steady him instead of letting him bowl into the fence.

Tommy Stack tried to put Scout into the picture, but I identified the real threat: L'Escargot. This was the winner of two Cheltenham Gold Cups, so his speed was not in doubt. He was a class horse, and he was making an impression. The measure of my horse's performance is the way he went away from him. At the second last, L'Escargot and Tommy Carberry came to mount a challenge. Red Rum was giving away a pound in weight to him, and I caught Brian looking round to assess the danger. He gave our horse one slap. This is how Peter O'Sullevan called the race for the nation:

'It's Red Rum with L'Escargot chasing him now, the two top weights, with Red Rum for England trying to compete that great double that hasn't been done since Reynoldstown, being pressed by L'Escargot for Ireland. Then comes Spanish Steps improving on Charles Dickens. Then Scout, and behind them Vulgan Town and then Rough Silk. They're coming now to the second last fence in the National. And it's Brian Fletcher on Red Rum being pressed by Tommy Carberry and L'Escargot. The two top-weighted ones at the second last in the National. It's Red Rum with a clear advantage there from L'Escargot, who jumped it second. Then comes Charles Dickens third, and Spanish Steps . . .'

At the last, Red Rum landed comfortably clear and I knew he was home and dry. So did Brian. He started to wave to the grandstands – and Red Rum quickened again as he mistakenly thought he was going to be hit. Brian had to grab the reins to prevent the horse from running away with him. O'Sullevan again:

'Tommy Carberry is trying to close the gap, but he's not going to. They come to the Elbow. A furlong to run, he's got a big weight remember . . . twenty-three pounds more than last year, but he's going to hold on. It's Red Rum from L'Escargot in second, Charles Dickens third, and Spanish Steps fourth. Racing up towards the line and Red Rum getting the ovation of his career . . . Brian Fletcher acknowledging the cheers of the crowds as he comes to the line! The winner of the National.'

As Red Rum passed the post he was seven lengths clear of L'Escargot. He really was some horse, wasn't he?

We did the round of interviews again; then, at the end of racing, I just wanted to escape the madness – a wonderful madness, but madness all the same – so I went for a wander around the course alone. I listened to the larks and I lost myself in thought until someone spotted me. 'Just taking it in, Ginger?' he asked. And I was.

But I'd forgotten that I had the keys to Stan's Rolls, and they weren't best pleased when they couldn't find me, I can tell you! They thought I'd gone on home, and it seems they were on the point of breaking a window when I strolled back. It seemed like a good excuse for a drink, anyway. After one or two, we drove to Stan and Carol's, then back to our place. It was the beginning of another memorable, memorable evening.

Our poor local bookmaker Stan Makin took a terrible hiding for the second year in a row. He had paid out a considerable amount twelve months earlier, but this was worse. You see, in the belief that no horse could come out of Southport and win the National twice on the bounce, they decided to stand all the bets placed on Red Rum. It took them the best part of a week to pay out. There were queues outside the place. They didn't lay off a single penny, on the absolute certainty that there was no way a second-hand-car dealer, training on Southport beach, could land back-to-back Grand Nationals. In theory, it was perhaps hard to fault their judgement – in theory. But I understand that the family had to sell some of the property they owned in Southport to settle their account.

WHEN WE HAD won our first Grand National, I'd received an invitation to attend a lunch at the National Sporting Club in London. I had reckoned it was too far to go to be bothered. But I later regretted that, and when I received my invitation this time I accepted, and asked Stan Wareing to be my guest. A chap who used to live a few doors down from my mum and dad's old house met us off the train in London. He said 'Well done' and suggested that we should go for a drink. I thought he was from the Sporting Club, and we took a taxi together to the Hilton Hotel on Park Lane. We proceeded to drink port and brandy – not a drink I normally touched. It was rather lethal, actually.

After several, someone came and touched me on the shoulder and told me that I was needed in the dining room in ten minutes. The fellow who was with us turned out to be nothing to do with the Sporting Club. Apparently, he had called home from London to offer his congratulations and Beryl had told him that I was coming off the train from Liverpool that morning. And there I was getting well oiled in the mistaken belief that he was our host.

We rushed through into the dining room, which was full of over four hundred men in dinner jackets. I was nervous, as I had to deliver a speech, hence the need for a little Dutch courage in the bar beforehand. One of the guests alongside me on the top table was Joe Bugner, who was good enough and brave enough to go the full distance with Muhammad Ali. He had to leave early as he had a fight on the horizon, and when he got to me to shake hands, I remember half getting up and realizing that my legs weren't quite what they should have been. Shaking hands with my right hand, I put my left on his forearm to steady myself. Drunk or sober, I thought, 'Jesus, that's like a shoulder of ham.' I don't think I reached my hotel bedroom until gone 3 a.m.

Back home, I was a bit subdued for a few days afterwards. But as Red Rum had come out of the National very well indeed, we decided to run him in the Scottish National at Ayr ten days later. Stan – who had a runner at the meeting called Explicit – offered to take us to Ayr in his Rolls. By this time, I was taking blacksmith Bob Marshall with us. It was a little on the expensive side, but I did not consider it a luxury. It was part and parcel of being professional.

Red Rum won the Scottish National in nice style, I must say. It was a unique double, a very special achievement, and the town council wasted little time in commissioning a statue of Red Rum for the racecourse.

1 9 7 3

Richard Pitman and Crisp bowl over Becher's. They were so far in front, the best I was hoping for was second.

But Brian Fletcher and the old horse had other plans. After clearing the last, they reeled in Crisp to win. Grand indeed.

And we knew how to celebrate. In 'The Upsteps' the day after.

1 9 7 4

Billy Ellison congratulates Red Rum the day after capturing his second National.

And 10 days after the Aintree win, Brian Fletcher and Red completed a unique double at the Scottish National in Ayr.

Enjoying a pint in a Yorkshire cricket club.

The Red Rum orchid.

Presented with the Freedom of Southport Beach.

Thousands cram on to Lord Street, Southport, to see the three times winner.

Placing his bet.

Receiving his Blue Peter badge.

Turning on the Blackpool illuminations.

Tickled pink at the opening of our new car showroom, with Ken Dodd and Jonjo.

EMPICS

Tommy Stack and
Red over the last
and on the way to
an historic National
treble.

The Guv'nor:
'What have you got
in the National?'
David Nicholson:
'What A Buck.'
The Guv'nor:
'What a pity!'

DAILY MAIL

The eve of the National. The moment of truth. Ted Greenway gives me his verdict. Red Rum will never race again.

After leading the parade, the old horse takes his final bow on the day of the '78 National.

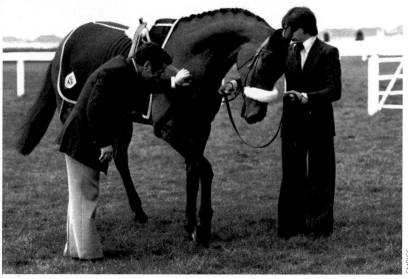

EMPICS

Red's withdrawal in '78 meant I could take Joanne and Donald to the
great race for the first time. And boy did we enjoy ourselves.

Even today, when we have a runner at Ayr, one of the lads always takes a bucket and a mop to give the statue of the old lad a wash. Anyway, the Ayr councillors were thrilled to see Red Rum deliver another stunning performance so soon after Aintree, and wanted me to attend a function or two. But, to be truthful, by this time it was all getting just a little bit much. I didn't want to cause offence, but I slid away to have a drink on my own at the hotel. I ordered a large Scotch and went and sat in a corner. The next minute I spotted Bob coming in, so I got him a large Scotch. Usually he drank beer, but he made no fuss of drinking whisky with me, and we just chatted in the way of two men who have known one another for a long time, through good and bad.

The peace could not last, though. Mr Le Mare had been on the phone to tell us he had arranged a party at the Prince of Wales Hotel in Southport. Stan gave me the keys and left me to drive us back in his Rolls. We'd be locked up today, but I did get us home in an incredibly short time. As we went to join the party, I glanced back at Stan's Rolls. It seemed to be sitting there sagging at the wheels, panting its head off. It was never ever quite the same car again.

But the party was a roaring success – and this was where I met Stan Markland, who became one of my greatest friends. He was over from his home in Jersey and we hit it off from the beginning. I didn't know then how true a friend he was going to prove or how important to my future he was to become.

THE WHOLE SCENE was incredible, if you think about it. From trying to find a winner on a wet Monday at Cartmel, I had now trained a horse to win the National twice while still running the car showroom. I just considered myself to be very lucky to have a horse like Red Rum. I honestly never gave a great deal of thought to the fact that I'd become a bit of a celebrity. I'm not saying I didn't appreciate never having to wait for a restaurant table in Southport, or the extra service or the drink on the house. I enjoyed all that immensely. But give or take a little success,

I was always just a Southport lad. I had got on very well with people before Red Rum – and our achievements simply meant I got to meet a few more folk.

Life didn't change that dramatically. When we started training we charged seven pounds a week to keep a horse, then we got a bit carried away and asked for a tenner. I suppose that when Red Rum won his first National we charged closer to twenty-five pounds a week training fees. But a stable lad was getting ten pounds a week and his accommodation was found, so we could hardly be accused of being expensive.

We never had a lot of problems with attracting staff at Southport. As opposed to most training centres – Lambourn, Newmarket, Middleham – there was always plenty going on at a seaside resort, and there were always plenty of lads coming out from Liverpool. And when the yard started to get some recognition, the lads knew how to capitalize on their standing in the town.

Our lads never had far to go for a pint. You turned right out of the yard and 150 yards down the road was the pub we called 'The Upsteps' – the pigeon men's pub. Another 250 yards on the right was the Blundell Arms. On the edge of the beach was the Fisherman's Rest, at that time an annex of the Palace Hotel. You would see the shrimp carts pulled up outside. That was my main watering hole, I suppose. But I never was a big pub man. My dad always drank in the Crown Hotel, six doors away from the family house in Liverpool Road. He wasn't a huge drinker, but he liked to go to the Crown for the last hour before closing time. People didn't have a television to vegetate in front of back then, and the pub was often at the heart of the community.

Even though Red Rum had made the yard better known, I have to say that we were never inundated with calls from people wanting us to train a horse for them. I think I was regarded as a one-horse trainer. I'd got a good horse and we'd done well together. No, we never had owners queuing up. I am conscious now that it could have had something to do with my approach to people.

I've been nice to people I thought might give me a horse, that goes without saying. But I wasn't any good at kissing bottoms and bullshitting like a lot of trainers. Rightly or wrongly, it was never an inclination of mine. I've always had a streak of independence – and Beryl thinks that has cost us. Yet I must say I don't think it has been a bad thing on the whole. I don't think I have ever been considered to be a really good trainer within the racing world – though in later years I may have changed a few opinions. Just Ginger – that's what they called me and that's who I am. Don't forget I was still selling cars as well.

And then there would be people gently laughing at us training on the beach. Some days they had a point. In the high tides during winter you could wait two, three, maybe four days before you could get on the sands to canter. And in winter there were gale force winds to contend with as well.

After we won our second National, I did seriously think about building a new yard. I'd seen some spare land close to the beach. If I could have obtained planning permission, there was the potential to have twenty or twenty-five boxes as well as room to build a house. Somehow, I never got round to speaking with Southport Council before the land was sold to a property developer. I regret that. If I had made a successful application, I'd still be in Southport to this day. We wouldn't have had to go through the traffic to get to the beach, and we could have stored equipment to prepare the sands more thoroughly.

To my mind, this was one of the nicest beaches in the country, perhaps in Europe. To illustrate this, I do believe that Major Henry Seagrave, a fighter pilot in World War I, rehearsed here for his attempt on the land speed record that he eventually captured on 11 March 1929 at Daytona Beach, Florida, where he drove at 231.567 mph. That's how good those sands were. Now the environmentalists have become involved, they have made a complete balls of this beach. As far as I am concerned the world has gone mad. I heard on the radio last year that a local farmer could expect a road to be made through the middle of the

11,000 acres he farmed. He had no say in the matter – but he made the point that if he had a pool with newts living in it there would be no question of the land being disturbed. It's got that ridiculous. Now, to protect natterjack toads, much of the once beautiful beach is today marshland, with star grass and mud everywhere. And there's no gain for anyone, as you never even get natterjacks on the beach. Mind you, in my day there were lizards in the sand hills and I used to get frustrated coming off the beach to be met by snotty-nosed girls out of college who told me I couldn't ride through there. They would be from some environmentalist group or other. Whenever that happened I used to blank them – or tell them to report me. One day they did come to meet us and I told them that I had been riding through those sand hills for in excess of twenty years, and that my father had done so before me. He never did, of course, but they weren't to know that. We never heard from them again.

On that beach, there were instances when we were ahead of the game, you know. Nowadays you would be hard put to find a yard without a horse-walker – a mobile carousel where the horses exercise on their own. We were walking horses to the beach and back again, and our horses were always out for 90–100 minutes. We were just different, that's all. Take Red Rum, for instance. After winning the National at Aintree, then the Scottish National, he spent his summer holiday in 1974 grazing in a field behind Stan and Carol Wareing's house. He lived with Andy, the donkey Carol had originally acquired to keep her own horses company. Red and Andy had a love–hate relationship – Red loved the donkey but the donkey hated him. Often you'd see Andy try to escape to a corner of the field to be alone. Nevertheless, someone wrote a book about the two of them and their special relationship. Mr Le Mare used to bring tubes and tubes of Polo mints to feed to Red Rum when he came to the field to visit him in the summer.

The Guv'nor was not Red Rum's only visitor, by any means. Carol remembers cars queuing up on the little road at the side of her house that led to the field where Red Rum lived with Andy. 'Actually, it became a little alarming from a security point of view,' admitted Carol. The old lad just captured people's imagination, didn't he?

Chapter Eleven

CHANGES AFOOT

'The number one reason the Grand National is still raced at Aintree today is — Red Rum.'
Mike Dillon, Ladbrokes

AFTER THE SECOND Grand National, it seemed to me that Jackie Grainger and Billy Ellison looked on themselves as celebrities. People were buying them drinks all over Southport and they were both drinking lads. They were playing up to the idea that they were the stars. They got above themselves, they really did. In his mind Grainger felt he was responsible for Red Rum winning two Grand Nationals. He had a hand in the success – I wouldn't query that for a moment. But he was one cog in the machine, no more.

Ellison was a silly lad, not a bad lad – but Grainger's influence on him contributed to his downfall. Even before we had Red Rum, Ellison had been exceedingly daft. One day I found a typewriter hidden in the hayloft in the yard. A typewriter! I went to the boys' flat to lay down the law. 'I don't know where this came from, but I want it off my property by lunchtime,' I said, angrily. Anyway, when I returned the typewriter had been removed. But that was not the end of the matter. The next I learned was that Ellison had been frog-marched into a police car and taken to a police station. It seems that he, along with another lad, had broken a shop window in a back street and pinched a variety of stuff. Their stupidity had been fuelled by alcohol. As I said, Ellison may have been silly, but I didn't think of him as no good. On that occasion I went to court to speak on his behalf, and he was released with a caution.

Grainger – a good horseman, no question – simply became more and more pig-headed. Along with Ellison, he overstepped the mark big-time on the day towards the end of 1974 that I found them asleep in our horsebox parked up in a lay-by. In the back of the box was Red Rum.

They had left a Yorkshire racecourse – I don't remember which one – ahead of me under instructions to return straight home to Upper Aughton Road. When I came across the horsebox parked beside the road, I wondered at first if they had had a problem. Then, when I reached the cab, I could see they were both out for the count. Furious, I banged on the window and woke them up. There was no way I was standing for them parking up for a rest with Red Rum in the back of the box. I cut into them like never before. And when they returned to the yard I cut into them again. The writing was on the wall from that moment. They had become too big for their breeches. This was the latest in a pattern of behaviour that was undermining discipline within the yard. In racing parlance, they couldn't stand the corn: when a horse has too many oats, it can begin to act a little crazily, and Grainger and Ellison had pigged out on being celebrities.

I was not prepared to let them become bigger than the yard. At the next outburst from Grainger I knew I had to get tough – or risk losing the respect of everyone else. Jackie had this great expression that he used: 'If you don't like what I'm doing, lick 'em and stick 'em.' It was a reference to a man's employment cards, which had to be handed over if you were to sack someone – but to do that you had to have their national insurance stamps up to date. In effect, Grainger was calling my bluff to fire him. He'd said this many times in the past without my taking any action. But this time I said to him, 'Jackie, stay exactly where you are.' I went into the office and asked for Grainger's cards. I came out and looked Grainger in the eye. 'I've licked 'em and I've stuck 'em,' I said. 'Now get out!'

Jackie was a good stableman, and good at feeding the horses. But that was his level – and he had overstepped the line once too often. Grainger spoke to me just twice again, and in both instances it was to abuse me. Once, years afterwards, I went to shake hands with him at the funeral of a mutual friend. He just spat and walked away. That was the kind of person he was. At the same time, I was saddened by the need to sack him. Beryl, I know, thought a lot of him. She never forgot that he had taught her a good deal about riding racehorses.

Later, I heard that he had Red Rum's bridle hanging on his wall at his home. I can well believe that, because Jackie would have taken it without saying a word. It was the bridle Red was wearing when he won his first National – and he'd had some of his sheets, too. Jackie Grainger died in 2004.

I made Ellison head lad after Grainger had left the yard. With his bonuses from Mr Le Mare, Billy bought his own house. It wouldn't have been that much – £600 or £800 – but it meant that he had his own little home for him and his wife. I forget her name, but she had a bit about her, she was blonde and bubbly and sang in the operatic society. The house was alongside the railway and they had a Labrador dog. The job had been going along all right, and he rode work on Red Rum as we prepared him for his third Grand National in 1975. But towards the end of 1974 Billy became increasingly unreliable. I heard another girl might have come into his life. I couldn't have cared less about his domestic arrangements, but I did care about him not turning up for work. After a couple of days out, he sent a message to say that he was ill. I suspected that was untrue, and I asked Beryl to go to his house to tell him I wanted to see him.

Beryl told me that when Ellison spotted her through a window, he grabbed a blanket and pulled it over his head before he came to the door in an attempt to convince her he had flu. Beryl said flatly, 'The Boss wants you in, Billy. If you don't come, he's going to send you your cards.' Beryl is convinced that when she called round Billy had been decorating.

His days with us were over shortly afterwards. Like Grainger, he became embittered towards me. He took me to an industrial tribunal, but failed to win any compensation.

From thinking themselves celebrities, Grainger and Ellison slid back to the level they had started out at. It was an unhappy ending; but, like I say, they couldn't stand the corn. Some years after they had been fired, it seemed to me they tried to get revenge by taking the side of a stable girl in a dispute that got me up before the Jockey Club in Portman Square. She had complained, after I had dismissed her, that she had been paid an unfairly low wage. I told the Jockey Club that she had been sacked as a result of performance issues, and that I'd paid her what I thought was a fair wage for her work. She was not entitled to higher pay as she was not qualified to meet the responsibilities of the job. But Ellison and Grainger went to Portman Square to speak on her side, but as far as I was concerned, they didn't tell the truth. I thought, well, now I know that they're bad men – because I knew how much money they had had out of us, and through the generosity of Mr Le Mare. They had just become bitter and twisted. I made a small out-of-court settlement with the girl.

Ellison worked for a time in Newmarket after he had left Southport. He also had a profitable sideline in selling racing plates that he claimed had been worn by Red Rum. I never had anything to do with him again – and the last I heard he was living in Blackpool, a shadow of the man he had once been.

With Ellison sacked, it was assumed by some in the yard that I would ask Christine Langhorn to look after Red Rum. Christine was the daughter of Jeff Langhorn, my old friend and partner in the little taxi firm we had started together at his grocery store. But I knew from working with Jeff at Frank Speakman's stables in Cheshire that he had very definite views on his horses, and in my mind that counted against Christine. Jeff frequently visited the stables, and I thought if I let her 'do' Red Rum I wouldn't be training the horse any more. Jeff Langhorn would be. I wasn't prepared to let him have that amount of influence through his daughter. Besides, I thought that I had a good lad for the job in Billy Beardwood; and so I gave him Red Rum to look after.

Jeff came and had words with me. I just explained that I thought the boy was stronger than his daughter, and therefore better suited to Red. It wasn't that Christine wasn't any good. She was a very good horse-woman. I just thought Billy would be better (and he was the only lad I rated as good at strapping a horse as Ellison). Simple as that. Christine only stayed with us for another few weeks and Jeff stopped coming after she had gone. But we did strike up our friendship again a few years later.

Beardwood was a Liverpool lad who supported Everton. By the time he began working with Red Rum the old horse was attracting quite a celebrity fan club. One day I told him Bill Shankly, the larger-than-life manager of Liverpool, was coming to the yard. Beardwood came in that morning wearing his Everton scarf, and placed another blue-and-white scarf round the neck of Red Rum. That amounted to a blue rag to a Liverpool man, of course. Shanks took one look at Billy stationed inside Red Rum's stable before he growled in his deep Scottish accent, 'Aye, son, an Everton fan I see. Well, that horse of yours has won more Nationals than Everton have won matches this season.' Pure Shankly.

On the eve of the 1975 National, I worked Red Rum on the sands with a horse called Wolverhampton, who was also to run at Aintree in the main event. Bill Davies, the property speculator who now owned Aintree, had sent Wolverhampton to me from Tom Corrie, who retired. He had paid something close to £20,000 for the horse, who had won his first three races with me.

As usual, Stan Wareing had come to watch Red's last gallop, and Richard Pitman was also with me that morning. Red and Wolverhampton strode out over five furlongs, and I can't say I was entirely happy with what I saw, so I decided to send the two horses back to have another gallop, just as I'd done previously with Red and Glenkiln. Christine was riding Wolverhampton and she jumped off with Red Rum, but after

200 yards she dropped out. I was following in the old Land Rover and I thought the horse was dogging it. I called to Christine to give him a slap, but just as I said that she pulled up. As we drew close, the horse quietly flopped on to the beach. When I reached him, Christine was already crying as she held his head. We took the tack off him as his eyes rolled around in his head. Then he went still. I asked Richard, 'What do you think's wrong with him?' Richard replied, 'I don't know – but he's dead.'

I tried to call Davies, but I couldn't get through to him at Aintree. I arranged for the horse to be picked up from the beach and to be taken to Liverpool University for an autopsy. I then went to Aintree to see Davies in his office. I accept that he was under pressure, as the National was less than twenty-four hours away and from all reports the race was in crisis. I asked Davies if he had insured Wolverhampton, but I could tell he was not listening to me. I thought, what am I doing here when he is not the least interested? It was his horse, but I was the one who was gutted. I hate losing any horse – but it is even worse when you lose a nice sort like Wolverhampton. Lord knows, we had precious few horses in the yard capable of winning races.

Yet if Davies was uninterested in what I had come to tell him, an aide of his suddenly jumped down my throat. He accused me of killing Wolverhampton by working him with Red Rum. I was steaming, and suggested that he might like to make the same accusation outside. 'We'll sort this out behind the stand if you like,' I said, angry beyond words with what he had said. He declined. Lucky for me, I reckon – I think he was questioned during police inquiries in a murder case a couple of years later.

That year the fate of the Grand National had been placed in the balance by Davies's brinkmanship. Allegedly, he had demanded money to stage the race, while alienating the punters by doubling the price of admission. The greatest race in the world was being brought to its knees. What bothered me no end was that the government was raking in £7 million in betting tax from the race, but would not assure the future of the Grand National by paying Davies £4 million for Aintree. You only had to look at the figures – a blind man could see the potential profit line for the government had they acted to bale out the Grand National, a source of serious revenue to them after all. But in my book politicians are mostly a thick breed. Had Aintree been south of Watford, I bet they would have poured in money to save the racecourse. But it seemed to me that in their eyes the north-west of England didn't have the so-called glamour of Ascot or Epsom. Where was the potential to win votes or claim prestige from saving Aintree from the bulldozers? Maybe I sound cynical; maybe I am.

So, instead of being bought by the government, the Grand National was left to fend for itself under the management of a man who, clearly, was more interested in constructing a housing estate than running this great horse race. It was an embarrassment that it had been reduced to this.

Like the FA Cup Final, Wimbledon, the British Open golf championship and the Derby, the Grand National is a jewel in the crown of British sport. And here it was, on its arse. Brave men and brave horses had competed in it since 1839, and yet to my mind it was being run near to extinction by a property speculator, short-sighted politicians and the inability of the Jockey Club to move a muscle to help.

I don't believe I am being conceited if I suggest that at that time Red Rum was the best marketing tool that Aintree had. Red Rum's success and his good nature won him ever-increasing fame. He was held in huge affection by the nation, he really was. Cards for him came by the sackload. People stopped outside the car showroom to snatch a glimpse of where he was stabled. Luckily, when the course did change hands the new owners made the best possible use of Red Rum's image – as you will see.

As well as all the turmoil around Aintree going on in the background, I had my own concerns in the countdown to that year's race. There had been heavy rainfall as winter turned to spring, and in the days before this National the ground had gone against Red. He was a horse that loved good ground and never really handled soft going. I did wonder how he would compete.

In front of a pitifully small crowd – the hike in admission prices had taken a heavy toll on the attendance – Red Rum jostled for position against thirty rivals at the start line. Once again Fletcher was in the saddle – and his strategy was not going to deviate from the one he had used to such devastating effect in the last two Nationals. Why should it? He would hunt round for a circuit, then he would edge Red Rum into the race. At least, that was the hope. But the heavy ground sucked the old champion's tank dry. In fact, he struggled so hard at one point that Fletcher later admitted he had thought about pulling up. But Red Rum plugged and plugged away and, through sheer endeavour and heart and guts, managed to get back into the race. His supporters yelled their encouragement for him. And at the second last, Red Rum and L'Escargot had the race to themselves. Now, for me, L'Escargot never properly received the credit he deserved. He was a very serious horse indeed. He had won the Cheltenham Gold Cup twice, and a Sun Alliance Chase at the Festival. And with Tommy Carberry sitting still and unflustered on him, he was galloping to take the Grand National from Red Rum. My horse was giving him 11lb in weight and L'Escargot ran away with the race, beating Red into second place by fifteen lengths. Yet to my mind it wasn't the weight that handicapped Red on this day; it was the ground. Still, two wins and a second was an enviable record for any horse to boast round the fences of Aintree.

It was to be the last time that Fletcher partnered Red Rum in the National. I had never had more than a professional relationship with him – they say he was a man with few friends. Through fate, Red Rum had given him a second lease on his career, which he had seized with both hands. Yet, towards the end of 1975, Fletcher was finding rides hard to come by, and in the autumn of that year my patience with him snapped.

We had taken Red Rum to Newcastle, and Fletcher was booked as usual. Now, I may be wrong, but I think Red Rum half-remembered the terrible hiding Tommy Stack had given him on his first visit there. Anyhow, the horse was never entirely happy at Newcastle ever again. On this afternoon, I had wandered down the course to watch him.

At the last, Fletcher had Red Rum bang upsides a horse called Tartan Tudor to contest second place. I expected Fletcher to pick up his stick, give him a couple of cracks and clinch second spot. Instead, Brian sat absolutely still all the way to the line and was beaten into third by a short head, I think. This infuriated me. It took me a while to walk back and by the time I got to the unsaddling enclosure Red Rum had been taken to the stables. But a crowd of excitable pressmen jumped on me. They said Fletcher had told them that Red Rum was no longer the horse of old, that he no longer gave him a good 'feel'. That was not all, chorused the newspapermen. In Fletcher's damning analysis, it was time Red Rum was retired.

'What do you say to that, Ginger?' someone asked.

Somehow, I maintained my composure. I told them that I would go home and give some thought to what to do next with my horse. Inside, I was spitting blood. I had no argument with Fletcher for having an opinion on the horse – but to my mind he was utterly out of order to say what he did to the press. He should not have spoken with them at least until after he had expressed his thoughts to me in private. But worst of all, I suppose, I had to deal with being told that my one serious horse was deemed over the hill by my jockey. I felt sick to my stomach.

As I drove home along Soldiers Road – the stretch between Newcastle and Hexham – I thought that I had one obvious option: to seek a second opinion from another jockey. Perhaps Red Rum and Fletcher had been to bed too often together; perhaps they knew each other's moves too well. Over the long drive back to Southport I assembled my thoughts. The next day I went to tell Mr Le Mare what I had a mind to do. As always, the Guv'nor trusted me to take what action I considered right.

I rang Fletcher and told him he would not be riding Red Rum in the Hennessy at Newbury, as I wanted to see how the horse felt to another experienced jockey. I already knew who I wanted to ride – Ron Barry or Tommy Stack, both good friends of mine. Fletcher took the news very personally and the conversation came to an abrupt end.

For the Hennessy I engaged Barry to ride. As it transpired, Gordon Richards had not long since told 'Big Ron' that he was on the downhill slope of a career that had twice – and in recent years – brought him the National Hunt jockeys' championship. What a state of affairs! Fletcher thought Red Rum should be put out to pasture, and a respected trainer like Richards thought Barry should hang up his boots. Ron, a man with a strong Irish brogue, was never the easiest to understand in English, but I do remember him telling one interviewer, 'In the circumstances, we will be lucky to get over the first fence!' Anyway, Red Rum ran a blinder under top weight to finish fifth. Ron gave him a good ride, and came back in to give me an encouraging report on the horse.

Now, as fortune would have it, I met Fletcher on the steps of the weighing room. It had always been my intention to put him back on the horse – I just wanted a second evaluation of Red Rum's condition, fitness and jumping ability. Pleasantly, I said, 'Hello, Brian. How are you?' He just walked past me. Well, as far as I was concerned that was the end of Brian Fletcher. He could forget riding Red Rum or any other horse of mine. It was his loss. He'd done well for Red, I knew that, but equally Red had brought him back into the game. And into the bargain, I knew how much he had earned from the horse because his bonuses from the Guv'nor had been the same as mine.

Fletcher did ride Red Rum again, at the end of that same year, when I gave the organizers of the Horse of the Year Show permission to invite him when they asked for my horse to make a guest appearance at the prestigious event. Two of my lads went down to London with Red, and they said Fletcher was rather unpleasant. Making excuses for him, I think he had a lot of personal problems at the time. Yet I never thought it was a coincidence that Fletcher and Grainger were good pals with one another. To my mind, they were similar kinds of men, rough and ready. I have never spoken with Fletcher again to this day.

JUST BEFORE CHRISTMAS 1975, bookmakers Ladbrokes came like the cavalry to the rescue of the Grand National. They signed a seven-year contract with Davies's company, the Walton Group, to manage the race. Whatever your opinion of bookmakers, there is reason to be eternally grateful to Ladbrokes. Without their intervention, I believe the Grand National would have died, and in all probability Aintree would now be a housing estate.

Mike Dillon – a public relations executive and still the face of Ladbrokes within the racing world – played a significant part in the company's strategy to keep alive this great institution of British life. Ladbrokes chairman Cyril Stein is also deserving of the respect of anyone with racing's interests at heart. In actual fact, Mike did invite me to express an opinion or two and he was aware from the beginning of the part Red Rum could play in keeping Aintree and the Grand National in the public eye. In the early days, I recall, he worked out of a caravan parked in front of the County Stand at Aintree; he had no option, as the offices had no electricity and no phone lines. The racecourse was derelict and neglected.

One day I went to meet Mike along with Liverpool footballers Emlyn Hughes, Terry McDermott and Alan Kennedy, all racing enthusiasts. We had an exceedingly liquid lunch – and quite possibly tea as well. I thought it only polite to suggest they all came back to Southport. But on the way we had to stop to feed some horses I kept in a field halfway between Aintree and home. Then we stopped at a Berni restaurant for a steak. When we reached Upper Aughton Road I couldn't find my door key – which wasn't surprising, I suppose, as by this time standing upright was challenging enough. I knocked on the door. Beryl had heard the racket we were making, but we did not hear her open a window. She slung a bucket of water on to the doorstep. With stunning accuracy. There were, three international footballers, the man trying to save the Grand National and the trainer of the two-times winner of the race, soaked to our boots. I think you'd call it a sobering experience – but that was Beryl!

Anyhow, with Ladbrokes as the driving force the race was on to save the Grand National. Prince Charles headed a campaign to keep the race alive, and a public appeal was launched. Buckets were rattled under the noses of punters to beg for loose change. It was demeaning to see the depths to which the National had sunk – but there was no time to moan. We all had to do what we could, and I was more than glad to muck in.

Mike Dillon has a generous recollection of those desperate days. 'It was Ladbrokes' intention to give the Jockey Club some breathing space by entering a management contract with the Walton Group that owned Aintree,' he explains.

'It is a misconception blurred by time that we sponsored the race. We never did. We managed it. During the period of the seven-year contract the Grand National was sponsored by the News of the World and Colt cars, for instance. But from the outset Ladbrokes realised that Red Rum had become synonymous with the race – and Red Rum had won the affection of the nation. We had planned to try to make what use we could of the horse. Where we were fortunate was that Ginger trained Red Rum. We were dead lucky to have such an accommodating man as him. Ginger always greeted any request I made to him about involving Red Rum with great enthusiasm. He was fantastic to work with and, clearly, would do all in his power to save the Grand National. Someone other than him could easily have told us to get lost. People say that this person or that organisation saved the Grand National. It's not true. The number one reason the Grand National is still raced at Aintree today is – Red Rum.'

It still makes me shiver to think that the race could have perished. But there were moments when the planning still fell apart; sometimes you were moved close to tears. Others times you had to laugh – like at the first meeting Ladbrokes managed in the spring of 1976. Mike had looked at films of previous Grand Nationals and noted that in days gone by, national flags had been flown along the embankment running alongside the racecourse. He thought it would be a neat touch to reinstate the tradition. He wrote to the embassies of all the countries that had signed to broadcast the Grand National requesting them to supply him a flag. The co-operation was total. On the first day of the meeting, the flags proudly flew over the course. But when Mike returned the next morning, they had all vanished. 'I went to see Liverpool play at Anfield the following week – and there on the Kop were all my flags,' he recalled.

To replace Fletcher, I asked Tommy Stack to partner Red Rum in the National. Tommy had finished fourth on Scout the previous year and I considered him a professional, intelligent jockey. He had that little bit of Irish mystique about him – he had been training to be a priest until he had a change of heart. He was sound rather than brilliant in the saddle, but a nice man with it.

Race day dawned bright and warm. Soon the course was awash with people again. Thousands and thousands came through the gates as the lure of the National bit deep. Eventually, the declared attendance was given to be 42,000. The race was not dead in the hearts of the nation.

Annoyingly, I was delayed saddling Red Rum. I had another horse in the race, Meridian II, whom I had bought for 6,000 guineas from Ken Oliver for a good friend of mine, Brian Aughton, who had a landscape gardening business. After I had saddled Brian's horse, I couldn't get into a box to saddle Red Rum for some time as another trainer was taking an eternity with his horse. To worsen my mood, when I eventually began to saddle Red one of the stewards said to me stiffly, 'McCain, get your horse in the paddock.'

I was furious. 'Fuck off,' I said.

Later, I was summoned to go before Lord Derby, chairman of the stewards. He was seated at the end of a long room and I stood to attention before him – it seemed like an echo of my days in the army. Lord Derby lectured me on my responsibilities, as he saw them. As the trainer of such a prestigious horse, he told me, I owed it to the public to let them see him as early as possible.

'With respect, I don't need you to remind me of my responsibilities,' I said curtly, and walked out.

I did think the whole episode was out of order. My horse had 12st to carry and I wanted to keep that off his back for as long as possible – though I would have had Red Rum in the paddock earlier but for the delay I encountered.

Brian Aughton is a grand man, great company at the bar and blessed with a wonderfully sharp sense of humour, and I was delighted that he had a runner in the Grand National. I remember an interview he gave to the *Daily Mail* just before the National, when he talked about the reasons behind his purchase of Meridian II.

'First, I fancy Ginger McCain's missus. Owning a horse at his stable is the only way we can be together. Second, I run this garden centre on the Ormskirk Road. And if my horse wins I reckon I'll clean up next Sunday flogging sacks of genuine Meridian manure. And third, Ginger told me a while back that there's only one horse in the field he's scared of for Red Rum, and that was Meridian. So I thought if a bloke like McCain thinks so much of the horse, I'd better be in on it. The only thing I made Ginger promise when I said I'd buy the horse is that Meridian will not be treated as a bridesmaid to Red Rum . . . they both must get top class treatment.'

Aughton had one question. 'When my horse wins, where do I go to lead him in? I mean, say I'm up in the stand . . . how do I get down?' I knew the answer to that one. 'You float,' I said. 'You step off the front of the stand and you float. It's easy, I've done it twice.'

While I wanted the best for Brian's horse, it is natural that Red Rum should have been my top priority. In a sense, the reputations of my horse and myself were on the line together as the runners went to post for that 1976 Grand National. Critics had been openly scathing about me – and, by association, about Red. To some watching at Aintree that afternoon, there was the suspicion that I was making one demand too many on the horse. I received letters of criticism from the public. But by this time Mr Le Mare was nearly ninety, and I felt a duty to him to run his horse. Red Rum had more time than the Guv'nor had. And anyway, I didn't let outside criticism get to me – Beryl always said that I built a brick wall around myself.

At least the ground was firm, as Red liked, I thought, as the race began with its usual cavalry charge to the first. Tommy kept Red Rum out of trouble on the first circuit, but at the thirteenth fence Meridian was brought down by the fallen figure of the Duke of Alburquerque, who had parted company with Nereo when riding hard at the front of the field.

By the time they passed us at The Chair in front of the stands my horse was round about tenth. Significantly, Rag Trade was fifth. As they went away from the stands down that avenue of fences beyond the Melling Road, Red Rum looked to be travelling awfully well. At Becher's, he was galloping beautifully and strongly, his place in the shake-up now looking to be assured. Another couple of fences, and my confidence was growing by the second. Four fences from home Red Rum jumped into the lead, just ahead of Eyecatcher being ridden by . . . Brian Fletcher. Side by side, Stack and Fletcher raced, but it was Red Rum that was moving more convincingly as the pace and pain of the race began to bite. Stack was barely moving a muscle. In contrast, Fletcher was riding for all he was worth. The crowd was yelling Red Rum towards the post, willing my old horse home. At least the public had not lost faith.

But then, from the chasing group, Rag Trade came to throw down the strongest challenge as six horses took the second last in with a chance. Yet I still sensed that Red was the one to be feared. He would get the distance, but would the others? For the third year running, Red Rum landed over the last in first place in the National. But, as in so many Nationals, the storyline was to be rewritten on the run from the Elbow to the winning post.

Rag Trade, carrying almost a stone less, came past my horse to take a decisive lead under John Burke. And yet . . . Red came hurtling back at Rag Trade. The gap narrowed . . . then narrowed again; but the winning post came just too soon, and he was beaten by two lengths. I don't mind admitting I had moist eyes as I watched his courageous fightback. How could you not admire what had unfolded? The old horse had battled to the end, and he was giving away a lump of weight. I think Rag Trade only ever won four or five races in his life. He was a boat of a horse that could miss a fence, but fair play: he got his act together that day, and John Burke gave him a wonderful ride. I was also delighted for trainer Fred Rimell, for whom Rag Trade was a record fourth Grand National winner. I was not to know that it was a record I would one day share with him. To me, Fred was one of the gods of the game: champion jockey before successfully transferring his knowledge to training, he represented everything that was good in National Hunt racing.

That summer Red Rum went out to grass with Meridian on land owned by Albert Wake down near the Southport–Preston bypass. One morning I was playing golf with Emlyn and Stan Wareing at Ormskirk Golf Club when a Ford Capri drove up near where we were about to hit our tee-shots. Inside was the assistant professional, who had come out to give me a message to call home, then ring Mr Wake. Instantly, I thought, 'Oh, shit, what's happened to Red Rum?'

I made the calls – and Albert told me that he had been watching the horses for a while and that Meridian had not moved. He went to investigate and found Meridian was as dead as a kipper. He died from an aneurism, possibly caused by redworm infestation as a youngster. Beryl and Albert both suggested I should immediately go home, as the press were clamouring for the story. But what could I do? The horse was dead and I was unhappy to be told the news, but there wasn't anything I could do that couldn't wait until after I'd finished my round of golf with my friends. Besides, I was winning. Oh, I got some stick for that.

Chapter Twelve

RED'S HAT-TRICK

HORSES GET KILLED on racecourses, yes. And sometimes a horse sustains an injury that requires it to be humanely destroyed. But those who call the Grand National cruel speak from ignorance. I have been associated with National Hunt horses for most of my life, and have missed the National just once since 1940 – and that was in 1949, when I was doing my National Service. In the circumstances, I feel I have some knowledge of this great race.

A Grand National horse is born and bred to jump hurdles and fences – though Red Rum could be named as an honourable exception, having just taken to the game of his own accord! But most horses in training have breeding going back for a number of generations designed to produce a horse physically and mentally suited to the task. As I explained in open correspondence in the *Guardian* with Carla Lane, a scriptwriter and animal rights activist from Liverpool, there is no point or purpose in entering a horse for the Grand National unless he is keen and willing to do what he has been bred to do.

From the day a racehorse is born, it is treated like the top-class athlete it potentially is. To do away with the Grand National would take away the opportunity for horses such as Red Rum, Golden Miller, Reynoldstown and other wonderful animals to reach the greatness to which they are entitled. Sportspeople have that opportunity. Why not horses? Very occasionally a horse is killed; but that happens over hurdles, it can happen even in Flat races. Sometimes working dogs on farms are hurt, or sheep are killed. But that doesn't make sheep farming cruel, does it? There is an injury rate on any racecourse. But because Aintree has the Grand National, all the do-gooders, including the RSPCA, have been known to climb on the bandwagon and condemn the race. They are completely and utterly out of order and they have no perception at all of what they are talking about. All the rubbish that is spouted does frustrate me.

A friend of mine said: you can put racehorses in boxes padded with cotton wool and the buggers will still hurt themselves. There's a lot of truth in that. One morning I found one of our horses, a very nice horse indeed, in his stable with a hind leg hanging off. How he'd done it nobody knew. We think he might have had a stress fracture that we hadn't picked up and for some reason he's kicked out at something and his leg's gone. Regrettably, it happens.

As I get older, I have far more time for racehorses than I have for politicians who jump on bandwagons. Politicians will do anything for a vote. So if a horse is killed on the racecourse, it is sad. Yet only for a period of time – because death has come clean and quick for the horse, and nobody is going to abuse them. It is abuse and neglect that are really disgusting. Think of what happened to Hallo Dandy, the winner of the 1984 Grand National. Some years later, he was found half-starved in a field where he had been turned out and forgotten.

Selfishly, perhaps, I find it more sad when a horse leaves me to go to the sales. I hate to see them go. Yes, they are expensive animals to keep in training, and owners have the right to make a cull on their horses. To be a successful trainer, you've got to be prepared to cull; to draft horses in and out. Yet it is not in my nature to do that – and I hang on to horses far, far longer than I should. I just cannot bring myself to get rid of them. I can't look a horse in the eye and say, 'You are going to the sales ring tomorrow.'

And I certainly can't tell them they're going to the knacker's yard.

All the years we were in Southport, where there was obviously no room to bury the horses, I wouldn't send them to the abattoir; if it was time for a horse to go, he'd be sent to the hunt kennels, put down and fed to the hounds sooner than fall into bad hands. But, in truth, we rarely had to destroy a horse at Southport. Nor, since we came to Cheshire, have I ever sent a horse to the bone man. Any horse that is shot on my land, stays on my land. I was lying in bed earlier this year wondering to myself where I would bury the next one who dies. There are quite a number here now. We have almost 200 acres and I like to bury them in various different places. I hire the contractor from up the road and he comes along with a digger and prepares a grave, so that the old horses can stay on the Cholmondeley Estate. Today, I think we have five brood mares who have become old-age pensioners, incapable of breeding any longer, and the abattoir would give you two or three hundred pounds to take them. But there is no way they will have them. My horses are put down at home and buried at home; it's as simple as that.

GETTING A HORSE fit enough to win the Grand National is very different from getting one fit to run in the race. Almost anyone can do that. To have a chance of winning the race you have to be focused on Liverpool – and that is where I was lucky with Mr Le Mare and Red Rum and, later, lucky again with John Halewood and Amberleigh House. I was allowed to prepare their horses with just one target in mind: the Grand National.

You can no more keep a horse super-fit for ever than you can a human athlete. Take a boxer. He needs plenty of sparring before a fight, but a trainer has to be careful not to overdo it. Too much sparring and a fighter can go over the top. It is the same with a racehorse. Timing is the key.

One great way of judging a horse's fitness is to see how he is eating. When a lad goes into a horse's box, he should automatically look in the manger. If a horse has left his feed, he should report it to the head lad or, depending on the size of the yard, the assistant trainer or trainer. It is a telltale sign that something is wrong. Perhaps the work is getting on top of the horse.

At Southport, the old pot boiler was lit in the cobbled yard at half past six in the morning on Wednesdays and Saturdays. Linseed was boiled until lunchtime, then you made your mash with oats and bran and a little of whatever else you might add. Afterwards you covered the mash with sacking and let it sweat until half past six at night. It was still warm when you fed it to the horses at evening feed. It was damn near an art form. Old stud grooms had their own little mixtures they used to make to keep a horse on his appetite. You checked your horse's droppings every day, too, and any change was an indication that something was not right.

Red Rum had his first feed around 7 a.m. After he returned from his workout, he would be given some hay before his midday feed. He would have his third feed around 6 p.m. and I would give him an extra bowl at 10 p.m. It's different now – we only feed three times a day. Some yards, I believe, feed just twice; that is difficult to understand, because a horse's digestive system is designed to cope with eating little and often. It was hard work making the mix in the boiler, but I still hated it when we did away with it. Times change, I suppose. Horses are fed in a less time-consuming way now – we feed cubes these days as well as oats, all very standard (though it's true that modern cubes may possibly give a horse a more balanced diet).

This has much to do with the way yards have expanded. In the years after the war, even a top trainer like Noel Murless would never have had more than forty horses in training. Today, the top trainers like Sir Michael Stoute, Mick Channon, Martin Pipe, Nicky Henderson and Paul Nicholls have far, far more horses. In my view, with the best will in the world there is no trainer alive who can single-handedly train all those horses 100 per cent, so you must rely on the quality of your staff. There are lots of artificial aids now, which, it seems to me, takes away some of the skill, the traditional horsemanship. Things like horse-walkers, treadmills and swimming pools are common at the bigger yards, and this lessens the need to have so many staff, as well as being a good aid to keeping a horse fit or assisting in its rehabilitation from injury.

With the job being so labour-intensive, I can understand the need to make yards more efficient. But within these big strings there are an awful lot of horses that do get wasted. I'd say that could be attributed to a lack of personal attention. Some yards have upwards of forty staff, and one bad lad can spoil a horse for life. If he does one or two things wrong, especially in the formative years of a young horse, that's it. All too easily, a negligent lad can give a horse a bad mouth or spoil his temperament.

I don't think it's a good thing for racing to have these big teams. I don't suppose for a moment it will ever happen, but I would like to see the Jockey Club stipulate that no yard can have more than sixty horses in training. In my view, you can't train more than that number correctly.

I always went round evening stables. Your boys stood to attention by the horse's heads, and the horses stood to attention and showed themselves properly. The manger had to be emptied and washed out. You would check the boys' cleaning kit, which had been laid out for inspection. Call it bullshit, but it never hurt to have standards. If I couldn't have my horses turned out properly on the racecourse, I wouldn't train horses. It's a quirk of mine. But it seems trainers don't think the average racegoer is as horseified as they used to be. I'd agree that the majority of owners would be pressed to tell if a horse was well turned out or not. But that doesn't matter. The trainer knows. That should be enough.

A shining example of this is the competition held before races when someone is asked to nominate the best-turned-out horse in the paddock. This is a well-intentioned idea. It's good that the kids who turn out the horses get a little bit of appreciation. But the whole process is devalued when you have the horses judged by the girlfriend of the man whose company is sponsoring the race. I've seen that, and I've made derogatory comments to the point where people think I am being rude. Yet I think it has to be said. I've seen the best-turned-out prize go to a grey horse, simply because of its colour, or be given to a horse because the boy leading it up is wearing pink socks!

This is unfair for the boys – and girls – who have worked hard to turn the horses out correctly. If they are going to have best-turned-out awards, then they should try and make sure that the person who is judging them knows what he or she is looking for. There's not just the horse to take into consideration; the boy or girl leading up should be smart and should be doing the job right. You see people dragging the horses round, stuff like that. Horses are only listless when they haven't been taught to walk out. The standard of horsemanship is nowhere near what it used to be.

When I was a boy in stables the tack was cleaned every day. Tack rooms used to be like little palaces. There would be a fire with winter clothing drying on racks, and a constant smell of leather and soap. The tack used to be oiled and gleaming. It's not like that any longer. Yes, I'm getting old and I'm getting grumpy, but that doesn't mean I am wrong about falling standards. Boys will put the same martingale on a horse of 15 hands as they will put on a horse of 17.2 and never bother altering it. Of course, staff won't take the treatment they used to take, either, which doesn't help if you are trying to instil standards.

An old horseman who had a horse with us at Southport told me some stories of when he had been a stable boy. He had been with Atty Persse – a hard little man, but a very good trainer who had trained The Tetrarch, a renowned sprinter known as the 'Spotted Wonder'. The old man recalled how, when Persse came into the box at night, you had to have your horse looking immaculate, with a quarter rug thrown over his hindquarters and his tack smartly presented. As a matter of course, you also had to say, 'Good evening, sir.'

One night, recalled the old man, Persse floored him with a punch under the chin that came out of nowhere and for no apparent reason. Persse then said to him: 'When I come in you say, "Good evening, sir."'

The boy claimed that he had done so.

'Well,' replied Persse, 'Say it louder next time.'

Obviously, you can't allow that to happen in this day and age, but there is something to be said about discipline. Captain Ryan Price was once faced with a strike in his yard at a time when he was training big-race winners. He asked who was acting as spokesman for the lads. When one lad identified himself, Price – who had been a Marine Commando – whacked him straight on the jaw and laid him out. There was never talk again of a strike in his yard.

You'd get arrested if you behaved in that manner nowadays – and rightly so. But it seemed like there was more affection for the horses on the part of the staff then. You had to be dedicated, because the wages and holidays were bad and you had to work all hours. In my experience, the average kid who comes into racing these days is gone within a couple of years. They arrive with stars in their eyes, thinking of becoming a champion jockey, and then find out the harsh realities of the day-to-day job. Yes, it is demanding and hard work – but it is also rewarding for someone with a love of horses and a willingness to dedicate themselves.

At racing schools now, youngsters are taught how the boss should address them and they are told what the boss is allowed to say and what he is not allowed to say. This is a funny old game. It's no good being polite to a boy when a horse is turning himself inside out and you know it's going to bury him. The language can be raw – but it's the language of the environment, like soldiers in a barrack room or footballers in the dressing room. A training ground is not always the politest place on earth! It doesn't have to be, and it's pointless to take offence. I put it to you this way: if you've bought a Rolls-Royce or a Bentley, it stands to reason that you would want a competent chauffeur. Almost certainly, he would be a mature man with a good driving record. Well, a trainer, especially one in the top flight, will give a quarter of a million pounds for a horse, which is a good deal more than you'd pay for a decent motor car. So, how is it the boy who gets to look after that horse often isn't capable of riding a bicycle properly, let alone a horse? There is something wrong here, isn't there? In the past, most yards had a good senior stableman around who would put the youngsters right as they served their apprenticeship. They are not about any more.

If I hadn't had my bit of luck, I would have been absolutely delighted to have a job as a stud groom or a head lad myself. I wouldn't have asked for any more, I seriously wouldn't. But the bit of luck that came my way happened to be of the bad variety – I married Beryl, and from then on I was getting kicked and spurred into doing things to progress in business and life. I truly would have been happy with a big dumpy wife who was a cracking good cook. And what have I got? I've got a rather attractive lady who won't get off my back . . . and I've had her for forty-four years! But the reality is she has been a driving force for good in my life – even if I have never liked being told what's to be done by ladies in any way, shape or form. Don't get me started about policewomen . . .

I don't like women in racing. There, I've said it. I came into this sport when it was a man's game. It's my sport. I am possessive of it. Now there are lady stewards, lady starters, lady this that and the other. They tell me there are lady jockeys, but I insist there is no such thing. There are women that sit on horses . . . of course, I say this tongue in cheek, and I think I have already made my admiration for Carrie Ford clear. I've had some good girls with me at the yard and I am appreciative of their work . . . But, dear, oh dear, I preferred it when you never saw a woman in the weighing room. It was a man's place, and in the years after the war most of the jockeys were senior riders who'd been in the forces, like Brian Marshall, Dave Dick and Dick Francis. They were *men*. And the weighing room was a man's domain, like a fighter's gym. You had that smell of men's bodies, sweaty and masculine. The toilet was a bucket in the corner that never got emptied until it was full. The odour added to the sense of place. Nowadays, you get girls walking in and out with their whips jutting out of their bags. And the weighing room smells like a poof's parlour!

Yet, for all of that, it's still a great, great game like no other.

On a spring day, Aintree is a picture in the sunshine, with grass as green as any grass you'd find anywhere in the world. But this game is also about dealing with life in the dead of winter. It's about days of driving rain and knee-deep mud, when tired horses and tired jockeys survive through breeding and courage. When you think neither man nor horse has anything more to give, you watch with admiration as somehow they keep finding a bit more, then a bit more again. It's about days when the lights go on before four o'clock in the afternoon and you've still got to wash the rain and mud from your horse before you load up for the long drive home. It's about pulling back into the yard when it's past bedtime, and knowing the alarm will go off again all too soon. For me, that is the essence and the magic of this sport.

RED RUM HAD not wintered that brilliantly on the racecourse that season from 1976 to 1977. He had been struggling under big, big weights, and park courses no longer motivated him. He had been racing that long, he acted like he was going through the motions. It was just a day out as far as he was concerned. He had probably lost a bit of his speed – what speed he had! He was showing signs of a small, gradual, but steady deterioration brought on by the passing years. Possibly he wanted five miles, not four and a half any more! But as the day of the Grand National approached, I was sure he was very fit. I was also sure that Aintree would bring a big race out of the old horse. Yet the odds were mounting against him, weren't they? Did we really have a chance? Or were the naysayers, who were beginning to murmur more loudly, correct?

Tommy Stack had publicly wondered if he had missed his chance to win a National when he had ridden Red into second place in the previous year. Some critics felt Tommy had been too conservative with the horse and should have applied some pressure a couple of fences out. But I never attached any blame to Tommy for my horse being narrowly beaten.

In the countdown to Red Rum's fifth National, we observed the usual rituals: Stan Wareing watched Red's last swinging canter along the sands, Beryl hosted a lovely party on the eve of the National, and we dropped into Stan and Carol's for a few glasses of champagne on the way to Aintree. As we drove to the racecourse in Stan's Rolls I knew we could not be taking our horse to Aintree in better condition than he was. All we hoped was that he would be stirred by the occasion, as he had been in the past. All we hoped was that we were right – and those who considered Red Rum to be over the hill were wrong.

Sadly, the smallness of the crowd at Aintree that year was pitiful to behold. Although it had been a decent crowd the previous year, the Ladbrokes rescue package was still in its infancy, and this great sporting institution was still in the intensive care unit. At least Red Rum gave the National some prestige, even if the place was on its deathbed. This year, Charlotte Brew was to be the first woman to ride in the race – and while I respected her courage, my views on women jockeys are now well documented. In my opinion, this is not a race for a woman.

After saddling Red Rum I left Beryl to her own devices and went to the top of the stand with my mate, Brian Aughton. As always, the start of the National makes the blood rush a little faster. As the tape flew up, I trained my binoculars on Red Rum and Tommy. At Becher's first time, Tommy had our horse hunting wide in the field and avoided the fallers at this first landmark on the course. Red Rum was jumping with his usual accuracy, and by the thirteenth fence Tommy had him in fourth position. At the front, Boom Docker was in a race on his own, but I didn't feel any need to panic. He would come back to us in time. As Red Rum passed us to jump The Chair, Tommy looked in serene control.

Out in the country on the second circuit, Boom Docker ground to a halt at the seventeenth fence, a horse out of gas if ever you saw one. He just refused to jump. This left Andy Pandy in the lead from Hidden Value,

What A Buck and Red Rum, who I thought was still travelling in cruise control. A horse called Nereo appeared in the picture but remained only briefly, falling along with Andy Pandy at Becher's second time.

Tommy could hide Red Rum no longer, and at the next he jumped ahead. Eight fences stood between my horse and immortality. But I wasn't thinking along those lines, not then. I was looking for any signs of weakness as I tracked him with my glasses. I had one worry: Red Rum was running in the company of a couple of riderless horses. Tommy asked him to quicken, and he quickened once, then again. Only a good horse could possibly do that after racing for more than three and a half miles over the most daunting fences in the game.

For a moment, Martin Blackshaw brought Churchtown Boy to contest the race with Red Rum as they crossed the Melling Road. But Churchtown Boy had won the Topham on Thursday, and there had to be a question mark over his stamina now. My horse still had to contend with the loose horses, but two fences out I saw Tommy pinch a look round. He had the race in hand – the Grand National was at the mercy of Red Rum again. The sun was shining. The ground was good. Red looked as though he was loving every minute. The further they go, I thought, the further he is going to win. It was wonderful to watch. I mean, the horse was twelve years of age! I knew it didn't get much better than this.

After landing over the last, Tommy pushed Red Rum out with hands and heels, man and horse in perfect harmony. He was not the same horse that had laboured through the winter on the park courses – the horse that some had said was finished. They were all wrong. He was relishing his work. He was bringing into play his ace: the Aintree Factor. The loose horses might have been a danger to him, yet in the end I think their presence turned out to be beneficial. They gave Red something to chase – and he pursued them like a hound after a fox.

All around me, people rose to acclaim him. The crowd may have been shockingly small, but that did not detract from Red Rum's performance. People understood that they were bearing witness to history. Running hard for the line, Red Rum was unstoppable, he was uncatchable. He was simply bloody magical.

On the BBC, commentator Peter O'Sullevan was telling the nation: 'Red Rum is winning the National like a fresh horse . . . in great style. It's an unprecedented reception for an unprecedented horse . . . Red Rum the little hero of Southport sands has broken all Grand National records.'

I raced to get down the stairs – with that bloody fool Aughton draped round my neck! So much for my theory about floating down from the top of the stand. At the bottom of the steps, my legs buckled and Brian took off. By the time I reached Red Rum, Tommy was wiping a tear out of his eye. He was not a sentimental man – but he had just climbed a peak that all jump jockeys dream of climbing and he was choking up. Why not? The Grand National affects you that way. As he walked Red Rum back through the crowds, people converged from out of nowhere to shower him with congratulations. No horse ever made so many connections as Red Rum.

Mr Le Mare had watched from his usual seat in the Queen Mother's Stand. He had spent all those years dreaming of winning the Grand National – and now he was headed towards the winner's enclosure for a third time. He had seen so much in his lifetime, had risen from nothing to make his fortune. But on this bright afternoon at Aintree he shook my hand with a smile that said all I wanted to know. The Guv'nor was the second happiest man at Liverpool – behind me!

At the winner's enclosure, BBC presenter Frank Bough pushed a microphone under Tommy's nose. 'He's a tremendous horse round here and anything I say won't do him justice,' said Tommy. 'I'm just glad to have been a part of him.' Bough came next to me, and I was all lit up now, of course. 'Never in doubt the way I saw it,' I suggested. 'He's an exceptional horse.' Hard to argue with that, isn't it?

That night we all went to the Bold Hotel in Southport, where owner John Craig had organized for a bevy of girls to join the celebration. John had said that if we won the National he would put on a meal at his hotel if I paid the bar bill. Red Rum was on the invitation list. By early evening, the news that Red was going to be at the hotel had spread all over town. Lord Street – the main thoroughfare in Southport – was blocked solid. Cars had to be diverted around the promenade and down Houghton Street. At 9 p.m., our horsebox was shown through the crowds by traffic police and pulled up outside the hotel. The ramp was lowered and into the night stepped Red Rum. Only five or so hours earlier, he had jumped round Aintree in the Grand National. Looking at him, you wouldn't have known he had had a race. He was bright as a new penny. He was led through the hotel's ballroom, but with half of Southport in his wake, I shouted to John Craig, 'Shut the bar, shut the bar!'

In the pandemonium, one memory sticks in my mind more vividly than any other. As I went into the hotel with my horse, with the dining room on my left and another bar on the right, people were yelling and applauding everywhere, but one fellow stood out. He stood on a table and he wore brown brogue shoes. I know this because he had one foot in the middle of his dinner. I could see the cauliflower on his plate curling over the sole of his shoe. Then I was gone – and I wish to this day I'd seen his face when he got down from the table.

Red Rum happily stood in the packed ballroom for some time before we sent him home. He thrived in the limelight, he really did. People just wanted to touch him or be in his presence. He oozed charisma. We stayed with the celebrations until gone 3 a.m. and Mr Le Mare blossomed, as he always did among good-looking women. It wasn't the smallest bar bill I've ever picked up, but I couldn't have cared less. Red Rum had gone to the party that he had created – and that was grand as far as I was concerned. It was the dead of night when I walked home alone along Lord Street, lost in my own thoughts. On the mile-long trek I passed a milkman or two and they offered a word or two of congratulations, but otherwise I walked with only my memories for company. It was a beautiful end to an unforgettable day.

RED RUM WAS now the people's horse, no question. Each post brought new requests for him to make an appearance. We had to keep a tight rein on his activities – he was still in training, after all – but one invitation that we felt we couldn't refuse came from Blackpool. Dignitaries in the town wanted Red Rum to switch on the famous Blackpool lights, and we accepted. On the night, he went into the Town Hall and walked up a big, wide flight of stairs. Ten thousand people were howling and shouting when they caught sight of him. Tommy Stack was in the saddle and I remember he said to me, 'I can't believe this, it's not happening, is it?' I turned Red round and led him back through a beam and as he passed the skyline lit up. He was such an intelligent horse. You could do things with him that you wouldn't dream of doing with any other horse. He was also a survivor, and he wouldn't put himself at risk if he wasn't sure of himself, so turning on the lights was all in a day's work for the old horse.

The year ended with Red Rum becoming a special guest of honour at the BBC *Sports Personality of the Year* show. To a rousing ovation, Red appeared in the studio on the second floor of the New London Theatre to take his place with the other celebrities of the nation's sporting universe. Unfortunately, Tommy had taken a very bad fall and was unable to travel to London. He had smashed his pelvis and spent weeks in traction. Yet his condition had sufficiently improved by the time of the show to enable him to appear, in his wheelchair, on a video link arranged by the BBC. As the studio guests started to laugh, Red Rum pricked his ears. Tommy smiled. 'He's thinking, I've met that fellow before some place,' he said.

Red was an intelligent horse unlike any other I have known. When he stood in his box at Southport, he looked out over the door at what was happening. Beryl and I could see him from the window of our flat, and he would be watching seagulls or airplanes overhead or following what might be going on in the yard. His ears would be cocked forwards as he took a real interest in what he was watching. Time after time, he would cock those ears to let me know that he was aware of his environment.

That was Red, star of the show and the star of my life.

Chapter Thirteen

MILLION-DOLLAR

HORSE

THE NEXT TIME Tommy saw Red Rum he partnered him at Haydock Park at the beginning of March 1978. He was just starting to ride again after recovering from the terrible injuries he had sustained the previous autumn.

I'd like to think that Red Rum provided Tommy with some inspiration to get back in the saddle. He wanted to be on him for another crack at the Grand National. His injuries had been caused not by an accident on the racecourse, but rather a freak incident in the paddock, when a horse slipped and rolled on top of him at Hexham, crushing Tommy beneath him and fracturing his pelvis in thirteen places. For the best part of three months, Tommy had been forced to lie on his back as his doctors adjusted a series of weights to realign his pelvis. He told me that the first time they wheeled him down the corridor to have an X-ray he asked the hospital staff to steady up: he had been motionless for so long, he said, it felt like he was doing 100 miles an hour. It says a lot for Tommy that after that kind of injury he came back to race again. A tough man, a brave man.

Tommy actually finished a long way back with Red at Haydock, but we weren't expecting them to set the world alight. The target, as usual, was Aintree.

It has never ceased to astonish me how much interest was shown in me, as well as Red Rum. For instance, in the week of the Grand National I was asked to be the subject of a column in the *Daily Mail* entitled 'One man's radio week'. Who would care what a car dealer from Southport listened to on the radio? But I answered their questions and the article began like this:

'Most of my radio listening is done in the morning. I switch on as soon as I get up at about quarter-to-seven and continue to listen in the car after breakfast when I drive down to Southport sands for the 7.30 gallops. Terry Wogan (Radio 2) is my morning favourite. I like his easy style, his choice of light music and, perhaps most important of all, the fact that you get an up-to-date racing bulletin.'

I also surprised one or two people, I suspect, by revealing that I enjoyed listening once in a while to poetry. I haven't the flair for getting the most out of it by reading – though I do have a love of books, with biographies at the top of my list – and prefer to listen to poetry on the radio. Richard Burton has one of my favourite voices, but for me there is no one to beat Sir John Gielgud. The paper asked – so I told them!

In Grand National week it was almost impossible to keep Red Rum out of the news. I never minded the attention he received; how could I? He was the lifeblood of what I did. It was grand that so many thousands of people – perhaps millions – showed so much interest in my horse. We tried to share him as much as we could without compromising him.

In fact, we had been nursing him along a little for a couple of weeks. He had a niggling problem that we couldn't get to the bottom of. At first, I thought he was getting a stringhalt, which is a contraction in the nerves in the hind legs. As we were well forward in our preparation, we were able to ease down his training. And we had him in the tide every day.

There was a great deal of media attention on him, because he was a reasonably short-priced favourite to win the National for a fourth time.

After news leaked out that he had a 'mystery ailment', medical bulletins were published on his condition during the countdown to the race. And Angela Rippon, at that time the best-known woman newscaster in the country, came to ride him on the beach for a feature on Red Rum to be broadcast before the race. I remember walking across Southport beach in the build-up to the National and seeing it smothered with hordes of newspaper reporters and television crews. I'd never seen so many people on the beach in winter!

We still hoped whatever problem Red Rum was experiencing was no more than a hiccup. Our vet, Ted Greenway, couldn't pinpoint anything specific, so we gently increased his work again. Before this Grand National, I made one change to Red Rum's routine. Instead of giving him his final gallop on the beach, I decided to take him to Liverpool. I thought letting him have a run over five furlongs at Aintree might give my old horse a little bit of motivation. He galloped beautifully – to the extent that Billy Beardwood, who was riding him, had to aim Red at the big fence nearest the stables just to check him. Red always liked to be in charge, and at his favourite racecourse he was full of himself. Again, there were reporters present. I was relieved. We were most certainly still in the game. I watched as Billy pulled up Red and headed for the stables on the course to take him back to our horsebox for the drive home to Southport. But just as he went through the gates into the stabling yard, I caught Red taking a short step. One other man noticed what I'd seen: Peter O'Sullevan. Quietly, Peter sidled alongside me and said, 'Ginger, did he take a short step?' I confirmed what we had both seen.

When Red arrived home, he seemed all right, and I was not unduly worried when I returned to Liverpool to watch the day's racing. On my return, Ted came to give Red Rum a final inspection. The horse was still walking 'short'. Ted – a good, good vet – did a nerve block to try to isolate where the trouble was. He soon deduced it was in his off hind foot; he thought Red had fractured a small bone.

Ted gave me the wisdom of his years. 'You could run him tomorrow,' he told me. 'But if the bone breaks, he would be crippled and he would have to be shot.'

Basically, the decision was made for us. It would have been unforgivable to let the old horse cripple himself after all the pleasure and success he had brought us. None of us wanted that on our conscience. Red was too much part of us all.

He would not run in the National. He would not run again.

As I listened to what Ted had to say, my mind went numb for a few moments. It was hard news to absorb. Red Rum had been central to all that we had achieved in the old game. We had just wanted to take him back to Aintree for one more shot – I was truly convinced he had one last big race in him. But Red Rum's welfare had to be our only concern. He deserved to be retired as the champion he was.

Now, this was huge news on the eve of the Grand National. And the *Daily Mail* secured a front-page scoop as they managed to get a photograph of the moment when Ted gave me his verdict. In the photo, we both look like we have just received word of a bereavement in the family. I took a call from a reporter on the *Mail* who offered me a monkey if I would delay making public the news of Red Rum's withdrawal for an hour. I guess they wanted a scoop. I agreed to the deal, as there seemed no harm in it. But I did call Mr Le Mare – and he completely endorsed the decision not to race Red Rum the next day. He cared about the old lad as much as I did.

Our eve-of-National party was transformed into a celebration of Red Rum's retirement. Plenty of champagne splashed about, I can tell you. After all, it was the end of a special, special time in our lives. Woodrow Wyatt, chairman of the Tote, told me at the party: 'You have made the right decision. It will be a bitter blow to millions watching the race, but the public would have been outraged if anything had happened to the horse.' The party went on to the small hours. Not far away in his box, at the top of the yard, Red Rum was sound asleep, oblivious to the noise and fuss he had created.

In the morning, the *Daily Mail* splashed this headline across the front page: 'Red Rum Out'. Below the headline was the picture of Ted giving me his diagnosis, with my horse in shot behind him. The story began: 'This was the moment last night when the incredible Red Rum was ruled out of today's Grand National by trainer Ginger McCain and vet Ted Greenway. McCain, Greenway, not to mention Red Rum, had done their best. After all, a 1970s Grand National without Red Rum would be like the Tower of London without the crown jewels.'

Apparently, bookmakers had taken £800,000 in ante-post bets on Red, mostly non-returnable. Really, I could have tried no harder to get my horse to race at Aintree. Without a runner, I took my children Joanne and Donald to the Grand National for the first time. Until then, the day was always too busy for me to have them around. It seemed right that they should at last get to attend the race that had shaped so much of their lives.

In a lovely gesture from Aintree, Red Rum was invited to lead the pre-race parade. To look at him, you would have thought he was as sound as a bell. He bucked and tried to do somersaults – and could not understand why he was not going to the start with the other horses. He was just being led back when Tommy Stack came upsides on his substitute ride. Tommy just wanted a quiet word with old Red. I think he had a tear in his eye as he spoke. It was rather a nice moment.

After the race, Ladbrokes chairman Cyril Stein asked me to join him for a drink. We chatted about this and that until one of his senior executives got to the point. He said to me, 'Ask Mr Le Mare if he will take twenty thousand pounds for Red Rum and then we will give him to you.' This seemed a very grand proposition for a thirteen-year-old gelding. I was told that there were no strings attached to the offer – but they made it clear that they wouldn't be disappointed if I entered Red Rum for the National again next year. They must have copped for a fortune in ante-post bets . . . I could see why Mr Stein had a reputation for being a shrewd businessman. The Guv'nor, though, had no desire to sell.

Red had ended his racing days as undefeated champion of the National, he was safe and almost sound, so I had no complaint whatsoever. He was intermittently lame over the next three months, but we never examined the problem further in any depth, deciding to allow nature to take its course.

RED RUM THE racehorse swiftly became Red Rum the full-time celebrity. Indeed, with so many pirates climbing on the bandwagon of his popularity we became concerned that there was a lot of garish tat being sold on the market under his name. A friend of mine called Peter Rougier suggested that the best way to protect Red Rum's image was to make him a limited company. So that's what we did. The Le Mare family consented to the plan and they had 50 per cent of the company, while I had 30 per cent and Peter had the remaining 20 per cent. I always had the final say about what the horse could or could not do – but the arrangement was very amicable, having been entered into primarily to protect Red Rum from being exploited. All officially endorsed Red Rum products had to be licensed.

Peter, who had been chairman of the hosiery company Bear Brand, though he was more or less semi-retired now, had been a friend for a fair time. He had had a horse called Implicate with me in my earliest days as a trainer (the horse, if you recall, that gave Beryl a broken cheekbone!) and I used to buy some company cars from him at Bear Brand. I'd pay £400 for one of their cars and if I was lucky might sell it for £500.

Peter's regular bookmaker was a man called Colin Jerram. I mention this because a few years before Red came into our lives Peter decided that his trainer and his bookmaker should go with him as his guests to see the Arc de Triomphe in Paris. On the plane journey down to London, I lost thirty quid at cards to the pair of them. Still, there was a big night ahead in town. Peter had the keys to the company flat in the West End, and we headed there to drop our bags before hitting the nightlife. Peter took us to the Eve Club – and from the reception he received it was apparent he was well known as a regular. There were some cracking girls dancing in the floorshow and, as I surveyed the scene, I couldn't help but feel I was flying a bit high for a working lad. Colin, I recall, got stuck into a big, blond Polish girl who came to our table. He was most uptight when she left him for an American sitting at the next table. Still, Colin took his revenge. When the American went to the dance floor with the girl, Colin helped himself to the champagne from his table. Peter was not impressed, but we drank it all the same.

Eventually Peter broke up the party, saying that he was returning to the flat. As he left, he said: 'I suggest you two don't waste yourselves in London tonight as we'll have a real night out in Paris tomorrow.' We nodded. Then I turned round to see Colin disappearing with another girl. At around 2.30 a.m. I left the club to go back to the flat. I intended to walk – as an ex-taxi-driver I hate to spend money on cabs! But when I got outside, a nice girl whom I'd spoken to earlier in the evening offered to drive me to where I was staying. As I had no clue as to the address of Peter's company flat, I politely declined her offer. I started to walk, following my nose I suppose. I do remember that I had to walk round mountains of rubbish in the streets as the London dustmen were on strike.

By sheer chance, I found the flat. And there, on the pavement, was Colin talking to the girl he'd left the club with – but by now he was no longer wearing his shirt. Peter had warned us to make a quiet return as the company chairman and his wife were also sleeping at the flat. When I arrived, Colin was working out how to get in, having locked himself out, and had just come across the answer. He had discovered a builder's ladder along the street and soon he had propped it against a first-floor window. With admirable cheek, he persuaded a policeman to help him.

Colin's plan was waterproof – but for one factor. The window he climbed through was the window of the bedroom where the company chairman was asleep with his wife. That did not go down very well. Anyhow, at least he was able to come downstairs and let me in through the front door.

The next morning we had an early flight to Paris, and my head was banging as we journeyed to the airport. John Oaksey, a significant and respected figure in British racing, was on the same flight. But when we landed, he found that he had forgotten his passport: so he was sent back to London on the next plane. Peter, who spoke French, had arranged for us to be met by a couple of his friends, a professor and a very elegant woman. Colin, I soon discovered, could also speak some French. I didn't understand a word of the language, but off we all went to lunch. I ordered partridge, which was a mistake. The bird contained more lead shot than meat.

Lunch went on for some considerable time, so we arrived late at the racecourse at Longchamps. Park Top was running in the Arc – and if I recall correctly she was unbeaten in England in 1969, winning the Coronation Cup at Epsom, and the Hardwicke Stakes and the King George VI and Queen Elizabeth Diamond Stakes at Ascot. She was owned by the Duke of Devonshire, who was in Paris to see his horse run, and Lester Piggott rode her. British racegoers piled their money on Park Top, in Paris and at home. Unfortunately, she got stuffed.

I had asked our friend the professor to place a bet in the next race for me. I was delighted when the horse romped home; but I was soon less than delighted when the professor told me that there would be no winnings to collect. 'I lost my courage,' he said. And I was fast losing my patience. Everything ran late – then I lost contact with Peter and Colin. I still had an aching head and I was generally pissed off. If this was French racing, I thought, I'd have a day out at Cartmel any day.

So I wandered aimlessly about Longchamps . . . until I came across a familiar couple pushing a pram. It was Albert Wake and his wife. I stayed with them until the professor and Peter found me. They had booked dinner in the city. The restaurant was owned by some French chap who had won the Tour de France – don't ask me to name him, but there were lots of pictures of him on his bike. Peter's most vivid memory of the evening was listening to me trying to explain to the elegant French woman the technique for castrating a horse.

SOME LITTLE TIME after Ladbrokes had made a bid for Red Rum, Peter was contacted out of the blue by a Japanese-American restaurateur called Rocky Aoki. He offered one million dollars for Red Rum.

Steeplechasing is not a big sport in America like it is in this country, and the first thing that struck me about Aoki's offer was this: Why would you pay that much for a thirteen-year-old gelding? I couldn't for the life of me work out how he could get a return on his investment. But, clearly, Red Rum was a very famous horse and they must have had something in mind.

Peter and I agreed that the offer was too good to refuse – Red Rum had to be sold. Peter went through the small print and it was decided Red Rum would spend six months of the year in America and six months here. I also spoke to Mr Aoki, who explained that he opened a new restaurant every month in America and that each one cost a million dollars to launch. So what was another million for Red Rum to him? Under the contract, I would go with Red to look after him when he was in America. And the best part of all was that after two years we would get the old horse back for nothing. It was a hell of a deal, it really was. At least under these terms I could still be with the old lad.

By this point the Guv'nor had turned ninety and his family had taken over the commercial side of Red Rum's affairs; and they were in agreement with letting him go. Mr Aoki flew to London and then drove to Southport to complete the contract. His Jaguar had a police escort when he pulled up outside the old showroom in Upper Aughton Road, as word had got out that Red Rum was being sold. A crowd of noisy protesters shouted their disapproval as I came to greet Mr Aoki, a small, very polite man. I was showing him to the front door when a big lady emerged from the crowd and took a swing at him with her handbag. 'Remember Pearl Harbor!' she screamed.

Now, what Pearl Harbor had to do with anything I never did understand – but her anger reflected the mood of those outside the showroom. And not just outside. The people booing on the pavement were not the only ones who objected to the sale of Red Rum. Beryl disapproved – and so did the kids. Joanne and Donald both had tears running down their faces at the thought of the horse leaving. Beryl came into the lounge, slammed the coffee and biscuits on to the table and walked out again.

What we didn't know was that some students had gone to picket Mr Le Mare's house as well. He did not know that anything was afoot – until then. But regardless of the protesters, we were going to agree, reluctantly, to do the deal. Mr Aoki had his lawyer with him, and to all intents and purposes the transaction was about to be finalized. After all, we were talking about a thirteen-year-old gelding that had finished racing; and we were only placing him in the hands of Mr Aoki on loan.

Then our telephone rang. Beryl answered it. She listened, and came back into the lounge. 'That was Mr Le Mare,' she said, dead straight, but I detected a sparkle in her voice. 'He said to tell you that Red Rum was not for sale at any price and that he stays with Ginger McCain for the rest of his days.'

The Guv'nor was always a decisive man. He might not have been running Red Rum Ltd on a day-to-day basis, but he was still the boss. No mistake. When he made a decision, there was no argument and no discussion. I must say Mr Aoki took the news with good grace.

Red Rum would stay with us until he died – and no one was more pleased to be told that than me.

*

REMARKABLY, RED RUM made considerably more money for all of us than the million dollars that Mr Le Mare rejected. One day this past spring David Elsworth called me on the telephone to wind me up because I'd said something or other about Desert Orchid. He told me that Desert Orchid, whose many triumphs included winning the Cheltenham Gold Cup for Elsworth, made public appearances for nothing. I tried to explain that we had to make Red Rum a limited company because otherwise he would have been devalued by a whole load of cheap memorabilia. Also, we soon found that whenever we did anything for nothing, people did not appreciate his presence, whereas if they paid £500–£1,000 (plus expenses) they seemed to value having Red Rum and treated him accordingly. Also, such was the demand for him that he had to have his own exclusive (and new) horsebox and two permanent staff to travel with him. You can't afford to do that very long for nothing. He was booked year on year by some organizations – and attended a Catholic retreat for eight years on the bounce. We also donated Red Rum to the charity Riding For The Disabled, and he appeared at functions on their behalf on a fairly frequent basis. Desert Orchid was loved because he was a grey horse. But he didn't have the charisma my old horse had.

Red Rum continued to be treated as he had been in training, just without all the hard work. And he certainly ate well – he loved the manger, did Red. The old horse opened supermarkets and bookmakers shops all over the British Isles. His head was sculpted in silver and bronze in limited editions – the six made from silver fetched £6,000 each. He appeared on fine china, tea towels and key rings. Business boomed: so much so that Peter opened a shop dedicated to Red Rum merchandise just across the road from the car showroom. All the while coaches would stop unannounced in Aughton Road just to allow tourists to have a glimpse of where Red Rum lived. Polo mints – the old lad's favourite – were sent to him by the box.

We had a whisky marketed in his honour, National Choice. We went to Scotland to meet the distillers, and brought home a fair few samples. Peter kept them in his office and sometimes – well, a fair few nights actually – we would end up trying them out as we chatted over the day. Beryl never liked me drinking whisky, though. She claimed it made me unpleasant. As if . . .

Red Rum made an appearance at the Highland Games, though I didn't go with him for that. He would be booked to attend Golden Wedding parties, birthdays and anniversaries. In the beginning, we would charge £250, but over the years it escalated in keeping with the times and the demand for him.

Every so often, Peter would give me a great lump of cash. I stashed it away, thinking I was dodging the tax man. Then, I must admit, I started to become embarrassed. I began to have a sense of guilt and feared that if I was caught I'd be thrown in gaol and they'd chuck the keys away. I think I ended up with £40,000 in cash under the bed. It wasn't earning anything and I wasn't spending it. Frankly, it was bloody stone cold stupidity.

I decided I had to tell Beryl and our accountant, and ask them for advice on how to get out of the hole I had dug myself into. They listened – then they burst out laughing. They told me that all the money had been already declared and the tax paid. So much for me thinking I had been nicking a few quid from the government!

One of my favourite Red Rum episodes took place at the Irish Royal Show in Cork. I went over with him and the lads in the horsebox from Liverpool. It was a big show over three days and Jonjo O'Neill was going to ride the horse. Jonjo was like a god in Ireland, so we knew not to expect a minute's peace. As good businessmen, we also loaded around £10,000 worth of Red Rum merchandise in a compartment inside the box. It was packed so tight there wasn't room for one more key ring.

Unluckily, we were stopped at Irish customs. And the customs officers said they wanted to see inside the compartment. Really, they just wanted to see Red Rum. But when they looked inside the merchandise tumbled out. Silence . . . then one of the officers started to talk about VAT. I had no idea whether he was expecting us to pay VAT, and I didn't know what the VAT implications were in relation to what we were doing. But I did know that I didn't like the way the conversation was headed. I started to fumble around and showed him a set of spoons and forks and a couple of other treasures. I said that if he liked he could keep them. With that, he waved us on our way.

At the show, Red Rum was paraded on all three days. We sold out of everything – and I mean everything: soiled goods, the lot. At lunchtime on the final day, we were packing up to make the drive from Cork to Dublin to catch the ferry home to Liverpool. We had to have Red Rum at an engagement in the west country the following afternoon. The organizers of the Cork show knew we had to make a swift departure, and Red Rum was being funnelled through a huge crowd back to my horsebox. We were making decent progress, until suddenly we came to a halt. Lying on the ground was a big man who was turning purple. Two or three people were attempting to treat him. In the crowd, we couldn't go forwards or backwards with our horse. We were stuck. And then someone near me said, 'Ah, Jesus, you've got to be getting away, haven't you? Don't worry about this fella, this fella's dead. Just pop your horse over him and be away.'

Only in Ireland, I thought.

Billy Beardwood was an absolute star with the horse. He coaxed Red Rum over the poor man's body and we got back to the box. We had nothing left other than empty cardboard boxes, but people were thrusting fivers at us to get their hands on anything that wasn't nailed down. People were still hanging on to the side of the box as we left, accompanied by a police motorcycle escort.

Once through customs at Liverpool docks – and we had to join a long queue, as there are stringent procedures involved in shipping animals – we then faced a marathon drive down to the west country. I admit I was a bit uptight after the long journey from Cork, and I did not take kindly to the manner in which we found ourselves ordered around when we got there. I didn't think the lads were looked after particularly well, either. Then I discovered we weren't getting one bent penny for our troubles. I told Peter there and then that was the last time Red Rum went anywhere for nothing, other than for our adopted charity, Riding For The Disabled. We weren't going to be treated like that and taken for mugs.

Red Rum's popularity never weakened, it really didn't. In Southport, John Craig renamed the Carlton Hotel the Red Rum Hotel in his honour. We had some parties in there, I can tell you. And one of the town's fire engines is still called Red Rum to this day. When he had engagements in the south-east, Red boarded overnight at the Horse Guards barracks in Knightsbridge, London. My travelling head lad, Harry Wright, a man I'd grown up with, and Billy were both welcomed in the officers' mess. One day in east London, our horse opened three pubs – and in all three the lads noticed the same chap, a smallish man with two big minders. It turned out to be Terry Ramsden, who later became a notable owner of a substantial number of horses. He also served 21 months in gaol in 1998 for concealing assets from bankruptcy proceedings.

On another occasion we were near Whitehaven in Cumbria. The town was so full of people I thought it must be market day; but no, the crowd had assembled to see Red Rum open a supermarket. Cars were parked everywhere, so dropping the ramp on the box required a bit of care. Once the ramp was down, we used to let the old horse stick out his head. He had the most elegant head, and he was always curious to see where he was, so the old lad would look around with ears pricked. The problem was trying to keep crowds of people from standing on the ramp. Every box we had ended up with the ramp bent, and everywhere we went policemen were needed to control the crowds. On this day, we witnessed another fatality in the crowd when a man just dropped down dead. I remember a policeman saying to me, 'That can't be a bad way to go, Ginger: see Red Rum and die.' It was sad, of course. But I could also see the policeman's black humour.

You know, we never sent the Le Mare family a bill for Red Rum after Red had retired. But, then, he always earned his keep. If I had thought for a moment that Red Rum didn't like what he was doing, I'd never have done it. But he was full of himself; he'd always been a showman. He'd loved racing, and now he was thoroughly enjoying his new life in the public eye.

The Guv'nor used to make occasional visits to the yard. He'd arrive in his big Daimler limousine to see how the old lad was doing, and then come in for a drink and a talk with me. He was never remotely interested in being in the public eye; it just wasn't his line of country. He had one or two other horses with me – Ballyath ran in the 1977 Grand National won by Red Rum, of course. He was a tremendous character and a gentleman of the old style; I had the utmost respect for him, and I did not know a soul who had a bad word to say about him. The Guv'nor had the satisfaction of realizing the three ambitions that he had set himself: he married a beautiful woman, he became a millionaire, and he won the National. He lived his final days on the Isle of Man, dying at the age of ninety-two, if I remember correctly. The funeral was supposed to be a family-only affair, but Beryl and I went anyway. I think his family appreciated that we had to pay our last respects. I will be for ever grateful to Mr Le Mare.

Chapter Fourteen

ON THE BRINK

I WAS STILL in business selling cars from the showroom in Upper Aughton Road with my partner Peter Cundy, who was not dissimilar-looking to me – tall, with gingery-coloured hair. People did mistake us for brothers, and we often used this to our advantage at the car auctions we used to go to regularly in Liverpool, Preston, Brighouse and Chorley – that one was a rough affair on Friday nights and chock full of old bangers. At the auctions, Peter would be on one side of the ring with me on the other. No one could tell if we were buying or selling. We would bid in harmony: Peter would nod one minute and I'd nod the next. No one knew if we were bidding for real or just running the car up to flop it on someone else's lap. So going to a horse sale was like water off a duck's back to me. Horse people think they are clever and pull strokes – but let me tell you they are babes in arms in comparison to second-hand-car dealers. The car trade is full of characters and plenty of villains, too.

Peter was a friend as well as a business associate. He was a drinking man, mind. At half past five every night, Peter was out of the showroom and down to the Fisherman's Rest. His routine was highly disciplined. He'd begin with a couple of halves of bitter, then move on to whisky and milk. The Irish landlord used to say, 'I'll buy in as much milk as Peter wants to drink whisky.' Peter had a clique of drinking pals at the pub – including me some nights – but he nearly always left at seven-thirty. One minute he was with you, the next he had gone. That was another aspect of his discipline.

One night I had not been long home from the Fisherman's Rest when there was a knock on the door. One of our cleaners had come to tell me that Peter had been in an accident not far from the pub. The law on drink-driving was not as tight then, but it was tight enough. When I arrived at the scene, Peter's Jaguar was parked in the middle of a wall, having bounced against the rear end of a van. He was still behind the wheel, blood running down his cheek from a mouth wound.

Someone had already telephoned for an ambulance and this had arrived. By chance, I had been at school with one of the ambulance crew. He asked me what had happened and when I told him, and added that Peter was my partner, he whispered, 'Is he pissed?' I nodded. My old schoolfriend assisted Peter into the ambulance in double-quick time to get him out of the vicinity before the police turned up. I followed him to hospital in my own car.

As he was helped into the infirmary, Peter's face was a bloody mess. The male nurse who came to greet him stopped in his tracks when he saw me. We knew each other too – from the days when I did some boxing and we had trained in the same gym. Again, I mentioned that Peter was my partner. 'Is he pissed?' he asked. I nodded. He said he knew a doctor on duty who disliked the police and rushed off to find him. The doctor duly came to casualty and told Peter that he needed stitches. He was about to go to work on Peter's face, when into the room burst a policeman short of breath from running from his car.

I knew him as well and, sure enough, I just happened to let slip that Peter was my partner. 'Is he pissed?' he asked. I told him that Peter might have had a couple. But before he could ask any more awkward questions, the good doctor threw him out of the room because he wanted to stitch Peter's wounds. Outside, my policeman pal told me to take Peter home and he would straighten out matters with his superiors.

We never heard another word.

According to Beryl, I involved myself in a lot of drinking sessions with Peter, much to her disgust. I dispute that I drank anywhere near as often as she claims – but she argues that I have a tendency to blank out memories that don't suit me. I can't remember ever doing that. But I don't dispute that I liked the craic of a few scoops with friends. For instance, John Wynne happened to be a director of the company that sold the William Lawson brand of whisky. Anyway, we'd be in our poky little kitchen some nights when John would arrive with bags of fish and chips and whisky. We did have a bit of an open house policy, and I remember a particular night when John was there along with Mick James, who had trained at Formby for Arthur Maiden. At midnight, we decided to have a contest to see who could run fastest. In the pitch dark, and full of whisky, we raced one another beyond the railway line. Silly really . . . and it was not as if anyone would remember in the morning who had won.

To all intents and purposes life seemed good. Trouble was, the motor trade had begun to turn sour – not just for me but in general terms. The income Red Rum generated allowed me to retain some independence for a time, though. Possibly this was not an entirely good thing. I never went looking for new owners as perhaps I should have done. When you have had a horse of the calibre of Red, it is hard to imagine how you'll ever find another one like him. I couldn't pay £20,000 for a horse. Nor did I have the numbers of young horses in the yard that the larger trainers had. I was still very much the poor relation.

Still, we had our moments. Emlyn Hughes and Terry McDermott, a team-mate of Em's with Liverpool and England, had a horse with me called Simmering at the end of the seventies after Red had retired. I retained a share in him. One day we ran Simmering when Em and Terry were abroad with the England team. I am guessing when I say this, but in all likelihood other members of the England team were persuaded by Em to back the horse as a good thing. I found out afterwards that Terry had called England to hear the commentary of the race and was relaying the news to the others gathered in his hotel room. As Simmering went past the post in first place Terry threw the phone so hard in the air that he broke the connection and screamed, 'We've won!' What he did not know was that the stewards called for an inquiry into the result. For five agonizing minutes, I had to wait to discover whether I had the winner or not. With winners hard to come by – and I was struggling to get into double figures after Red Rum had retired – I was relieved when the stewards announced that the result stood. So were Em and Terry, as I suspect they'd had a right touch at odds of 100–8 – but they never knew about the drama of the inquiry until they spoke to me after they had come home.

With a maximum of eighteen horses in training – and invariably two or three of those would be on the sick list at any one moment – my debts began to mount. Only the huge demand for appearances by Red allowed us to remain training, if I am truthful. At second-hand-car auctions, when I made a successful bid the auctioneer would say, 'Knocked down to Red Rum!'

Yet I remained conveniently oblivious to the truth of our predicament. I admit that while we had this ongoing success with Red Rum I cocked a blind eye to what was happening with the cars. The worst thing we ever did was to go into new cars – but at the time it seemed such a natural development. We even had Ken Dodd open our new showroom in a blaze of local publicity. He was appearing in his own show at the Floral Hall on the promenade, and I called on the off-chance that he might have heard of me through Red Rum. A lovely man, he said he would be pleased to open the showroom. He did not want a fee, asking us instead to buy two or three hundred pounds' worth of tickets for his show for local children. Ken, a big Liverpudlian celebrity, built his comic routine around an imaginary place called Knotty Ash that was inhabited by 'Diddymen', imaginary little people with 'tickling sticks'. He arrived around 1.30 p.m. – and wouldn't go home! My mum and dad were both present, along with Jonjo O'Neill and Ron Barry. Red Rum made an appearance, it goes without saying. All in all, it was quite a big event for our little part of the world. I even sold Jonjo a new car!

Our car business had very humble origins. But with this grand opening, it really felt like we were on our way in the trade. We had become an agency for Austin Rover cars, with a new showroom and a new servicing department. The Austin Rover company had made a U-turn in policy, opting to reinstate small agencies across the country, yet even so our first application to join forces with them had been rejected. My response was to write a personal letter to the company chairman. I told him that we could take on an agency for a Japanese car company, but that I wanted to sell English cars. Within a few days, people from Rover came to meet us and the contracts were drawn up and signed.

Soon we were on the mailing list to go to exotic locations for new car launches, receiving invitations to places like Monte Carlo and Marbella. We paid £250 towards the trip and Austin Rover collected the rest of the bill for a couple of nights away. I had membership of the company's 'One Hundred Club' – for selling 100 or more units a year – but I think I was given preferential treatment on these launches as I suppose I was reasonably well-known at this stage. Certainly, Beryl and I always had top-standard accommodation. These occasions were really glitzy affairs, with stars like John Cleese making the presentations. When the new car appeared out of a cloud of smoke, you thought to yourself, 'I'll have a dozen of those.' Cars were placed at your disposal to test. It was a seductive sell.

But we had stretched ourselves beyond our financial limits. The showroom alone had cost £30,000 to modernize. And to get the new car agency we had to have a service department. Each time a new model came out, you were automatically committed to stocking the spares that went with it. We haemorrhaged money.

At least I'd had the vision in the good times to buy three properties that came up for sale across the road from the showroom. That meant I had some collateral in bricks and mortar, and that kept us going for a while. I also had Red Rum to take to the bank. His earnings persuaded the bank manager to lend me money as the car trade ran into difficulties.

I wasn't alone – the business as a whole was going into decline. We just weren't selling enough cars, and the pressure was building. Before I knew it, the bank had the deeds to the properties across the road and the overdraft was still getting bigger.

By 1982 we were sinking fast. We were £100,000 overdrawn and the bank, in the unstable economic climate of the times, wanted to call in the loan. Our assets nowhere near met our liabilities. We stood to lose everything that we had worked for.

Now, my partner Peter and his wife Marie seemed immune to the hardships that we had started to endure. They lived in an expensive part of Southport and owned a new caravan, drove a smart car and holidayed abroad more than once a year. As Beryl pointed out, they had brand new carpets and a washing machine; she wanted to know why she had to buy these commodities second-hand. I didn't pay that much attention – but Beryl did. Beryl had waited for years even to have a carpet on the stairs, as any money I had was most definitely spent on horses. Beryl did cut into me over that. She even went to see my mother, crying as she bemoaned the fact that my horses always took precedence over anything else. Beryl asked my mother if she could help – and I don't think she was best pleased when my mum laughed at the very thought of having a word with me. She knew what a waste of breath that would have been.

But even if I wasn't too bothered about domestic niceties, I could no longer ignore the crisis in the car business. Our bank manager made it plain that we had reached breaking point. Still, Peter was as liable as I was. Or so I assumed. As the true scale of the problem surfaced, I said to him, 'The way things look, the bank manager will soon have the roof off our heads.'

Calmly, he replied: 'They won't have mine.'

'How's that?' I said, puzzled.

'Our house is in Marie's name.'

I was speechless. He had acted to look after himself without mentioning a word to me. We were meant to be partners. That's not what the word means to me.

Finally, I said, 'Bollocks to you.'

After this, to my mind, our partnership had no future. Beryl suspected that Peter had been working some scams for some while, and that he had been creaming money off the business for his own account. Marie, I'm certain, had nothing to do with it. I don't think they were terribly large amounts of money, but they would have added up and exacerbated the seriousness of our position. We never pursued him for the money – I suppose I was too soft. As far as I was concerned, it was Peter's betrayal of my trust that was unforgivable. Even so, I had to accept some of the blame, as I had not paid proper attention or heeded the warning signs. Beryl insists that she told me we were struggling, but that I didn't listen. She probably has a point.

Luckily for us, as the crisis deepened Stan Markland was over from Jersey staying with us for a few days. Since we'd met at the party after Red Rum had won the Scottish National, Stan had become a valued friend of mine. A proper man and a proper friend, he was one of those handful of people that you meet in life, if you are lucky, who will do absolutely anything for you. He had made his fortune in the steel tube industry in the north-west. One of my owners, an oldish man in the fruit and veg business, told him that he had a horse with me and Stan liked the sound of that; so he took half-shares in two horses with the old man and I trained them. But then another acquaintance of the old boy began training, and he wanted to take the horses out of my yard and send them to this other stable. Stan wanted to stay with me – so one horse left and the other remained. Quick Half she was called, and she was a decent mare who won three or four races. Stan was a half-pint-of-bitter man – but he had an ability to drink halves all day and all night!

Beryl and I became regular visitors to Stan's home in Jersey. He had taken on a big pub–restaurant on the island called The Harvest Barn, which could seat 200 people. He said he didn't really want it, but he had ended up with the place in the way that wealthy men make investments. I happened to be present when Peter Greenall – later Lord Daresbury and chairman of Aintree Racecourse – and his father made an offer for Stan's pub. The Greenalls were a brewing dynasty, of course, and they could see the commercial sense of having a large pub on the island. But Stan told them that he would not sell to them. Why? 'Because I think your beer is crap,' said Stan.

We had some good, good times with him in Jersey. I had to go into training myself before we went over: the hospitality was that fierce, I wouldn't have a drink for a fortnight! Stan's local pub was across the road from his house, but he took the car because he always said that he would be too pissed to walk home. He had his own set of keys to the bar. I became a member of the notorious Wednesday Club. We would meet for our first drink at around 11 a.m. and take it from there. Mostly, we drank halves of bitter, but if we did bother with a meal in the evening we would have some wine. With two or three of his friends, Stan took particular delight in spotting those holidaymakers who thought they could take a drink. Usually, they ended up sliding down the bar.

I've got a picture of me slumped on the stairs at Stan's house, eyes all over the place. Someone has written a caption in a bubble coming out of my mouth: 'Wednesday, bloody Wednesday!' I couldn't go the gallop with them. They had nothing to do on that island but eat and drink. Money was no object to Stan. He complained that he couldn't get decent fish and chips on Jersey, so he thought nothing of flying his plane to Blackpool to have a fish supper and flying home again. He did love his fish and chips. One summer when we just couldn't afford the fares over to Jersey, Stan sent his plane to collect us. That was the measure of the man's friendship.

So it was a stroke of luck for us that Stan was in Southport when it became evident that we could not escape from the financial hole that we had dug. Beryl was at the end of her tether, and she was crying at the prospect of losing the roof from over our heads. Years earlier, I had had to deal with bailiffs at the door, because Beryl had delayed paying a bill as she juggled the money around. I chased them off the premises with an axe handle. We never saw them again, and the bill was paid, albeit a little late. But the bank's threat to foreclose on us was not something that we could dismiss.

As we worried what our next move could possibly be, Stan just came into the showroom and wrote out a cheque for £30,000 to slice the overdraft almost in half. He never asked me to sign a scrap of paper and the money was never mentioned again. Yet without that money, we would have gone under.

Of course, after the rescue package we couldn't continue as we were with Peter, otherwise there was a real possibility we could have gone back to square one. Even though he was empowered to sign cheques on the business, we had no formal written partnership. He said that all he wanted to do was to walk away. I agreed to that – and I took on the debts.

I did train Stan's horses at a discount, but I was still a bit naughty. I was buying horses when I should have been paying Stan back . . . but it all worked out awfully well; Stan never badgered me for his money, even though in the end it did take me over five years to repay him.

Sadly, Stan died about fourteen years ago, and since coming home from his funeral I have never had the heart to return to Jersey. Much as I love the island, it would not be the same without him.

AFTER PETER WASHED his hands and walked away, I was left to chip away with the cars as well as the horses. Eventually, I took on a salesman called Eric Jones. He had been a professional footballer, and I think he was on the books at Everton at one time. He was a nice enough chap, but he liked to spend much of his day in the bookie's across the road. He couldn't sell furs to an Eskimo. He knew how to do a deal for his friends, though: he would get them a good car – and take a right load of shite in part-exchange. Clearly, he was not the answer to my prayers and had to go.

I left Beryl, who did all the book-keeping for the business (sometimes not finishing until the early hours of the morning, all while she helped with the horses and brought up two children), to place an advert for a new salesman. One of the two applicants turned up in a T-shirt and jeans, which hardly impressed Beryl. Yet, discarding his casual appearance, Beryl saw something in Paul Nolan that she liked and we offered him the job. No one was more surprised than Paul — or more disappointed !

Let Paul explain:

'The long and short of it was my wife got me to take the job — I thought she had to be joking. I had been living and working in Jersey, and I had been told that if I signed on the dole I would get a tax rebate on money that I had earned when I worked in England before. I reckoned that had to be worth about nine hundred quid. But as I signed on I was asked if I had registered for a job. I said no, so she directed me to the job centre. Someone said, "What do you do?" I told them that I was a sales manager, and I artfully suggested that they wouldn't be able to find a job like that for me. I was told that they had an interview for me to go to the next day.

'I thought that this was not going to plan. I didn't want a job. That was why I turned up in a T-shirt for the interview. As we chatted away I thought, lovely people as they are, they really don't know that much about cars. Ginger had half an inkling, but they didn't know much about the value of cars. I mean Ginger had been around with Peter and had done bits and pieces, but not on a daily basis.

'Ginger gave me the job and went off to Jersey the next day. All I could see around the place was this terrible load of dross. Oh, I can remember them all. There was a Rover that had come from a local farmer called Croppers that was stood on the books at three and a half thousand quid and was worth all of thirteen hundred, or fourteen hundred tops. I looked at the dire stock and I realized the entire load of crap had to go. We had to reconcile ourselves to taking a big hit before we could start buying stock at proper valuations.

'Once Ginger knew what I could do he was terrific to work for. He backed me — throwing money at me to go out and buy cars. Sometimes he was making me buy cars I didn't want. "You'll sell them, cock," he said. "You'll sell them."

'At Brighouse auction one day there was a new limited edition Mini that had come out, an attractive car, but pink. I figured we could go to nineteen hundred, no more, but I thought it would make a higher price. I duly came out of the bidding at nineteen hundred quid. I said to Ginger to leave it alone, it was too dear, and I went for a bacon butty. Now, the auctioneer, Arthur Smith, knew Ginger very well. And he also knew that sometimes I'd drop out and that Ginger would take over behind me. It was a sort of game between them. So I'd gone to get the bacon sandwiches and I could hear this Mini going on two thousand two hundred . . . two thousand three hundred . . . and I came back and asked Ginger, "What fucking dealer bought that?" And he said, "We have!" I had it on the forecourt for about six weeks and we made about eighty quid profit.

'I did fall in love with the place on sight, because it was beautiful with the horses and the cobbled yard out the back. It was fabulous and coaches continually stopped outside and you could see the driver telling them all about the home of Red Rum.

'We managed to turn the business round in the first year, I think we transformed a hundred thousand pound loss into a two thousand pound profit.'

Paul is still to be found at McCain's Showrooms – only the business is his these days, and he leases the property from me. He has a lot of modern BMWs and Mercedes for sale! He also has a share in a horse with me.

Chapter Fifteen

THEY SHOOT HORSES,

DON'T THEY?

WE JUST BATTLED on, as the little yard with a small amount of ammunition to fire against the big boys, until one day in 1983. I had long since accepted that life is never short of surprises. I was at home doing mundane jobs when I answered a knock at the door to find two attractive ladies on the doorstep. I had never seen either of them before. With them, though, were two men, one of whom I did know: Jeffrey Samuels had a horse with me.

Jeffrey, a little Jewish fellow, knew everybody and anybody. He had been in a wine bar in Southport when he came to meet the women, he told me. The women were in the company of John Halewood, and Jeff had engaged these ladies in conversation and joined them for a drink. Later, one of them had come to Jeff's rescue by making an emergency repair when he broke the zip on his trousers during a visit to the toilet. Jeff said that the conversation eventually turned to horses, and he told them how he had a horse in training with me – and that he suggested he could show them Red Rum. That was how they all – Jeff, John and the two ladies – came to be on my doorstep.

Beryl happened to be out, so I was alone to entertain them. They were bonny girls, ex-air hostesses, and John was engaged to one of them; Ann, the other woman, was his personal assistant. I got out our Waterford crystal and opened some champagne. Doesn't that sound grand! Actually, there is an amusing little tale as to how we came to get the glasses.

As I've explained, we tended to run Red Rum in the Greenall Whitley Handicap Chase as his final prep race before the Grand National. The wife of the chairman of Greenall's was a big fan of our horse and was always asking me to dinner. Naturally, I said I would be delighted to join them, but somehow the years passed without me making a visit to their home in Cheshire. Finally, I accepted an invitation to have dinner with them, but, rudely, Beryl and I arrived at their old-fashioned farmhouse thirty minutes late. They were the perfect hosts and waved aside our apologies as we had pre-dinner drinks with their other guests. Just before we went to sit down, I was asked to accept a gift as a token of their appreciation for Red Rum running so often in the race they sponsored. When the chairman had finished speaking, I was given a beautiful Waterford decanter. His gesture sparked pangs of guilt for having delayed coming to dinner with them for so long. I had just finished thanking them for their generosity when I was told that the other seventy-four pieces of the set were boxed and waiting for me in the hall. Not much later, my good friend Brian Aughton offered me £500 for the lot. I've got to say I was a little tempted – it was a good deal of money at the time – but Brian was always a bandit and I reckoned the set was probably worth a good deal more, so I refused. He never missed a chance to try and pick your pocket!

We rarely used the best crystal, but I decided such attractive guests had to be treated properly. After a few glasses had gone down, they asked me to show a video of Red Rum winning the Grand National. I do remember that John, who was in the wine business, knocked over and broke one of the Waterford glasses. He was most apologetic, but we'd had a good craic and that's what counts most at the end of the day.

Before my unexpected guests left, John said that he would like to have a horse with me and that I would hear from him in the near future. I said that was a good idea – but privately I never supposed anything would happen. How many times had I heard that after a few drinks, I wondered? As it turned out, that chance meeting with John was to lead to a friendship that exists to this day. But it is a friendship that, as well as bringing us an enormous amount of fun and the ultimate success on the racetrack, has on occasion brought me to the edge of despair.

I FORGET HOW many times John came back after that, to discuss horses and have a few glasses, but it was a fair few and we got on well together. One thing I do remember is that he ended his relationship with the woman he was with when he first turned up on my doorstep. He had switched horses, so to speak, to go out with Ann, who, I must say, was really lovely. It also became evident that John was serious about having a horse, and so, after one of our sessions together, I arranged to meet him at the next scheduled sale at Doncaster. John arrived with his mum, an Irish lady, and his dad, who had been an officer in the merchant navy. I took John to stand in the left-hand side of the balcony area in the sales ring, where I had stood when I bought Red Rum. Maybe the little bit of luck I had had that day would rub off. From there, you can lean over the balcony and see the auctioneer and the opposition. By now, I had an idea just how competitive a man John was – he did not concede defeat easily – so it promised to be an interesting experience.

We had a specific target in mind: an unbroken store horse that I thought would make 6,000 guineas, maybe 8,000 at worst. But as the horse was walked round the ring the bidding kept escalating and John kept offering more. Finally, the horse was banged down to John for 15,000 guineas; in 1983 that was a tidy sum, and I'd never been associated with a horse of that value. Now we had to have the horse vetted. On inspection, the vet found a little mark inside one of his eyes. He informed us that he didn't think that it would affect the horse's vision on the racecourse, but he was unable to pass him as sound. I thought that this gave us a chance to renegotiate a new deal and I told John that he should pay no more than 6,000 guineas for the horse – but his enthusiasm to strike a deal led him to buy the bugger for 10,000 guineas.

With the horse bought, we went to the bar where John's father was waiting. We ordered in some champagne to celebrate, and that was when John's dad suggested that I should buy his son another horse with the 5,000 guineas that had been saved. There was one that I'd seen go through the ring that took my eye, and it hadn't made its reserve price. I managed to buy it for 5,000 guineas. So John had gone to Doncaster to buy one horse and come away with two. And I had two good horses for the yard where I was training around a dozen or so others. These horses that John had acquired were definitely a damn sight better material than the breakdowns and cast-offs that I was having to work with now that Red Rum was out of the picture.

John named the second horse Highland Gold and I sent him to Sedgefield for his first race, but Beryl went rather than me. She arrived later than the horse and was met with the news that Highland Gold was a non-runner. Beryl went to find our lad Norman, who was with the horse, and asked what had gone on. Norman told Beryl that Highland Gold had been withdrawn on a vet's instructions as the horse was 'choking' in his box. Highland Gold wore a muzzle, but he was a clever horse and he had tried to remove it by scraping it on the floor of the box. As a consequence, he had a ball of straw stuck in his gullet. He had thrown himself around in a panic and looked in a desperate state, with mucus coming out of his nose. Yet by the time Beryl had arrived Highland Gold had calmed down. Norman had sponged water into his mouth and the problem had been resolved. The vet wanted to inject a muscle relaxant, but first asked Norman to trot him outside his box three or four times. All the discharge had gone and there was no sign of a cough. Beryl hurried Norman into getting Highland Gold ready to race.

In the meantime, Beryl called me to tell me that our horse had been withdrawn and asked whether she should try to run him anyway. I expressed total confidence in Beryl to manage the situation as she saw fit. She rushed off to tell the stewards of the meeting that Highland Gold was perfectly capable of racing – and after they had inspected him, the horse was placed back in his race. Jockey Kevin Doolan was told to pull up the horse at the slightest hint of a problem with him. Instead he ran beautifully to win in some style. So that was an afternoon when we had a winner with a non-runner!

There was a postscript to the day: John had family commitments and didn't go to the racecourse – and, to be honest, I hadn't given him any suggestion that the horse had a chance of winning. Shows how much I know! This was in the days before we all had mobile phones, of course, so John found out that Highland Gold had won at odds of 20–1 from the results service on television. Later that night, he mischievously rang to ask me how his horse had run. I told him that he had won. He continued to press me about the horse's performance and convinced me that he had not heard the result. Eventually, I lost patience and shouted down the phone: 'How many more times, John, the horse fucking won!' John began to laugh . . . he'd done me. Highland Gold, in fact, won several more races.

The other horse that John had bought – called Halewood Vintner – also proved a success. He was versatile, getting placed on the flat, over hurdles and over fences. Jonjo rode him a couple of times for us, and Sally Aston gave him a good ride in the Ladies' Diamond Stakes at Ascot when he ran an absolute blinder, galloping on strongly at the end.

By now John had been bitten by the racing bug, and he wanted to find a horse to run in the 1986 Grand National. We went to Ireland together in 1985 to see a horse called Dudie that was trained by Paddy Mullins. I have to say, when we observed him walking around the paddock at Fairyhouse he looked a miserable, dark little horse. But we would reserve judgement until we had seen him race. Dudie had run in the National the previous year and had jumped off like a scalded cat. He made the running for the first circuit – and a story later circulated that he had been backed to be in front passing the grandstand first time.

Once at Fairyhouse, John and I had a nice few whiskies before the race. With three to jump, Dudie moved into contention with the leading horses and I can remember telling John that I didn't think we would get him now. But in the closing stages Dudie visibly tired, and he tailed off to finish eighth. Afterwards, we established that the horse was still on the market and John paid around £8,000 to bring him home. So Dudie would represent John and me in the National. Unfortunately, Dudie proved to lack the Aintree Factor. The place scared him to death. He fell at the fourth; jockey Kevin Doolan remounted, but then he fell for a second time a couple of fences later. It was a classic case of a horse losing his bottle.

John was by now married to Ann, who formed a sentimental attachment with their horses; a fact which was to prove significant to us in the coming months. For, sadly, we were about to experience the downside of the game.

Jonjo finished second on Halewood Vintner at Wolverhampton over fences, and blamed himself for not winning the race. The horse's next race was at Uttoxeter with Kevin Doolan in the saddle, and it appeared that there was no way he could be beaten. I couldn't believe it when he finished second again. But there was worse to come. When I went to meet the horse at the unsaddling enclosure I discovered that he had cut through his tendon. It was a dreadful injury, and it was plain to me that the horse would have to be shot. But the vet at the racecourse, a youngish man, decided that the horse should be given a chance. He had his girlfriend with him, and I think he wanted to impress her with his 'sensitivity'. But no matter what his reasoning was, I knew it was a completely wrong decision to load the horse into his box to be driven to the veterinary hospital at Liverpool. The vets there took one look at him, and immediately decided that the only humane option was to shoot him. I was mad, because the vet's false sentiment at the racecourse had unnecessarily subjected my horse to the pain of travelling. Hard as the job is, the horse should have been put down on the spot. And as if this wasn't bad enough, our luck was about to worsen.

Highland Gold had won five races for us now, and looked like making a beautiful novice chaser. Then one morning I went into his box and found that he had broken his pelvis. These things can happen – it only takes a horse to roll around awkwardly. We managed to get him to his feet and, after calling the vet, I let John know about this latest terrible occurrence. To be perfectly fair to John and Ann, they always put the welfare of their horses ahead of any financial considerations. Their instructions were to do the best that we could for him. So we patiently got the old horse together again. He must have been at least three months in his box in the yard before, once he was on the mend, we brought him out and walked him. We had just reached the point where he was well enough to be ridden quietly on the road when I came in one morning to find him down once more. He was a beggar of a horse to roll, and in doing so he had managed to fracture his pelvis for a second time.

I rang for our vet Ken Wrigley, who worked with Ted Greenway. As soon as he had examined the horse, Ken told us that he was dying. I rang John and told him what had happened, and that our vet felt Highland Gold had to be put down. At this time, John lived in Wakefield, which was at least an hour and a quarter's drive from Southport. He asked me not to do anything until he got to the yard. By this stage John was my premier owner, with four horses in my stables, so I wanted to respect his wishes if at all possible. Yet when I discussed the position with the vet, he told me that the issue was out of our hands. Highland Gold was bleeding internally and, in his opinion, would be dead within half an hour. We couldn't even get the horse to his feet. So the vet shot him to spare him further pain.

But when John and Ann arrived, they were furious to discover that Highland Gold had been put down contrary to their wishes. I couldn't seem to get through to them. The job had had to be done, I told them. And it had been. I was gutted, too. I'd lost two good horses within a few months of one another. There's nobody softer than me when it comes to horses; but this is a tough old game, and there are times when hard decisions have to be taken.

Ann, however, was not in the mood to listen to reason. She was very distressed, and she sat in our kitchen and told her husband that she was not prepared to put up with this any more. They had two young sons now, and she argued that the money would be better put aside for them rather than invested in horses with all the risks that that entailed, not least emotionally. I could understand her point of view, but that didn't mean I agreed with it.

John and Ann decided there and then to put their remaining horses on ice. I disagreed with that strategy, and I said so. John can be quite hard when he wants to be – you don't build a company as he has done without breaking some eggs – and I knew I had my back to the wall. They thought I'd been too quick to shoot Highland Gold and told me that I should have waited. I told them I'd had no choice. As the temperature in the kitchen rose, I told John to take his horses and stick them up his arse.

Actually, that is John's version of events; still, although I don't recall saying that, it doesn't mean that I didn't. Emotions were running high, after all. And it does sound a bit like me, I admit. I was as distraught as John and Ann, as I'd really thought we were getting somewhere with Highland Gold. He was a good, nice-natured horse. I know I get too attached, which means events like this hurt me just as much as they do the owners. But I also know what is right for the animals.

In the event, regardless of anything I could say, John had his three horses removed from my yard: Dudie went to Reg Akehurst along with another horse whose name I forget, and Miss Club Royal was moved to Jimmy Fitzgerald. At least they had gone to good trainers, I thought, as if that was any real consolation. And my reputation never suffered as a consequence of the moves, as John wasn't that well known in racing then. The real damage was losing three horses out of a yard that had no more than eighteen horses in all.

This job is a great leveller. It brings you into line very quickly if you get above yourself. John and Ann were relatively new owners, and it was understandable that they should become emotionally attached to their horses. It's also fair to suggest that I was a little more bolshie back then, as my confidence was still inflated with Red Rum's triumphs.

As well as losing my best owner, I also feared that I had lost a friendship that I valued. But gradually, John and I started to speak to one another again. One night over a meal, he told me that he owed the bank £800,000 on his business overdraft. That shocked me – after all, I'd almost gone to the wall when I was £100,000 in debt to the bank. But John thought that to owe that amount of money was no more than a natural phase in building and expanding a company on the scale he envisaged. He was a man who knew the direction he was taking in life, and he would not be deflected. One day he said that he would have a dozen horses with me. I said, 'Yes, John, and three bags full!'

Anyhow, some time later John called on the telephone and told me that he had been offered the chance to buy a certain horse (I am afraid it is asking too much of my memory to recall the name). He asked for my opinion and I suggested he should buy it. 'I'll only do so, if you'll train it,' said John. We were back in business – for the moment.

BEFORE JOHN HAD entered my life, at the beginning of the 1980s, we'd had a horse called Hallo Dandy. He was owned, along with two other horses in the yard, by Jack Thompson, and we had some success with him. Thompson – Black Jack, as he was known for the colour of his clothes – was a wealthy man (at one point he would help to bale Aston Martin out of trouble), but he was also a bit of a wind-up merchant, and when his horses were unfit he would call me and demand: 'Why aren't my horses running?' On one such occasion I told him that they had problems. Jack wanted them taken to a veterinary clinic in Market Harborough. I told him to save his money; I explained that the vets would say: 'Shoot that one, fire that one and rest the other one.' Jack didn't want to listen, so the horses went to Market Harborough anyway. He was told to shoot one, fire one and give the third (which was Hallo Dandy) some physiotherapy. After this Jack took Hallo Dandy away from me and gave him to Gordon Richards to train.

A bit later Jack was back on the phone to me, having been made an offer for Hallo Dandy, asking me to assess his value. 'Ask Gordon, he's your trainer,' I said. Jack said that Gordon was not as good a judge of a horse's worth as I was. I told Jack I thought Hallo Dandy was worth £20,000. He thought the same, and told this City chap that was the amount he wanted. Four days passed before the City slicker came back on to confirm the deal. 'I want £24,000,' said Jack. The would-be buyer said that he thought he had been quoted £20,000. 'Ah,' said Jack. 'That was the price four days ago; this is the price now.' Jack got his price – and then Hallo Dandy went on to win the 1984 Grand National for his new owner.

Jack was not downhearted, however. He had landed a huge gamble on Hallo Dandy and he held court in the champagne bar at Aintree after the race. I was with Stan Markland, a man of greater wealth even than Black Jack. When Jack asked Stan to get four bottles of champagne in, he happily did so. He did it a second time, but when Jack asked him again, Stan let him know he was not a complete mug. His language was tasteless, but Jack took the hint and didn't take any more liberties.

Owners can be a strange breed. Around 1986 I sold an unbroken young horse called Rinus for £6,000 to a businessman named Bert Proos. He was a lovely horse and won a lot of races, but one day out of the blue Bert rang to say that he was moving the horse to Gordon Richards. I don't think Gordon had anything against me, I really don't! I reminded Bert that I had sold him Rinus – and another horse called Balmatt – on condition they stayed in my yard. Bert thought that a payment of £500 would sweeten my mood. Well, there was not a chance in hell of that happening. 'Bert, you are not a man of honour and you are not a sportsman,' I bellowed. 'And you can stick your five hundred pounds.' It was yet another blow to take on the chin. Rinus was good enough to finish fourth in the Grand National.

Time moves on, though. Now I train a couple of horses for Bert's son David, who has an ambition to win the Grand National. In the summer of 2005 David invited Beryl and me to stay with him at his home in Portugal and to play some golf. His son Harry is a very talented golfer – and David showed us great hospitality.

In 1986 we had two runners in the Grand National: Dudie, and a horse called Imperial Black who belonged to a man named Tom Webster. Imperial Black won fourteen chases for us. Tom entered into an unusual arrangement with me, in fact. He said that when Imperial Black won four races he would give me a set of golf clubs; and he also gave me six golf balls for every length that the horse was in front at the winning post. As he often won by ten lengths I soon had enough golf balls to open my own shop! Michael Dickinson – later to outshine his father Tony as a trainer – won several times on Imperial Black, a big horse that Tom and his wife Sally, a good horsewoman, had paid less than £5,000 for in Ireland.

One summer's day, Tom rang me out of the blue to say that he was going to apply for a trainer's permit. I was amazed – as far as I was concerned, all Tom did was drink. However, he seemed serious, and thought that I should write him a reference. He was most surprised when I refused. I explained that I would write a letter on behalf of Sally, but I could not bring myself to give him a reference as he was not in the least qualified for the job. I might occasionally dull the truth, but I have never told outright lies. My advice to Tom was to go in through the back door: to start point-to-pointing and then go hunter chasing to give him a foundation for applying for a training permit.

I don't think that was what he wanted to hear, as his response was to threaten to take Imperial Black out of the yard if I wouldn't co-operate. I told him that he must do what he felt was right, but he wouldn't be getting a letter from me.

So Tom began to call round. One of his first calls was to Michael Dickinson, to whom he offered Imperial Black to train. Michael declined, telling Webster that he couldn't take the horse as I was a friend of his. It takes a good, honourable man to take such a position. Later Tom told me that he had asked Michael who he recommended should train the horse. 'Ginger McCain,' he had replied.

But Tom was determined to find someone else to train the horse in return for a reference. He finally found someone who agreed: Neville Crump, who said he would write a letter of recommendation that Sally was competent to hold a training permit – which is what I had offered to do. I was very surprised at Neville, but I think that by this time the job wasn't going all that well for him. Imperial Black won two races for him, I seem to recall.

Tom was in partnership with a man called Tony Lunt, who took over ownership of a horse named Kumbi. This was a horse that I trained to compete in three Grand Nationals in 1984, 1985 and 1988. Kumbi never completed the course, but he did have a good deal of success elsewhere. Like Imperial Black, Kumbi won fourteen races. It was a remarkable record for two partners with only two horses.

I'll admit I probably wasn't too polite to Tom during this time, and things were more than frosty between us for a while. Yet before then, when things were all going well, Tom and Tony would come down to the beach on a Saturday morning to see the horses work. We used to be on the beach for the first lot at about eight o'clock. By the time they'd finished, we would have emptied three bottles of champagne. Then we would go to the little café at the end of Lord Street and have a full fry-up. The boys would by then have been home for a bite of breakfast themselves, and we would be back on the beach to watch them work the second lot. Lovely, lovely days.

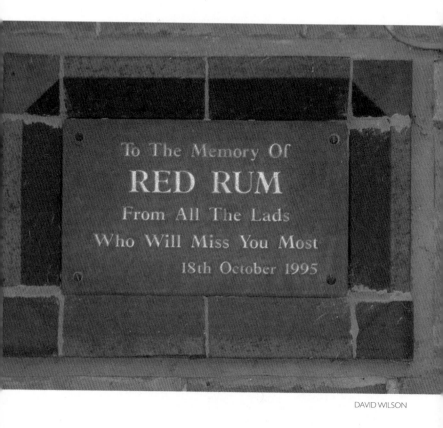

To The Memory Of
RED RUM
From All The Lads
Who Will Miss You Most
18th October 1995

A fitting tribute at Aintree.

EMPICS

Red Rum's final visit to Aintree on his 30th birthday. He was, and always will be, the 'People's Horse'.

MIRRORPIX

Jackie Grainger salutes the old horse at his grave on the Aintree finish line.

Amberleigh House in Red Rum's old box on the
Cholmondeley Estate. A worthy occupant.

The gallops at Cholmondeley. A long way from the view
outside the car showroom in Southport.

2 0 0 4

Takagi falls at the Chair but Graham Lee and Amberleigh House avoid the trouble.

Graham and Amberleigh time it to perfection, moving past Clan Royal and Lord Atterbury to snatch victory. My fourth National. Bloody magic!

My good friend John Halewood celebrates his horse's victory.

'You done us proud, Graham.'

I wasn't always confident of victory on the day.

Jonjo, Clan Royal's trainer, offers warm congratulations after being pipped at the post. A quality man.

Years before that 2004 triumph, Stan Markland bailed us out
and set us on the road to success again. A true and proper friend.

Fish and chips? No problem. We'll hop on the private plane.
Stan with his wife Phil, and Joanne and Donald.

At Stan's house in Jersey after the notorious Wednesday Club. First drink
by 11.00 a.m.

Donald's first ride, at 16 years old – honest.

Me and my angelic grandkids: Ella, Toby, Noah and Abbie. The respect they have for me is clear, don't you think?

Joanne leading Donald on Sure Metal to his ride in the '96 National.

Joanne and Red Rum.

Red Rum. 3rd May 1965–18th October 1995.

Yet they couldn't go on, because we were coming off the beach pickled every Saturday morning. Tom could drink for England – but Beryl didn't approve (again) and in the end I ran out of arguments to justify our behaviour.

Eventually, Tom did send Imperial Black back to me, and he was in place to win his fifteenth race when he cut through his tendons and died on the racecourse. Imperial Black was only ten – a terrible shame as he was a good horse.

ON A MORE amusing note, I must tell you about Beryl's experience riding in the Ladies' Derby at Ripon. It was in 1988 and Donald, who at this point was working for Luca Cumani at Newmarket, happened to be at the meeting. Beryl was slow out of the gate and never managed to get into the race on what was not the quickest of horses. She came towards the post racing Geraldine Rees – on another horse that was no good – for last place. After the race we were taking tea at the racecourse when we heard an announcement over the tannoy: 'Mrs McCain to the stewards' room.'

Dutifully, Beryl went to see the stewards. She came out of the meeting looking like death. 'They've fined me two hundred pounds,' she said. I told her that I would go to have a word with them on her behalf. I went to see Lord Halifax, chairman of the stewards, and asked if he could put me in the picture. Politely, he invited me to watch the replay of the race. And there was Beryl beating her horse like a carpet, then pulling her stick through to her other hand and doing the same on the horse's other flank.

'Well, Ginger, what do you think?' asked Lord Halifax.

'M'lord, I think you should have fined her twice as much,' I said.

Donald remembers returning to Cumani's yard to be teased by the other lads. They had christened his mother 'The Lancashire Lasher'.

Chapter Sixteen

CHICKEN NUGGETS

FOR ALL THE difficult days in this game when the fates conspire against you – or your luck is on the floor along with some bad-legged horse you have nursed to get on the racecourse – it just takes one winner to erase the bad memories. Some winners are more special than others, though. Red Rum is an obvious case in point. But the story I'm about to tell you is the tale of a horse that in all probability you have never heard of; yet he too had his own special day. And I'm including it here because I think it illustrates the magic and excitement that the sport brings – the reason I love it so much.

He was a big horse I bought in Ireland for 3,000 guineas and shipped home. In time I sold him to John Singleton and Alan Orritt, who were – and remain to this day – business partners and friends. They have a processed-chicken plant in the north-west and trade under the name Champ Chicken. Not unnaturally, they named their new horse after the company. No one could have guessed how the four-legged version of Champ Chicken would become a legend in his own modest lifetime. After all, this is a story with a very unpromising beginning.

For his first ever race we took Champ Chicken to Uttoxeter to run over hurdles, and booked Jonjo O'Neill to ride. As we sometimes did, we offered to meet Jonjo at a motorway service station where he could park his car and continue the journey to the racecourse with us. On this afternoon, it must be stated that we travelled more in hope than in expectation. My friend Tony Stannard, who was not a stranger to the bookmakers, had come with us for a day out and a punt. This was just a typical day's racing, one like a hundred others over the winter, and there was a smallish crowd at the racecourse. It was the sort of day that makes the old game tick over. Jonjo's brief was to give Champ Chicken a decent ride and let him enjoy his work. Anything more than that would have been a real bonus. Jonjo understood the score, yet without placing our horse under any pressure he had Champ Chicken positioned to make a challenge as they turned into the straight. But as the contenders pushed on, Champ Chicken seemed to stall just a little and Jonjo finished with him in mid-division. Quite honestly, I was not unhappy with the horse's performance. Yet as he dismounted, Jonjo made a point of letting me know that he had been responsible for the horse fading from the picture. 'I made a bad mistake at the first fence in the straight,' he admitted. 'I'd have gone awfully close if I hadn't done that.' I appreciated his honesty – but that was typical of the man. You always knew where you stood with Jonjo.

Back at the motorway service station, Tony had to get out of the car to let Jonjo clamber across as I was driving a two-door coupé. Jonjo leaned over to me as he left, and, in a voice designed only for my ears, suggested: 'I meant what I said about that horse. If I hadn't hit that fence in the straight I could have won.' His words struck home. Did we trust in Jonjo's instincts and go for a 'touch' next time out? John and Alan didn't need any persuading that Champ Chicken should be laid to land a coup.

We entered him for a modest race at Bangor. The challenge now was to keep the betting market unaware of the gamble that was going to be staked on Champ Chicken. To that end, the money could not be placed on the horse until twenty minutes before the race began. I think I agree with Jonjo when he later declared that the bets on the horse were placed with military precision. John and Alan, under direction from another friend of ours called Ronnie Mentha, asked their management staff to spread the money across as many bookmakers as possible in order not to arouse suspicion. I think bets were struck in Preston, Liverpool, Manchester – you name a town and there was money riding on Champ Chicken. I had not known a 'touch' on this scale before.

John and Alan were at the racecourse with their wives Di and Trish, naturally. No one connected with the horse wanted to miss out on the fun or excitement. I gave Jonjo a leg up, and he cantered to the start knowing what was at stake. Being the superb jockey that he is, Jonjo delivered a faultless ride. The opposition was outclassed. In the stand, our hearts never missed a beat. Champ Chicken sluiced up . . . and unsuspecting bookies were clobbered far and wide.

We took over the bar and called in the champagne. We opened the bottles with as much abandon as those racing drivers in Formula One and the corks whizzed around. The bar at Bangor was lined with a foam-like material – and for years afterwards you could still see the holes that the flying corks had made. We drank them out of champagne. And we all sang that soppy song that was a popular hit . . . 'Didn't we have a lovely day, the day we went to Bangor!'

Naturally, we had to stop at one or two pubs on the way home. Days like these you don't want to end, and if they do you don't want to be sober to remember when they ended! John and Alan, good, good friends and very loyal to me by keeping horses in my yard through the lean years, love to tell the punchline to the story. According to them, their staff and friends who had gone round the betting shops on foot or on bicycles to lay the money returned to collect their winnings by taxi!

I believe that the bookies were taken for in excess of £30,000 – a lot of money in the eighties. It was talked about in our part of the world for quite sometime afterwards.

While on the subject of John, I must recount another 'sting' he was involved in – but again I must stress that the coup was an entirely legitimate case of getting one over the bookmakers. In the early 1990s John owned a horse called Hey Cottage – probably one of the best horses I have had my hands on. As it happened, he had only taken on Hey

Cottage after a friend of his, a man called Bob Diamond, had encountered some financial problems. Singy didn't pay a lot, and I had recommended him as a grand horse that was going forwards. I think he won his two bumpers, ridden by my son, Donald, if I am not mistaken. After Hey Cottage won a hurdle race on his next appearance, we decided to go chasing with him over the National fences at Aintree. In fact, the horse's reputation had begun to reach a wider audience, and Richard Dunwoody rang up offering to ride him. Now, when a champion jockey like Richard calls, you'd better let him ride.

Unfortunately, Hey Cottage belly-flopped over the first fence, knocking all the wind out of him. He was a distance behind and I thought Richard would pull him up. But, no, he sat on the horse quietly, quietly, like the good horseman he was. I can remember thinking, 'Well done, old son, at least you are giving him a ride.' Richard eventually finished third, albeit a long way back. In his next race at Chepstow, Hey Cottage had Carl Llewellyn up, and beforehand I had a real belief that the horse would win. In the paddock, I told Carl to hold up the horse as he had had only one run and I considered it best that he arrive late on the scene. However, I was proved wrong. Quite clearly, the horse had the stamina to stay – but Carl obeyed my instructions to the letter and held him back; in the event, Hey Cottage did not quite get to the winner and was beaten by a neck.

At the time we hadn't really got a talking horse in the yard – one that made people take notice of us – so I was mightily encouraged by what I'd seen from Hey Cottage. We decided we would take him all the way down to Ascot to compete in what looked like a modest chase. I wanted Graham McCourt in the saddle, but he had been offered the ride on another horse in the same race. We squeezed and pulled out all the stops to get Graham to change his mind – including, if I am truthful, a little emotional blackmail in implying that if he didn't ride Hey Cottage he would not get the ride on Hot Plate in the Grand National. Reluctantly, Graham agreed, but his decision was made late in the day and the next morning's papers had Graham Bradley down to ride Hey Cottage. Brad had been our fall-back plan.

John Singleton had gone to stay at the Windsor Castle Hotel, not far from Ascot, along with a friend, John Gray. From there, early on the morning of the race day, Singy called me on my mobile and asked the question he likes to put when asking about a horse:

'Is he fit?'

I politely pointed out that I wouldn't be sending him to the races if he wasn't.

Singy's next question was more direct. 'Will he win?'

'I think he will run very well,' I replied.

'Do you know what price he is?' asked Singy.

'No.'

'A hundred to one!'

Bugger me, I thought. The papers aren't usually that far wrong. I was beginning to lose my bottle, I don't mind admitting.

Singy came back again. 'Who rides him?'

'Graham McCourt,' I answered.

'The papers say Graham Bradley is down to ride.'

'The papers are wrong,' I informed him. And that was that.

Maybe an hour later, my phone rang again. Over breakfast, Singy and his friend had decided that Hey Cottage represented serious value for money. Now Singy told me that they had got on the Tote, and then they had placed yet more money on the horse with bookmaker Victor Chandler. By this time, what little bottle I had left had gone totally awol.

At the racecourse, I tried to go about business as calmly as the circumstances permitted. But it wasn't easy. In the secondary paddock prior to the race I had noticed Rough Quest, the horse we'd persuaded McCourt to desert, and he was a good-looker. The bookmakers also thought him to be the class of the field, as they had installed Rough Quest at 7–4 favourite on the course. Honestly, I felt a pang of guilt for twisting Graham's arm to give up that horse to ride our 100–1 outsider.

Even so, I also felt a sense of excitement. I said to Singy, 'This is better than sex, isn't it?'

Singy shot me an earnest look. 'I'm not sure about that . . . I'll let you know in ten minutes.'

As the horses swung round Swinley Bottom to jump the second last, Hey Cottage came to tackle Rough Quest. I could see that John's binoculars were shaking in his hands. 'What about this, John? Better than sex?'

Still shaking, Singy muttered, 'Fucking hell, Ginger, you're right!'

Well, our horse won by about three lengths from Rough Quest. Beryl ran to meet Graham McCourt. He leaned out of the saddle to kiss her. 'Your husband can walk on fucking water!' he said, smiling. I hadn't had a single penny on the horse – but John and his friends were soon properly pushing out the boat in the champagne bar. We were drinking those Jeroboams of champagne and Jenny Pitman came over to join us for a drink. 'Ginger,' she said. 'They should lock you up.' Graham Bradley also stopped at our party. 'Everyone keeps saying to me, "Great, Brad, what a ride you gave him."' I think half the racecourse was getting pickled.

Then someone introducing himself as an employee of Victor Chandler sought me out. He handed me a slip of paper and said, 'The Boss said to give you this, Ginger, and thank you very much.' It was a betting slip for how much he had been taken for. It was for an awful lot of money.

As we were finally leaving the course, a taxi came screeching to a halt. The door flew open and Bob Diamond almost fell out. Bob had seen the horse win and hurried to Speke Airport in Liverpool to catch a flight to London, then jumped in a taxi to Ascot. Singy had put £100 on Hey Cottage for Bob, and he had arrived to collect. We went for dinner at the Windsor Castle Hotel, an establishment with quite a formal dining room. Soon, we had the place in uproar. Grown men were singing,

'Who got a hundred to one? We did!' It was the 'touch' of a lifetime. Yet if Hey Cottage had won at Chepstow, he would have gone off second or third favourite at Ascot. It wasn't the horse's fault – it was mine. Beryl and I left the party in full flow, as, sadly, we had to return home for the funeral of a friend, Alan Percival.

If I am honest, I thought Hey Cottage was going to be my next National horse with a serious chance of winning – a thought only encouraged by the fact that Rough Quest won the 1996 Grand National. But by then we no longer had Hey Cottage. Tragically, the horse got colic and the vet found that he had a twisted gut. He was only eight years old when he was put down – and that was a sad day for us all, as he had been a horse with serious, serious potential. That's racing, I suppose. You have your highs and you have your lows – yet some kickings take a little bit longer to get over. But what can you do? That's always been the nature of the job.

RIGHT THROUGH THE eighties I was still in the car trade, and although Paul Nolan was now managing the day-to-day business, I still went to my share of car auctions. One day, when we had finished at an auction at Leeds, I said to Paul that we could get to Sedgefield in time to see a horse of mine in the three o'clock race. Paul looked at his watch and told me that it was ten past two, and we'd never make it. I persuaded him that we could. I never thought much of it, but Paul's recollection of the drive is still vivid.

'Ginger had a rotary-engined sports car, a very fast little job. I mean very fast. Ginger was doing a hundred and thirty miles an hour up the A1. I tell you what, Jackie bloody Stewart couldn't have done the journey any quicker. I spent the whole way under my seat spluttering, "I'm too young to die!" Ginger was a good driver – but God Almighty we must have broken all records in getting from Leeds to Sedgefield in not much more than forty-five minutes.'

In actual fact, we drove up alongside the course just as the horses jumped off for the three o'clock. We saw my horse come down to the second . . . and topple over!

There was rarely a dull moment. Red Rum still attracted a host of visitors – from the Duchess of Westminster to the cast of *Coronation Street*. Almost every day a coach would pull up outside the showroom and thirty old ladies would get out. Mostly, they marched right in as though our stables were a public monument rather than a place of business. Still, no harm was done and we had a very happy yard. In the summer, at the end of the working day I'd often put out some bottles of wine and the lads would get stuck in. All right, the wine might have been on the cheap side and slightly corked, but no one cared until later. There was a church up the road and some nights you would find bodies draped all over the place as the wine took its toll.

I remember coming into the yard once and thinking I must have had one scoop too many, considering what I was seeing. But I was stone cold sober; we'd just come back from a day out racing to be greeted by Red Rum's home undergoing an unplanned makeover. I couldn't believe my eyes. As I have explained, the stables behind the showroom were set in a rectangle on a beautiful cobbled yard. It was like a Victorian street. But as we turned in that day we found one of the girls who worked for me stripped to her bra and pants and concreting the yard from a cement mixer. She was doing the last bit when we walked in. What had possessed the silly bloody Irishwoman I'll never know, but you can assume that she didn't stay on the payroll much longer.

Over the course of time, I'd expanded the yard as best I could so that we could accommodate more horses. But I was beginning to grow less enamoured of the suitability of the area for training. Traffic was building up and the environment people were interfering with us. There had also been a revision of council boundaries so that we now came under Sefton Council rather than Southport. That never made sense to me. Southport is a conservative town, whereas Sefton includes Bootle, which in those days was a really rough neighbourhood. To merge us with Bootle was bureaucratic bollocks.

Anyhow, having applied to extend the number of boxes we had in the yard, we had a visit from a busload of councillors, and the upshot was that we had two timber boxes erected – though not without some bother. One woman at the back of the yard did object, claiming that her son was having nightmares because of the noise the horses made. Horses don't make a noise at night; in fact there is nothing quieter than a stable yard at night. And she wasn't the only one giving us grief. Some people tried to prevent us from taking horses out through a rear gate by putting dustbins in our path; so we just kicked them aside and went out anyway. Then I had a run-in with a woman I knew only as Mrs Clarke. She came round to tell me that my horses were attracting flies. I told her that she was a liar and that she shouldn't make such accusations. I said that in my view our horses were looked after better than her or anyone else in her family – and I added that I thought they were entitled to be as they were far better bred.

These were minor inconveniences; the real problem lay with the two timber boxes in the yard. The council decided they had to be taken down as they claimed that we did not have planning permission for the boxes that we had built. The dispute hinged on a technicality – were they to be considered mobile buildings or permanent ones? We appealed, and the matter dragged on for a very long time. Finally, another coach party of councillors turned up outside. Before they arrived, we temporarily moved Red Rum from his usual stable into one of the timber boxes. To ensure there was no mistaking the horse in residence, we even transferred his name plaque and screwed it over the door of his makeshift home. Bugger me, given what Red Rum had done for Southport I thought they should have built him a palace. After he had won his third Grand National, he had been given the Freedom of Southport Beach. And hadn't 10,000 people filled Lord Street, hanging from buildings and roadside trees, to see Tommy Stack parade Red through the town behind three brass bands? Now there was a rumpus over him living in a timber box.

What the inspection party cost the council I cannot imagine, but there were too many councillors to count filing into the yard – and all to see two boxes at the back of Ginger McCain's car showroom. I can tell you, I didn't invite this lot in for a drink. Not long afterwards, I received a letter that rejected my appeal.

This was the final nail in the coffin. With the gallops already being ruined by local environmentalists, we had been shopping around on the quiet looking for somewhere out in the country. Now, in the late eighties, we stepped up the search. We went to look at Fred Rimell's place, The Racing Stables, at Kinnersley some fifteen miles north of Cheltenham. Fred had died, and his wife Mercy wanted to stop training altogether. The property belonged to the insurance company Sun Alliance, which sponsored two big races at the Cheltenham Festival. Stan Markland offered to fly over from Jersey to view the stables with us, and John Singleton joined us too.

The old stable yard was run down, and the house was a tip (Fred and Mercy had not lived there, but in a bungalow further away). There were two cottages and a very good all-weather gallop that Sun Alliance had put in, as well as a schooling ground that, admittedly, had seen better days. The yard itself was square, with olive trees that keep the flies away. I cannot be precise, but I think there were around thirty boxes; they were not in a good state, but there was bags of potential. I was prepared to uproot from Southport, as the place had a track record. Four Grand National winners had been trained there; Gold Cup winners, too. You knew that, given the horses, the facilities were good enough, even though the place required a substantial amount of investment to bring it up to a modern-day standard.

I understand that there had been twenty-three applicants to rent the stables – and I found that I had made the shortlist of three. We discussed the finances, and I was invited to an interview. The other candidates were Jim Wilson, who had been a champion amateur rider and had taken up training somewhere the other side of Cheltenham, and Simon Christian, who had been assistant to Fulke Walwyn and George Owen. As explained to me, what the owners were looking for in a new tenant was a trainer of some standing who was financially sound and who had a mature family to provide some continuity.

Wilson had only just started training – and I didn't think Christian had a family. He had also acquired a reputation when he was in Lambourn as someone who spat the dummy when things went against him. As I headed south for the interview I was in an upbeat frame of mind because I supposed I had to be in the pound seats. But when I walked into the room I could not believe who I saw among the interviewing panel: Mercy Rimell. What was she doing there? Who was she to judge me or anyone else? After all, she was out of the ball game now, as the yard was nothing to do with her any longer. For two pins, I felt like saying, 'Thank you, gentlemen, I won't bother wasting any of your time. I'll see myself out.'

But I didn't do that, as I was keen to take over at Kinnersley. Afterwards, I felt the interview had gone well, but for a while I didn't hear anything. We were staying with Stan in Jersey, in fact, when someone from Sun Alliance tracked us down. A voice on the other end of the phone said, 'I am awfully sorry to tell you this, Mr McCain, but you haven't got Kinnersley.' I asked him if he would mind telling me who would be moving in. I was told the successful applicant had been Simon Christian. I was shocked. I was mad. And I was sickened, because I had set myself on getting the yard.

I asked the man from Sun Alliance which of the criteria Christian had met. It didn't appear that he was as financially sound as me; after all I had my properties in Upper Aughton Road, a car showroom that was now turning over a profit again, and horses in training. He wasn't proven as a trainer. I said, 'Simon Christian is everything that you didn't want.' I forecast that Christian wouldn't last more than three or four years.

From what I remember, he was in the job little more than three. He had some winners, but it's a hard old game. I've spoken to him a little since, and he is a nice person. But I think that he found there is a big difference between being an assistant trainer and being the man held to account for everything. As an assistant you don't have to pay the bills – and you don't take the flak.

Swallowing my disappointment, I went on with the search. It led me next to Neville Crump's place, which had come on the market at Middleham in Yorkshire. Neville was getting out of the game. Beryl and I went to have a look at the yard to see if it would suit us. I liked Neville and, to be honest, I think he was keen for us to have it. The yard was old-fashioned, a bit dark and dour, but again it was a place with a good track record. The timber boxes were not quite falling down, but they were rotting. Neville intended to have a bungalow built on a plot of spare land, but I had no problems with that as I could have lived with a fellow like him around. I would have respected and taken his advice.

The asking price was £380,000. I didn't bid him. I know I could have raised around £180,000 – without selling any of the properties we had in Southport – and I thought the bank would have lent me the other £200,000. But I had one reservation. At that time the stables shared the gallop with a handful of other trainers. That meant that if you arrived with your horses at the wrong moment, you might have to wait for two or three strings from other trainers to finish work before you could start. I also remembered being told that in a training centre – like Lambourn, like Newmarket and like this place in Yorkshire – there can be difficulties on holding on to your staff. If you give a lad a bollocking, it is all too easy for him to go down the road and get another job. With such doubts in my mind, I thought I had better keep on looking.

Our wait was worthwhile. In 1990 we moved from Upper Aughton Road to Bankhouse, set in 192 acres on the Cholmondeley Estate in Cheshire. I was keener than ever to make a fresh start, as before we had left Southport I'd taken another hammer blow with the death of a horse called Honeygrove Banker. I still believe this was the second-best horse I'd had my hands on. I'd bought him outside the ring at Doncaster for £4,000 when he failed to make his reserve as an unbroken horse. He was a tall, elegant, long-striding horse and when we schooled him over fences he looked impeccable. But we were never to find out how good he was. In his final race over hurdles at Uttoxeter, when he was carrying 12st 7lb, he fell. I knew he was dead as soon as he hit the ground . . . he had broken his neck in the fall.

Our fortunes had to improve in Cheshire. I had been a stable lad in this area as a young man, of course, but it was when I sent a couple of mares to be covered by a stallion Terry Hall stood at Castle Stables, not too far from Bankhouse, that I came to appreciate what was on offer. As we didn't have the facilities at Southport I'd leave a mare with Terry, and I'd go over to see him once in a while, and over five or six whiskies we'd put the world to rights. I never received a bill from Terry so, just occasionally, I'd get struck by my conscience and send him £500. By this time Terry had had a public licence for a couple of seasons, but training wasn't his strong suit. I just loved those stables, though. Russian Hero was trained from there to win a Grand National.

Terry knew my feelings for the area, so when he learned that a neighbouring dairy farm was about to become available he rang me with the news and told me to contact Strutt and Parker, the agents. Beryl and our daughter Joanne went to see Bankhouse and, cliché or not, they were over the moon about the place. With dairy farming very intense in the locality, the agents had advised the owners of the property, the Cholmondeley Estate, to seek to diversify if at all possible. Our proposal to train racehorses was obviously just the kind of attractive alternative use of the land that the agents wanted. Beryl and I were swiftly invited to attend an interview at the London offices of Strutt and Parker in Berkeley Square, Mayfair, where we met Lord David Cholmondeley. To our great delight, we were told that same afternoon that we could have the tenancy.

From that point on, everything moved quite fast. The dairy equipment, farm stuff, carpets and curtains were valued at £25,000. I thought this a bit steep, but we were that keen to get into Bankhouse we bit the bullet and didn't dispute the valuation. When we held a sale of all the equipment, we lost £20,000, a fair old lump if you had it in your hand. Before we even moved in, I had some land ploughed at the beginning of November to put a dirt gallop down. But with the first heavy rainfall, the gallop resembled a ditch, and I realized I'd need an all-weather gallop. The company I spoke with quoted me £10,000 a furlong, and we had just over four furlongs once we had scrubbed out a dry ditch in a hedge. I beat them down to £7,000 a furlong and left them to it. One day after racing, while we were still at Southport, I decided to look in to see how things were moving along. As I went up the long, winding drive, all I could see was masses and masses of equipment. I thought they were building an extension to the M6 – and then I remembered that I was paying for it.

Eventually, we moved into Bankhouse in the darkness of that winter – and we didn't have to wait long for our first power cut. Suddenly, I was dealing with generators and a way of life far removed from what we had been used to at Southport, with its street lights and conveniently local Chinese chip shop, off-licence, chemist and paper shop – not to mention the three pubs on the doorstep. All at once we were seemingly in the middle of nowhere with nearly 200 acres of land that we didn't know what to do with. At heart we were basically townies uprooted into the country – yet we have never looked back.

Chapter Seventeen

ROCK BOTTOM

WE HAD STUCK our necks out by taking on Bankhouse – especially in the financial sense. Our annual rent was £26,000, and we knew we were all in for a lot of hard graft. Even I was riding out – something I hadn't done for a considerable time. Our children Joanne and Donald had both left home before we had moved out of Southport, but we had hoped that they would come and join us in Cheshire, as – unsurprisingly, perhaps – both had become involved with horses.

As a small boy, Donald hadn't been keen on riding, but his sister had shown an interest quite early on. In fact, I bought one of her first ponies from Sir Bobby Charlton. We'd met one evening at a sports function when Joanne was about thirteen and, when we began to talk about our daughters, Bobby casually mentioned that he had a pony for sale that his daughter had outgrown. He explained how the pony had competed in the Prince Philip Cup, the top Pony Club mounted games – at which point I told him to behave himself as I couldn't afford that quality of pony. But Bobby insisted that he was more interested in finding a good home for the pony than making money.

When I got home I mentioned this conversation to Beryl, and she thought she should take Joanne to have a look at the pony. It was called Gambol and stood at 13.1 hands. They took an instant liking to him, and I had a deal with Bobby for around £200. Considerately, he let us have the pony's headcollar and the night rug as well – but then, I always have driven a hard bargain! Joanne started to go round the local Pony Club shows and gymkhanas, and that in turn encouraged Beryl to have a ride on him. She had hardly ridden since she'd had the children, and the experience on Joanne's pony enticed her to begin riding racehorses again. Then we persuaded young Donald to get in the saddle; and he became hooked. Gambol was a grand pony, a cracking hunter. I can remember watching with some pride as Joanne pinged a big ditch in a cross-country event for the first time.

Yet it is a fact that the kids were sort of supplementary to the horses in the McCain household. Indeed, sometimes before the children arrived I think Beryl herself felt that way. On several occasions she took off without telling me where she was going, and I wouldn't see her for two or three days. I'd be distraught . . . though that is not the way Beryl remembers the episodes.

'You were not in the least distraught, but sometimes I just got to the end of my tether with you. Once I did go away when Joanne was about two and a half and I was pregnant with Donald. I remember wheeling her pushchair and wondering, "Where am I going to go?" I ended up taking the train to Surbiton, Surrey, and I stayed with a friend before stopping with my brother Len. I suppose in a blunt way I was trying to make you miss me, or at least not to take me for granted. The thing was I always came back on a Friday so as I could make out the wages for the staff.'

While I never dispute that the horses took precedence, that does not mean that we did not attempt to do our best for our children. When they were old enough, both of them went to Merchant Taylor's, a fee-paying school at Crosby, about ten miles away. I had never imagined being able to afford to do that, even if I had felt so inclined. After nursery, Donald started at Linaker Street School in Southport. One day I had gone to pick him up and I found myself standing outside the gate with other parents whom I can only describe as rough. Some had never done a stroke of work in their lives – or at least, that was the impression I had of them. In no way, shape or form can I be branded a snob, but I thought I wanted something better for my son, and we soon switched Donald to a private school in Formby. It was a good move for Donald, as the school taught children manners, discipline and sportsmanship. I can't think of three better principles to teach a boy. After Donald had passed an entrance exam to leave to go to Merchant Taylor's when he was eleven, the senior master told Beryl, 'Your son will get on in life because he is a nice person.' I like to think that he was correct.

If I am honest, I'd have loved him to be a top-class jump jockey. He had his first race ride on the Flat at Haydock Park when he was fifteen – that was under age, but we told a little white lie on the forms. Given his size, he was always destined to be a jump jockey, and he was good. Yet we never had the calibre of horse to give him the rides that he was entitled to expect. In the event, we decided that if he wasn't going to be a professional jockey, there were other options in the racing world, such as training, and that it would be best for him to learn at other yards, rather than our own. I arranged for him to work at Luca Cumani's stables in Newmarket. I knew from the beginning that he would have it tougher than most, for the simple reason that he was my son. I could imagine the head lad telling Donald, 'You are not with Ginger McCain now.' But I also felt that it would be good for Donald to get an insight into how other trainers operate.

There was a possibility that he could have been fixed up with a job in an American yard – to broaden his education still further – but it just so happened that at the time this proposal was being discussed the racing authorities in this country decided to explore the possibility of schooling horses to race over hurdles on the all-weather gallops. They introduced some trials – but some daft buggers set the hurdles in ground like concrete. Donald was the only amateur rider involved, and the jockeys were given all sorts of hairy horses to ride. The professional riders were insured, but as an amateur Donald was not. As bad luck would have it, another horse brought down Donald's, and he snapped the cruciate ligament in one of his knees. At the time, I did not realize how serious an injury that was. He was taken to hospital in Newmarket, where he was treated by doctors who were used to dealing with footballers and rugby players with the same condition.

It had not crossed my mind that we had a case for compensation, but that was what I was advised by the Jockey Club's medical officer. He felt that Donald should have been entitled to insurance along with the other riders. The advice was sound. Donald received £3,000 compensation – but he has been left with a niggling problem in his knee. Even so, in his time he rode over the big fences at Aintree on at least seven occasions, I think, without having a fall, and that includes riding Sure Metal in the Grand National. Donald is over six feet tall, but he got down to 10st for that ride. If he had stood in the sunshine, you could have seen right through him. He finished fifth on a horse called Harley in the Foxhunters' Chase at Liverpool – a race run over the National fences – and I recall hearing Richard Pitman's BBC commentary with a certain amount of pride. 'They're going down to Valentine's and that's young Donald McCain in the picture, really coming of age,' said Richard. I mean, it's a fact that most fathers expect more of their sons than they should do, so it was a bit special to hear such a compliment coming from a knowledgeable horseman like Richard. Donald also came third on Dudie in the Kim Muir Chase at Cheltenham.

He was never the bravest, perhaps. But he was a good jockey, and he was good round Liverpool. I think he rode getting on for forty winners under Rules. Other trainers were probably apprehensive about putting him up in the mistaken fear that he might try to pinch their owners.

After a couple of years Donald moved from Luca Cumani's to ride out for Sir Michael Stoute for a summer, then he went to Lambourn to work for Oliver Sherwood. He was there until we moved to Bankhouse, when I called and said I needed him with us.

When Joanne first left home she went to study animal science at Brighton Polytechnic, and she found work riding out at Charlie Moore's stables. As Joanne's a diabetic, I wasn't entirely happy about that. But I suppose my real concern as a father was that I thought Brighton was a bit too much of a party town for a girl on her own. Joanne is not the ugliest girl in England, so in my own old-fashioned way I didn't like her being down there. I also understood from her letters to me that she was feeling homesick – Brighton was a long way from where we lived and where she'd grown up, after all.

After a time, she left Brighton and took a job with Nicky Henderson, a top trainer in Lambourn. She also did some secretarial work and rode out for Jenny Pitman, who also trained in Lambourn. Joanne was disappointed that the Jockey Club would not give her a jockey's licence because she was a diabetic, even though a man with the same condition was considered fit enough to play professional football. It might have been a wise decision, but in some ways it was a shame that Joanne wasn't give the opportunity, because she was good. She was stylish, strong with good hands and plenty of bottle. But as you know, I still think race riding under National Hunt rules is not a profession for women. I include my own daughter in that category.

In due course, Joanne left Lambourn for Newmarket to work with Shippy Ellis, a respected jockeys' agent; then I was delighted that she came to join us in Cheshire, where we had enough work for us all and more besides.

Back home, when she was twenty-four, Joanne became involved with a boy who worked in a point-to-point yard near Shrewsbury. He wasn't a bad lad – but as a father you are always hoping for your daughter to find someone better. So we had a right ding-dong argument. I told her what I thought, and I said that either she stopped seeing the lad or she got out of the yard. She's a hard-headed person, and I can remember I was doing Red Rum in his box when I looked out to see Joanne driving out of the yard. Her car was loaded with her stuff and her little dog Errol was in the passenger seat.

I have never told her, and I have never told Beryl, but as I watched Joanne's car disappear I was shattered. But I suppose I am every bit as hard-headed as her, and I wouldn't back down. Joanne found a job as head girl with Mrs Sheila Crow, who trained point-to-pointers not too far from us. Probably a few months had passed, with Joanne talking to her mother, but not me, when we all met at a local point-to-point meeting. I'd missed her and I made a point of speaking with her; and quietly, quietly she came back into the fold.

Now, when we had moved into Bankhouse, the Mitchell family who farmed neighbouring land had made us especially welcome. I noticed that Arthur Mitchell's son Andrew came to help us whenever the possi-bility arose. He was a nice lad and a real grafter, and I thought to myself: Why can't Joanne get saddled up with a fellow like him? Well, sure enough, Andrew asked Joanne out – and suddenly, I found the boot was on the other foot. Cheshire farmers being Cheshire farmers, the Mitchells didn't approve of their son taking out Joanne. These farmers like their sons to marry other farmers' daughters, so there is a bit more land to be exchanged. Well, that was my opinion at the time. Anyhow, I am certain the Mitchells didn't think my daughter was good enough for their son. I happen to think my daughter is good enough for anyone. But I also recognized that it would be a brave man who took on Joanne McCain! Andrew proved to be that man – and he married Joanne in June 1996. I guess we'd been forgiven for Glenkiln's victory all those years previously.

Beryl may not have wanted children, but once she had them there was no better mother. I spoilt them, as dads do when they are trying to make up for what else they don't do with their children. But Beryl has to take the credit for the way Joanne and Donald have turned out. In the environment they grew up in – and through Red Rum, of course – they have met a lot of successful people, titled people and celebrities, and they know how to be polite and well-mannered. But they are not over-awed in such company. At the same time, Joanne would have made a good fishmonger's wife! Oh dear me, she can stand her corner with anybody. Donald is more polite and withdrawn. But overall, they were good kids who have become lovely adults and parents. I'm proud of the pair of them.

*

I MUST ADMIT I'd expected when we moved to Bankhouse that we would be in a rich catchment area to attract new owners. I was hopelessly wrong. We hardly drew a horse from this part of the world. I suppose I'd been used to owners who had made a few quid and knew how to spend it. Farmers seem to be conservative by nature – and farming as a whole had been going through a tough time, making it harder and harder to make a decent living. But if new owners were not beating a path to our door when we moved to Cheshire, worse news was about to strike.

John Halewood's marriage to Ann had begun to unravel by the time we came to Bankhouse. She was intensely preoccupied with their two sons, while John's time was consumed with the impressive business empire he had built. However, our friendship had recovered and, as he had a sumptuous home not too far from our new yard, I began socializing with him more. One day close to Christmas I dropped him off at home and John found that he was locked out. I felt this was a bit extreme on Ann's part; OK, give him a bollocking, but I don't think you can lock a man out of his own house, as I keep telling Beryl. Then the next I heard she had taken the boys and left. We invited John to stay with us, and he did. The second day he was with us a chap arrived on the doorstep to serve John with divorce papers.

At this time, I knew an attractive woman called Judy Eaton who was also at a bit of a loose end. Judy was from Southport – sometimes I had taken her to school in my taxi – and I knew her father quite well. In fact, he had a nice set of gates off me from Upper Aughton Road and I don't remember him ever paying! He claims otherwise, of course, and we often joke about it. I thought Judy and John would be good company for one another – and I suppose I rather threw them together. Beryl and I had gone to the Grosvenor Hotel in Chester after racing one day and Judy was in the bar. In my usual diplomatic fashion, I said something to Judy along the lines of, well, you're spare and John's spare, why don't you two get together? I felt like a Good Samaritan – but Beryl felt otherwise. She warned me that if Judy became involved with John she could have an influence on him with regard to his horses. Judy had trained on a small scale and once ran a horse called Harley in the Grand National.

Judy's sister Lisa was married to a Cheshire farmer, Mark Williamson, who had begun with a few liveries and then taken out a licence to train point-to-point horses. Lisa was good friends with Joanne and they had ridden ponies together. Anyhow, Beryl's fears were confirmed when, not long afterwards, I received a call from John. He told me that he wanted his horses to be moved to Lisa. We were at full stretch financially in Cheshire – and the cars were not walking out of the showroom in Southport. John took four horses out of the yard, Old Redwood, Kentucky Gold, Chalie Richards and Flinters, plus Dudie who was in retirement. It left a big hole in our stables, and in our resources. We only had around twenty horses in all, and John's were the best. We'd bought Chalie Richards for him in Ireland, he was a lovely unbroken horse, a great big fella standing 16.3. I'd go into his box when the boys had strapped him out and just look at him. He filled my eye. I had great expectations of him, but he had a wind problem, so I had him what they call 'hobdayed' – an operation that involves taking out the valve in the throat that the horse breathes through, giving him a clear passage of wind. We ran him twice at Liverpool and Donald rode him both times with implicit instructions not to be hard on him. He finished second in both races with very quiet runs. He was going to make a lovely horse.

Old Redwood had an amusing story behind him. I bought a horse at Doncaster sales for 10,000 guineas with my own money and as I was driving home I wondered – not for the first time – where the money was going to be found. On the M62 I realized that I had to pass close to John's place at Wakefield. I took the necessary small detour off the motorway and John made me welcome as usual. We had a few drinks and ended up in the sampling room. There were vats of sherry the size of gasometers and men walking round busily in white coats. It was very impressive. Well, we carried on sampling and we finished well pickled. If the police had stopped me on the way home, I'd have hung. I had deliberately gone to see John to sell him the horse I'd bought at the sales, of course. But in the morning I couldn't remember if I'd sold the horse or not. 'You bloody did,' confirmed John. He took the horse on for ten grand – but he was a nice horse with a future. We fired him purely as a precaution. Well, he was now gone. Miss Club Royal (who had returned to my yard when John and I had mended fences) was the only horse that John left with me.

I'd lost four big chasing types. I don't know what happened, but when they left my yard they were three weeks off running I reckoned, but not one ran for many months and not one fulfilled the promise I thought they had shown when I was training them. I accept that they had problems in the past, but when they left my yard they were in fast work and close to running. Michael Williamson is believed to have taken one of them out hunting and the story goes that the horse broke a hind leg and had to be shot. Williamson said he was opening a gate and that the horse got his leg jammed. I never understood quite what happened and why he would have been in the situation to shut a gate on a high-quality horse like that. Donald struggles to speak to the Williamsons to this day. He was extremely upset by some comments made by them on the soundness of the horses when they left our yard, and he rang John Halewood to tell him in person.

So John and I were adrift again. I felt bad. After all, I had been best man at John's wedding and was godfather to one of his sons. I can remember walking into the house and telling Beryl and Donald that I was going to pack up training. I am a man who sets great store by friendship and loyalty – and I thought a friend had just kicked me in the guts. You get disillusioned, you get disenchanted. There have been some owners that I haven't always got on with, but John was a close personal friend. What he did flattened me. I really didn't feel like I wanted to carry on with the job for a day longer. I was at rock bottom.

Chapter Eighteen

GOODBYE RED

BERYL AND DONALD would not hear of me packing the old game in, of course. I was down – but I was not out. I might have lost four good horses and my best owner, but I had other horses that needed my attention. I'd climbed from the floor before and I could do it again.

It was a case of working hard to keep our heads above water. It also seemed a natural time to refocus exclusively on training. Paul Nolan had been running the car business in Southport for years, so it was not too much of a jolt to sell out to him. I retained the premises, but he now traded alone, although he never changed the name of the showroom. And of course Red Rum still earned his keep.

We had slowed his regime down, though. At first we restricted him to two engagements a week, then we cut him down to one. The old lad was getting on – and out of respect I actually retired him completely towards the end of 1991. But it was clear from his restless behaviour that he missed the buzz of being the centre of attention, and so we began to accept invitations again, on a limited scale.

He had already had a health scare before we had left Southport. Lesley, the last girl to have ridden him out regularly on the beach, reported to me that Red kept going lame in a hind leg. He would sweat up and sometimes become a little distressed. Vet Ted Greenway came to examine him and deduced that he had a blockage in an artery. From that moment, Red was on a daily dosage of Warfarin.

He had handled the move without a hiccup. At Bankhouse he had paddocks to roam, as he was no longer being ridden. Yet in 1992 Red had another setback, and this time he was taken seriously ill. He was placed on a drip in his box, and we were convinced that he was nearing the end of his days. He was never uncomfortable, but he was extremely poorly and there did not seem much hope for him. He was barely eating or drinking, and we discussed putting him down. It was sad to watch the old lad go downhill, but age is something that none of us can fight for ever, can we? While it was a terrible thing to contemplate ending Red's life, I have always felt that I have a duty to my horses that goes right up to dispatching them. I cannot see them in pain. Red was no exception – his welfare had to come before any sadness I might feel about losing him after these years.

The affection in which he was still held could be gauged by the fact that every day on the dot of nine o'clock for over a week the phone used to ring in the house. On the other end of the line was Lady Beaverbrook, whose family had once owned the *Daily Express*, seeking a bulletin on Red's condition. If I wasn't there to take the call, she gave me a bollocking! Hundreds of get-well cards and messages came to the yard, while other well-wishers sent cheques or postal orders to be passed on to the Injured Jockeys' Fund.

Remarkably, Red fooled us again: he made a surprise recovery. True, he always appeared just a shade hollow after that; but he enjoyed a decent life for over three more years. He was a horse who loved people and attention. Every horse in the yard was eating Polo mints, as we were sent boxes and boxes of them. We just continued to care for him and take pleasure from him for the time we had left with the old lad. Age was his greatest enemy – as it is for all of us.

Like an old person, he just slid into decline as time passed. Remember, he'd had a hard life, as hard as any racehorse before or after him. He had raced over a hundred times over distances as short as five furlongs and as long as four and half miles. He was a tough horse – but we knew death was drawing near and it was something I dreaded.

There was a horrible predictability about the moment when Donald came into the kitchen one morning and said, 'Dad, Red's down in his box and can't get up.'

With Ted Greenway having died, John Burgess had become our vet and he was at the yard by 7.30 a.m. By then, the boys had managed to get the old lad on his feet. But his head was down and he looked almost like he was drunk. John inspected his gums and took Red's pulse. Solemnly, he reported, 'Ginger, he's dying.' If you are a horseman, you know the score. You don't leave an animal to die. You want death to be short and quick. I told the boys in the yard what had to happen and one by one they came to see him. They all had tears streaming down their faces as they gave him a last pat and said goodbye. Old Red took a Polo or two as well.

Shortly, there were just John and me left in the box. I was devastated. I didn't know what to do. What to think. Here was my old friend, who had been with me so long, seen me through so much, given me so much, dying. And I didn't know how to say goodbye. Shamefully, at the last minute I bottled out and asked John if he had any objections to my waiting outside. He told me that would be all right. I stood outside his door. I just couldn't be there at the end. I was an emotional wreck . . . I accept that leaving his box was unforgivable – I should have stayed with Red until the job was done. But I just couldn't steel myself for what I knew had to be done. Instead I walked outside and waited out of sight.

Pop.

That noise told me that John had put Red out of his misery. I swallowed very hard and walked back inside. What I found choked me more than anything ever has before.

When you shoot a horse, it flops to the ground. But if ever there was a scene-stealer it was Red Rum. John was still looking at the old horse in disbelief. When he was shot, Red had slid down with his back to the wall and propped himself against the big bank of straw that we kept in the box. His bloody ears were still pricked and aimed right at me. I don't weep easily, but that just made me crack. He had been a part of my life for twenty-three years, and now it was over.

FOR MANY YEARS, a plan had been in place for Red Rum to be buried at Aintree. But it had been ages since I'd last discussed this with the management of the racecourse, and so I wasn't entirely sure what kind of reception I would receive when I went to call them to tell them the news of Red's death. I need not have worried: from the moment I was put through to chief executive Charles Barnett, matters were put in hand with speed and efficiency. He promised to have a horse ambulance to us within an hour and a half, and told me that Red would be buried alongside the winning post. Kindly, Charles told me to leave all the details at his end to him.

When the ambulance arrived we had half a dozen lads congregated to help get Red on board. I wasn't going to have my Red Rum winched out of the box with a rope tied round his neck. We dropped the ramp on the ambulance and we laid a bed of straw as far as the door of Red's box. Then between us all we eased him along the straw in as dignified a way as we could. He was lighter than in his prime, but I imagine he still weighed seven hundredweight or thereabouts. Slowly, the ambulance inched down our long drive and Red Rum was on his last ever journey to the place where his legend had been born.

Joanne and Donald left a couple of hours later for Aintree. Obviously, they were cut up. He'd been an even bigger part of their lives than he had mine. After all, they had known nothing but Red Rum since they were tiny. And the kids came home from Liverpool to give me a message from the groundsman at Aintree, a lovely big, bluff man from County Durham called Bob. I'd got to know him during his time at Sedgefield racecourse. Bob had told the kids: 'Tell your dad we have buried Red Rum with dignity, and facing the right way.' Now that choked me as well. But it was the perfect resting place for the old lad. I cannot think of a more appropriate place for Red Rum to be buried, bang on the winning line at Aintree.

Seven years earlier, a life-size statue of Red had been unveiled at Aintree by the Princess Royal. I have loved the bronze statue, sculpted by former jockey Philip Blacker, from the moment I saw it. Philip has captured the character of the old horse in a manner that I don't think any other sculptor of horses has quite managed. It is the perfect monument to Red.

The day after he died he was front-page news on what seemed like every national newspaper. He was on all the television newscasts, and the tributes to him were gracious and generous. I would suggest Red Rum was the People's Horse. Does that sound a bit prejudiced? By that I mean, he didn't belong to Mr Le Mare and he didn't belong to me. He belonged to everybody who loved him. Sometimes, as I drive across England, I think that my old horse has been seen in every one of the houses I pass. Millions and millions saw him, you know.

His death was a relief to us in one way. We knew that, at thirty years old, he didn't have that much time left, so it was better to have faced the reality of his passing than to have to keep fearing the day. I suppose we all tried to put on a brave front, but the whole family was hit hard. A thumping great lump of our lives – not just mine, but Beryl's and the two kids' – had just been buried with Red Rum. He was a complete one-off. He had everything. He had confidence in people. He had an ego. I'd say, more than anything else, he had charisma. And he had become a part of me, all that I represented I suppose.

How many winners have I had now? Not that many, because we are not and never have been a big yard. But perhaps the number reaches 700, and that's winners that have been obtained despite the fact that I've had a lot of bad horses. When you've got bad horses they pass through your hands that much more quickly, you know. They come and they go; yet at the same time, good or bad, I've far more time for horses than I've ever had for people.

Until Amberleigh House won the Grand National for me for a fourth time in 2004, there were those who thought I was a one-horse trainer. I wouldn't ever say that Red Rum and I were meant for each other. Yet I would say we were good for each other. If I hadn't got him – and I don't say this in a boastful fashion – he probably wouldn't have lasted in racing much beyond the age of nine or ten. Where would he have gone from there? He would never have made a good hunter because Red Rum was Red Rum. He wouldn't jump a bloody twig if he didn't want to. And so he was out of this world for me. So, when they said I was a one-horse trainer I said that they were probably right. But I did make a good job of that one horse, didn't I? And I can never be anything but eternally gratefully to the old lad.

On his grave at Aintree are written the lines:

Respect this place, this hallowed ground,
A legend here his rest has found.
His feet would fly, our spirits soar.
He earned our love for evermore.

Rather nice, that, isn't it?

Whenever I am at Aintree, I always go to pay my respects to the old lad. I just love to be alone with my memories. I think of that first Grand National in 1973, when Richard Pitman seemed to have the race won on Crisp. Years later, Richard said that he was so far out in front that he was listening to the race being called over the loudspeakers on the course. He said that he made a mistake after jumping the last when he put his whip in his right hand and gave his horse a tap. He has no cause for self-recriminations, he really doesn't. Crisp was damn near going up and down on the spot before his horse failed to turn right at the Elbow. He was a great big, long-striding horse, but he had shortened his stride as he tired under the weight of carrying 12st. At the end of the day, basically Crisp was a good two-miler, so his performance had been quite brilliant until my horse came and passed him. But the next year my old lad carried the same weight and he won it going away. You didn't see him staggering around or running off a true line.

So many wonderful memories.

After one Grand National, I went to see the old lad and then walked across to the water jump. All the parties were over, almost 100,000 people had headed homewards, and there were four ducks swimming in the water as if it was their home. Red Rum will never be forgotten for as long as they run a race called the Grand National.

He was not born to be a star, and in his earliest days he was treated hard. That is a truth of the old game. Horses that are not stars possibly run on days they should not. But if you have a good horse, you can assess your possibilities more easily, you can draw back a little as you know there is always another day. You take much more care of a star. I'd be a fool and a liar if I said otherwise.

Red Rum made himself into a star to bring light and joy wherever he went.

Chapter Nineteen

BAD DEBTS AND VIAGRA

I HAVE BEEN lucky with most of my owners. Down the years men like Mr Le Mare, John Halewood, Stan Markland, John Singleton, Alan Orrett, Tony Stannard, Eric Chapman, Gary Salters, John Glews, Emlyn Hughes, Ronnie Mentha, Tommy Rathbone, Les Morgan and Jack Clayton became good friends.

Yet I cannot imagine I am alone among trainers in having had one or two owners go seriously sour on me. So much is done on trust – and people do have stars in their eyes when they buy a racehorse. And buying a horse is just the start. The real cost of owning a racehorse comes in the training fees, and that is not something everyone appreciates. If a horse gets injured – and it's an injury-prone sport – the bills still have to be paid. When someone's horse is not running, or his shoes get tight in business, it seems the first person he doesn't want to pay is the trainer. To my mind, no matter what regulations are supposed to be in place, it still remains too easy to move horses from trainer to trainer before bad debts surface. But I have always believed that as a trainer I have to rely on my judgement, and I have never been afraid to chance my arm.

Just occasionally, I got it badly wrong. One man who conned me was a member of the Wednesday Club in Jersey. He seemed to me to be Stan Markland's gopher; Stan sent him to go for this or to go for that. He built a bond of trust to the extent that Stan lent him £17,000. Then the man disappeared. Eighteen months later, Stan received a call from him out of the blue telling him to come to England to be repaid. Stan flew in his private plane to an airport on the south coast and collected his money. He was back in his Jersey pub inside three hours.

Some time after that episode, this same man rang me to find him a racehorse. I'd just got a nice horse over from Ireland, and I sold that to him for £22,000. Not satisfied with one, he instructed me to buy him another for £30,000. I thought he was in a bit deep and told him so. But he said to me: 'Are you buying it for me – or do I get someone else to do it?' As buyers with that amount to spend didn't grow on trees I went to Doncaster sales and did as I was requested.

He was now into me for £52,000 – and although he'd promised me the money, I hadn't seen a penny. It was at a period of our lives when we could not afford to catch a cold like that – Red Rum was still working to a pretty full diary, but the job was hard in those early days after we had moved to Cheshire and John Halewood's horses had gone. I had to pay Doncaster and suddenly the whole thing was becoming unfunny. After making repeated demands for the money that I was owed, I was taken aback when he suddenly agreed to meet me in the Bold Hotel in Lord Street. We sat in a corner of the restaurant and there, to my astonishment, he paid me in pound notes. I never questioned where the money came from – and I didn't want to know.

We resumed training his horses, but another twelve months passed without our being paid a bean. I suppose I was thinking that, as he had coughed up the last time, he would do so again, even if it was in his own time. But his debt got bigger and bigger until he owed us around £40,000. We were stretched to the point of breaking. In fact, when I look back, we were in Queer Street and no mistake. Again, he made a stream of unkept promises. I couldn't fathom out what was going on, but Stan said that this fellow was into something involving so much money that if it came off I would get two dozen new horses from him. Now, Stan didn't need any involvement of that kind. He already had a fortune. I often wonder if this guy picked Stan's pockets as well.

Anyhow, this man asked to meet me when I next came to London.

He had a limo waiting at the station for Beryl and me. I thought he was flying a bit high, but I accepted the lift to the National Sporting Club. While I was there, he took Beryl out to dinner at a very fancy and presumably expensive restaurant. She still remembers how the head waiter came up to the man and put an open menu in front of him and said, 'I'm not sure if you like this wine, sir' – actually, he had been discreetly delivering a note to tell the fellow that his wife had called. Beryl still chuckles at the thought of being considered a scarlet woman!

He may have bought her dinner, but he still never paid his bills. After a time, I turned his three horses out into a field. Eventually, I sent them to the sales and bought them back for buttons, because a horse out of training does not look as good as one in racing condition. Then, unexpectedly, we received a bank draft in the post for £15,000. It wasn't enough, but it was something. And we desperately needed it. Beryl stuck it in the bank and it was instantly swallowed by our overdraft. A couple of weeks later we were informed by Barclays that the money we had banked was part of a £250,000 stolen draft. There was talk of the money being reclaimed from us, but that was an impossibility as it had been used to reduce some of the debts we had. We had done nothing dishonest. We had been paid and we used the money accordingly, and the banks accepted that.

This con artist had come very close to breaking us – and Stan was disgusted. And do you know what amused me most? His brassneck cheek. Having disappeared off the face of the earth for years, he called me in April 2005. He wanted to know if he could have a horse with me. Fortunately, Beryl took the call . . . otherwise I might have been tempted to sell him a very nice horse indeed; one with no past and even less of a future, if you understand me!

My other really bad debtor was a man whose business had grown pretty quick and who was making a nice few quid. Donald rode his horse at Carlisle one day and he'd pulled clear going to the last, only to fall. When Donald came back he apologized to the owner, of course – to which the owner said, 'That's OK, we only had ten thousand each way on the horse.'

Actually, I had sold them some new Austin Rovers from the showroom in Southport in the days when we had gone up in the world. They left a low deposit and had hire purchase up to their eyeballs. That was not my concern, but I understand that the cars were never paid for.

I was on the beach at Southport one morning and the fellow came along to see the horses at work. As we watched them gallop, he told me that he needed some money to tide him over. Stupidly, I told him that I had a few quid he could have. I asked him if £10,000 would get him out of a hole. Not long afterwards, he rang me to say that he would like to borrow the money with interest. At least I had his horse as security, I thought. In reality, his horse had a 'leg' and was none too special. Still, I lent him the money; and that was the last I ever saw of it. His bills went unpaid, too.

It was stupid of me to have been taken in. You do meet a lot of wide boys in this business – and if I have a weakness it is that I might be too keen on occasion to get horses to train. But they were people I quite liked; all right, they were a bit quick, but being in the car trade I was used to being with people who were quick. I have been badly conned twice, yes. But I don't think that makes my judgement too bad.

LIKE MOST OF US, I always took my health for granted. Before we came to Cheshire, I'd only seen the inside of a hospital twice. The first time I went in for a routine hernia operation; but on the second occasion I was taken to hospital in excruciating pain. I think I'm pretty tough, with a high pain threshold, but this had me rolling around the bedroom floor in agony, vomiting non-stop. Beryl called for an ambulance, but I felt so awful, I couldn't wait for the ambulance to arrive. By chance, Brian Aughton had called in to see us and he bundled me into the back of his Rolls-Royce. At the hospital I said to the nurse,

'I don't care what you do to knock me out – cut my throat if you have to – but take this pain away.'

I was kept in hospital for almost a fortnight – don't ask me which year it was, because I have erased it from my memory – as I continued to run a high temperature. But after doing a number of scans and running innumerable tests, doctors admitted that although they suspected I had gall bladder trouble they could not find any evidence to substantiate that. I was allowed to go home and advised to stick to a fat-free diet. Later I went for a further examination at Fazakerly Hospital, where they found an abnormality at the end of a bile duct and removed it by laser treatment.

Some time after our move to Cheshire, the symptoms returned: vomiting, pain, jaundice. Once again I was admitted to hospital – and once again the scans produced negative results. However, the surgeon was convinced that my problems stemmed from my gall bladder, and said he intended to perform keyhole surgery. But before that procedure was booked, it was discovered that I had a stone in my gall bladder the size of a walnut, and I was immediately booked into theatre for a conventional operation. It seems my gall bladder and liver were scarred because of past infections.

After that, I was as fit as any horse in the yard until early in 2000, when Beryl noticed that I had a persistent loose cough and that I appeared unusually tired. She made me visit a doctor – and that was how I discovered that I had an irregular heartbeat. I was admitted to a coronary care unit for a week and given a course of drugs to return the heartbeat to as near normal as possible.

About twelve months later I began to have problems in the water-works department. I began to pee too frequently. Naturally, I assumed that I had a problem with my prostate gland. After having the necessary X-rays I was informed that I needed an operation. Did I have prostate cancer – or was it benign? On the day I drove back to hear the result of the biopsy, I thought, 'Bugger it, Ginger, whatever they tell you, you've had a great run.' And I meant it seriously. If it was bad news, I just didn't want to become an incontinent old man who was useless to anyone. If necessary, I wanted to be taken round the corner and shot.

Beryl, Donald and Joanne talked me into going 'private', reasoning that we thought nothing of spending £2,000–£3,000 on a vet to examine a horse and treat it. I was against the idea as I've always had a very high regard for the level of care and the quality of nursing in the NHS, but it was a fair point and they won the argument. I saw a specialist at a private hospital in Chester and they told me that they would be able to operate on my prostate within a few days. I was told that the operation, plus anaesthetist (and a bloody brass band for all I knew), was going to cost over £3,000. Oh, and they wanted another £500 to insure the operation in case anything went wrong. You also had to pay up front – in case you snuffed it, I assumed. All this upset me greatly. I did take a liking to the consultant surgeon, though. On the operating table, I said, 'Hang on, Mr Powell, this is bothering me, having to bloody pay for this operation. We'll have a deal. I'll give you a racehorse if you do the operation for nothing.' Those were the last words I spoke before I went out cold. During the operation it seems my heart went haywire again.

The next day Mr Powell came to see me on his rounds. He examined me and as he went to leave, he said, 'Oh, by the way, about that deal.' I looked at him blankly. 'What deal?' I asked. He didn't tell me until much later about the proposition I had made – and by then the bills had been paid.

Within a couple of weeks I was back in hospital as I had become very short of breath. Doctors had to find a way to get my heart to slow down. I can't remember the sequence of events once they got me into hospital, but I know they were anxious to get my heartbeat to a normal rhythm. As far as I understand it, they stopped my heart and then restarted it. I am told they had to do this twice. Beryl swears that she never offered the specialists £500 not to restart it, so I must assume I dreamt that under the anaesthetic! I can recall all the tubes that were stuck in me and, with typical diplomacy, I told the doctors that their machine was telling them 'bollocks'. I felt sure there was nothing wrong with me. They thought otherwise – and guess who was right? It seemed to take an awful long time for my heart to come down to whatever pace it should be at. Finally, the doctor told me that I would be allowed home the next day. He informed me of a long list of things I couldn't do – and that included drinking alcohol. I knew Beryl had told the doctors that I drank whisky, something she never liked, so I suspected her of being a snitch.

I said to the doctor, who was Asian: 'Are you a Muslim?'

'What's that got to do with anything?' he replied.

'Well, you know bugger all about drinking. I do.'

The doctor wasn't impressed and I can't say I blame him, but I'd had enough of hospitals. I take my prescribed pills on a daily basis and don't look any further than that. As far as I know, I haven't yet been classified useless. I still work as hard as I ever did and rarely do I miss a morning on the gallops, though I am the first to acknowledge that Donald plays a hugely significant role in the day-to-day running of the yard.

Beryl was with me when I went back for a check-up with Mr Powell – yes, the same consultant who had previously operated on me – and he reported that he was pleased with my progress. Politely, he asked me if I had any problems. 'Only the one,' I said. 'You did warn me that I would experience problems having sex, Mr Powell. Well, to be fair, it's not bothering Beryl, but my girlfriend's getting upset!'

Quite seriously, he asked me: 'Would you like some Viagra?'

Chapter Twenty

BACK IN THE FRAME

AT THE BACK of my mind, I always hoped that I might get to work with another real Aintree horse one day. I'm not saying for a second that I thought I could win the Grand National again – I just wanted the chance to go back to Liverpool with a realistic chance of competing. It was an ambition that I knew John Halewood shared.

With time, our friendship recovered; I really do like and admire John, even though every now and then he manages to give me a good kick where it hurts most. By the 1990s he had become an extremely wealthy man, and as the years passed his wine business and financial institution continued to expand, to the point where Halewood International employed over 1,500 people. He had horses in training with various trainers, and wherever John went there was always someone trying to sell him another one. In fact, that still happens.

With Donald working hard at my side I was training a respectable number of winners, and we continued to scour the sales catalogues in search of that special horse; yet, as ever, we lacked the ability to compete at the sharp end of the market. But that was about to change, in just one conversation with John. It was the spring of 2000 when he said to me something along these lines: 'Look, Ginger, you're getting on a bit and I'd like you to have another Grand National winner before you turn up your toes. Try and find me a horse to take to Liverpool.' That was music to these old ears.

Shortly afterwards, I went to Ireland to stay with my good friend

Sean Byrne. Beryl and I have stayed with Sean's family for years during race week at Punchestown, a grand festival held a couple of weeks after the National meeting at Liverpool. As well as high-class racing, Punchestown provides Irish craic at its very best. On this particular visit we saw a horse called Amberleigh House win. But I must confess that the horse's attractive woman owner had been the one to fill my eye most! Oh dear, oh dear. She was around six foot two, with legs that you would dream about. She was American and her name was Amber, and as well as having magical pins she was an awfully nice person. She lived with her partner – who had grey hair tied in a pig-tail – on an estate-like property that they called Amberleigh House, which had its own pub. It's hard not to like that kind of style – and it does cut out the risk of getting breathalysed on the way home. We had been invited to a couple of functions at the house and, as you might expect, we'd been shown typical local hospitality.

Over drinks I had asked Sean to keep an eye out for a horse with the potential to go to Aintree. He told me that Amberleigh House was scheduled to go to the Doncaster sales. As I thought about the horse some memories were stirred. I knew that he had jumped over all the big courses in Ireland. I also recalled that he had been beaten only a neck by Florida Pearl, a horse that in his time had been good enough to compete honourably in the Cheltenham Gold Cup and the King George VI at Kempton Park. On the day Amberleigh House was beaten by Florida Pearl he had received almost 2st. I formed the opinion that he was the kind of horse better suited to getting weight from good horses rather than giving weight to bad ones. He was just not big enough to be saddled with a heavy weight himself.

I thought it was worth letting John Halewood know that the horse was coming on the market as he seemed to have credentials that might suit us – and suit Aintree. John listened to what I had to tell him when I came home from Ireland, and he instructed me to go and buy the horse in the sales ring at Doncaster. But our plan was thwarted when Amberleigh House was withdrawn from the sales. If I am honest, I suppose I thought that was that. Then, some months later, Sean called out of the blue to tell me that Amberleigh House was on the market again. It seems that the couple who owned him had separated – I must say from where I was looking that pig-tailed man must have been mad!

As Sean knew the horse and the owners, I thought it made sense for him to liaise with John over the purchase. John agreed a price in Irish punts equivalent to £75,000, and once Amberleigh House had successfully passed a vet's examination, it was arranged for the horse to be booked on a ferry to England.

On 4 November 2000 I was in bed when I heard a horsebox drive into the yard. I looked at my clock – it was almost 3 a.m. I put on my dressing gown and went downstairs. It was raining stair rods as the driver dropped the ramp on the box. I looked inside and there was this little horse shivering and shaking in the corner. It was winter and he was without a rug, his coat standing out like a coconut mat.

I said to the driver, 'What the bloody hell's that?'

'It's Amberleigh House,' he replied.

'That's not the Amberleigh House I saw win at Punchestown.'

'Boss, I don't know what you saw win at Punchestown, but that's Amberleigh House.'

When he came out into my yard in the rain, you have never seen a more utterly pissed-off and dejected horse in your life. I stabled him in Red Rum's old box, the prime spot in the yard, because he was the most expensive horse we had ever had. I like to think Red would have liked the idea that we might at last have found a suitable horse to take over his old home. Even so, the signs were still ominous. Amberleigh House didn't look any bigger in the stable than he had at the back of the huge horsebox. Anyhow, I put a rug on him and gave him a meal and walked back into the house for a cup of tea feeling a bit sorry for myself.

We Englishmen all know that these Irishmen try to stitch us up with horses. They go to bed dreaming about burying us. Yet back in bed, I wasn't dreaming at all; I was having nightmares. I couldn't sleep – I just lay awake thinking that I'd done £75,000 of John Halewood's money. I've always enjoyed a pretty good relationship with the Irish – yet it weighed heavily on my mind that I hadn't gone across to Ireland myself to see this horse at close quarters, as I should have done. The next day I went to have a look at him before breakfast and he looked a little bit better than he had in the middle of the night – but he still didn't look very big. No matter which angle you looked at Amberleigh House from, you couldn't make him look any larger. Later that morning I discovered that the horse had been sold without the knowledge of his trainer, Michael Hourigan. He had not even been told that the horse was on the market, so it was a total surprise when he found Amberleigh House being loaded to leave his yard in Limerick. Michael was gutted – so the horse travelled as he stood. That explains a bit of it, I suppose.

John didn't rush over to see the new horse that I had bought for him. By this time he had a string of horses in training, mostly with Lisa Williamson. In fact, he had bought them a new horsebox with Halewood International printed on the sides. That rather got up my nose; silly, I know, but it did. The Williamsons had John's nice horses and it seemed a shame that they were to all intents and purposes being wasted – in my view, anyway – while we were having to struggle with horses with much less potential.

But Amberleigh House was plainly in quite a different class from the other horses we had; so we badly wanted to do well with him for John. I think, too, that it was as important to him as it was to us that we had some success. After all, John had placed his faith in me by getting me a serious horse to take to Liverpool again. Of course, we put a fair bit of work into Amberleigh House at home, where Donald rode him. But we also felt it important to have an early look at him on the racecourse, so we placed him in a two-mile chase at Wetherby just eighteen days after he had arrived shivering in the yard. He finished last of five runners – but we weren't too concerned, as we always appreciated that he was a horse that needed a far greater distance than that.

We did not run him again until the following February, when Warren Marston was in the saddle for a three-mile chase at Haydock. He was seventh in a ten-horse field. Two weeks later, he was pulled up over the same distance at Uttoxeter. John, a sportsman who might have made a professional footballer, accepted these performances without complaint. He is a man who knows that owning a racehorse requires riding with the punches. Amberleigh House was pretty highly rated in the handicap and had carried nothing less than 11st 7lb, so we were not too disheartened.

Liverpool was his target and, quite truthfully, we went to Aintree for the 2001 Grand National with some optimism. Our horse had won round Leopardstown and run big races at other Irish courses. Yet to win a National we all know that you need to have a share of luck as well as a talented, fearless horse and a good jockey – and Amberleigh House's luck deserted him on his Aintree debut. He was in the air on the take-off side of the Canal Turn when a riderless horse hit him amidships. Amberleigh landed on his belly on the other side of the fence, but quickly scrambled to his feet.

Unfortunately, Warren was no longer in the saddle. As other horses came over the fence, you could just see his legs sticking out of the spruce. It was unclear what shape Warren was in. But as he was in the line of fire, another jockey, Jim Culloty – who went on to have such a wonderful association with Best Mate as they won the Gold Cup three times – came to his aid and dragged him to safety by his feet. Had he been a footballer, he wouldn't have moved until two physiotherapists and a stretcher crew arrived on the scene! It does upset me when I see the theatrical behaviour of modern-day players, who get paid £90,000 a week and act like prima donnas. They get a tap on the leg and then roll around on the ground as though they'd been shot by a sniper in the stands. It's absolute rubbish – but no one does anything because they are supposedly superstars. Spoilt, over-pampered and over-paid actors, more like. I'd tell them to get on their bloody feet or get off the pitch.

While Warren walked away unscathed from the misfortune, our horse returned to the stables with a cut leg. It was only a small wound, but it would not stop bleeding. The duty vet insisted that the horse remain at the course until the bleeding had been stemmed. Donald was with Amberleigh House, so I left for home. The wound was bandaged, but this did little to prevent the bleeding and there seemed nothing that Donald could do other than wait . . . and wait. It had gone dark before, finally, they were allowed to leave the racecourse, and I suppose it was almost 10 p.m. when they drove into the yard. As Donald had reported that the cut was still a problem we had made a call to the emergency number of our vet John Burgess to get someone to examine him on his return. It was a wise precaution, because when Donald opened the box to lead the horse out there was blood all over the floor.

Quite often, blood pumps faster from a wound immediately after a race as the horse's heart is beating so fast. But after the horse has calmed down, and his pulse rate has reverted to normal, then any bleeding tends to stop. And yet Amberleigh House's cut just kept bleeding and bleeding. How could such a small cut cause the loss of so much blood? Horses don't often bleed to death – unless they're out in a field somewhere and nobody finds them. In the event, the vet who had come out to us applied fresh bandages and said that we must take Amberleigh House to the veterinary hospital on the Wirral straight away. Donald went with him.

It was a worrying time for us all. I don't recall a horse ever losing so much blood from a cut that wasn't all that much bigger than a scratch. We anxiously waited news from the hospital. When the telephone rang, we feared what Donald would tell us. We were frightened that

Amberleigh House might catch an infection through the wound. To our relief, the news was good. When the vets had removed the bandaging, they found that the bleeding had finally stopped. Even so, they wanted to keep Amberleigh House under observation for a few days. No one wanted to explore the wound too deeply as it was close to tendons, so the best course of action was deemed to be to clean the cut and wait. He received first-class care, I have to say. Fortunately, he had no reaction and he made a full recovery.

Seven months later Marston rode him to win the Becher Chase over three miles three furlongs at Aintree, beating Smarty, the horse that had finished second to Red Marauder in that year's Grand National. It was my first winner over the National fences since Red Rum had won the last of his three Grand Nationals twenty-four years earlier and it was marvellously uplifting because I'd convinced myself that I would never train another winner there. I felt I'd had more than my share of luck for one lifetime; and I suppose I was beginning to feel that I had forgotten how to train. You get downhearted, disillusioned, even sick at times – but the good days make you forget the rest. We knew for certain now that in Amberleigh House we had a horse with that Aintree Factor.

It was a boost for Marston as well, as he had been struggling at the time. But in all honesty I was never that keen on Warren. I didn't think he showed that much loyalty. We didn't fall out, but within a year I stopped using him. He would jump off one of your horses and tell you straight that it was not fit. He had a very intense manner. Now, if I have learned anything after all these years in the game it's this: you have to be able to laugh in adversity as well as in triumph. If you don't, it will break your heart. I don't want a jockey coming to me and saying that a horse is not fit. You can phrase it differently. You can say that the horse isn't as straight as you thought he was, boss. After all, he was only offering an opinion. Did he not think I might have some clue as to whether or not my horse was fit?

*

I WAS SO convinced that Amberleigh House would run a big race in the 2002 Grand National that I backed him, because I was disgusted by the odds on offer: 40–1. It was a bloody insult in my book after the way he had won the Becher Chase. But I never got the chance to rub the bookies' noses in it – because Amberleigh House didn't even make it into the race! In a way I was hoisted with my own petard, I suppose. Some while after the Grand National had been restricted to a maximum field of forty runners, I had campaigned that the fairest way to decide the field was to take the top forty horses entered in the handicap. That was the system now in operation – and Amberleigh House was out of the handicap.

When I'd backed that system, I had not anticipated someone like Martin Pipe having eleven horses entered. With no disrespect to Martin, I thought it was bloody silly, what he was doing. He had entered a number of horses, some of them from France that had never jumped an English fence in earnest. In my opinion, he was making a mockery of the National. For him to have had 25 per cent of the runners in 2002 and probably the same again a year later was totally out of order. Half of them had only won round courses in the west country. They are not Liverpool horses. The Grand National is a great race and an institution – it is entitled to proper respect. Amberleigh House was a Liverpool horse, and he was in the form of his life; but he was going to be deprived of a chance to race in the greatest steeplechase in the world. I felt it was a disgrace – and said so. Right or wrong, I said my piece as I saw it. I was at an age when I knew I wasn't going to have a lot more chances to win a National.

Martin Pipe has as many winners in a week as I have in a year, so there is no way I am going to criticize him. But his style of intensive training is not my style, and I wouldn't want to go down the road he has taken. He has an enormous turnover of horses. It is not unusual for horses to last in his yard for just two years before moving on somewhere else. He tends to have a lot of smaller horses that have a limited life in racing. His team is brilliant at getting the best out of those horses while they are with them.

Now, I was asked for my opinions on Martin Pipe for a television programme called *The Cook Report*. I would not criticize Martin for his training methods, and not a word of what I said made it on to television. It is well documented that Martin takes a scientific approach to the job, regularly taking blood samples from all the horses in his yard. That's all there is to it. He is just a bloody good trainer. You can't say any more than that. But I like to enjoy my horses and I love my horses – so that approach isn't for me.

Yet the truth is, if you don't have the material you can't do the job. Martin Pipe is fortunate enough to have an owner like David Johnson, who seems to have a bottomless wallet; Howard Johnson has Graham Wylie's huge investment at his disposal; Jonjo O'Neill has the backing of J. P. McManus. So I was grateful to John Halewood – but the handicapper kept Amberleigh House out of the 2002 National and that was a travesty of justice. With luck in running, they would have had to shoot him to have kept him out of the top six.

With Amberleigh House excluded from the big race, we ran him in the Topham Chase at Aintree instead. That race is staged over two miles five furlongs and he finished sixth, running on strongly. He jumped a lovely clear round, never put a foot wrong, but he never quite got into the contest as he needed that extra one and a half to two miles. It's not in my nature to be bitter – but I was pissed off.

In November that same year, we returned for the Becher Chase again. By then I'd decided to part company with Marston, and Tony Dobbin rode Amberleigh House, giving him a flawless ride to finish second to Ardent Scout.

Four months later I caught the train from Crewe to London with Beryl to attend the annual lunch hosted by Martell – sponsors of the Grand National – to announce the weights for that year's race. It is a grand day out, and part of the ritual of the occasion calls for a number of trainers to submit to an interview over the course of lunch. When I was asked for my opinion on the 2003 National, I said: 'If nothing else, we've proved that the handicappers are bribable. After we couldn't get in last year I sent a dozen cases of red wine, and we have been given a very comfortable weight and we are certain to get in this time.' It was all tongue-in-cheek stuff, but sometime later Bill Smith, the official handicapper for the race, told me that he had been subjected to an official inquiry. He hadn't been, of course, but in future, Bill asked me to be careful what I said. Some chance at my time of life . . .

In fact, Amberleigh House had been given 10st 10lb for the National and I thought that was a weight that made our horse most competitive. We felt we were going to Aintree with a hell of a chance. This would be the horse's fourth time over the National fences and he had never put a foot wrong; on the occasion when he was knocked over he had been an innocent victim of circumstances.

You'll know by now that I'm not a person to let things bother me unduly, but when you have only one shot to fire there is a tendency to get a little nervous as the race gets closer. Every bit of work over the last few weeks is scrutinized. At the back of your mind is that fear that the horse might give himself a rap. At that point, you are too close to going to Aintree to recover fitness and get that bit of edge into your horse that you need if you are to succeed. If something goes wrong at this stage, you're done for.

You have to be focused on the National and nothing else. The trick is timing. You can't hold on to a horse's fitness for ever. Like Red Rum, Amberleigh House was constitutionally sound. Like Red Rum, he would stand plenty of work and come and eat up. But unlike Red Rum, as Amberleigh House attained fitness he stopped eating his midday hay. That told me the work was getting to him.

As I explained, Donald rode all his work. And although he is supremely fit, Donald has to weigh over 13st. You can waste flesh, but you can't waste bone. And both my kids have good bones, it runs in the family. If you look at Amberleigh House, he isn't that much bigger than a pony. And yet Donald never looks out of place on Amberleigh House; he rides a big horse. I would say, too, that it is beneficial to have someone in the saddle who has the strength and ability to hold a horse properly. You can balance a horse so much better without pulling or mauling him about.

For me, the eve of the National is when I feel most calm. After Amberleigh House had completed his swinging canter over five furlongs on the all-weather gallop, which I get to by driving my battered old Range Rover uphill across the fields from the yard, I felt the job was done. There is nothing you or anyone else can do from this stage on except deliver the horse safe and sound to Aintree.

Donald and his wife Sian went in the box with him on race morning, along with my travelling head lad, Wizard. Sian looked after Amberleigh House, and she had plaited some strands of Red's hair into his browband before he left the old horse's former stable. When Red's mane was pulled we always used to keep the hair and send it to his fans when they wrote. Beryl had found some and thought it would be a good idea for Amberleigh House to carry some of the old horse's hair round Aintree. It was a sentimental gesture – but it was nice to think that just a little of the old lad would be galloping past once again. Donald and Sian can play a tune on Amberleigh House.

You live a horse – you have to if you want to get the best from him. You have to know a horse's phobias, his whims, and his likes and dislikes. I don't say you pander to him for twenty-four hours a day, but, silly as it may sound, you need to create a personal, one-to-one relationship with him. For my money, that's how it should be, especially if you are going to compete for a big race.

Luckily for me, now that Donald is so heavily involved I am able to go to Aintree and meet with friends and thoroughly enjoy the craic. I don't think I am being immodest when I say that I am well known at Aintree. From the moment the man on the car park shows me into the course, all I hear is, 'All right, Ginger?' I never get blasé, though. I love the fact that people know who I am at Liverpool, and the older I get the more I look forward to a little bit of banter and a laugh. I haven't got that many more National days left in me, so I am determined to enjoy them as much now as I have in the past. Even in the hard years when I never had a horse in the race or, if I did, it didn't have much of a chance, my love for Aintree and the Grand National never diminished.

After a wander around, I made a short appearance in John Halewood's box at the top of the Queen Mother Stand. No doubt his guests are astute businessmen, but I do get impatient with answering the same questions over and over again. I sound like a parrot. So as soon as I can, I nip across and have a drink with Derek, who manages the stable yard at Aintree. As I've said, he has always looked after my interests: each year he reserves the same stable for our horse – the one that Red Rum always occupied.

After a chat and a couple of drinks in Derek's office, it was time to look at my horse, who by now had been led down to the saddling boxes beside the paddock. Saddling a racehorse is an art, I think. I used to work in conjunction with Harry Wright, my travelling head lad, who came to work for me after Jackie Grainger and Billy Ellison had gone. Harry had been in the army with me and before that we had been order boys together as kids working for the provisions company. Later, he worked for me for a while when I had my small taxi business. When we saddled up, the job was done quickly and cleanly, A–B–C, just the way I like. Amberleigh House is a horse who gets a bit tense when he is being saddled, so Donald likes to apply the same principles. Once saddled, I ensured Amberleigh House had his mouth rinsed out and his eyes sponged. Then I stretched his legs to be certain that the girths were not pinching him. Even if my horse wasn't worth a carrot, I'd want him to enter the parade ring looking a picture. I think on the day Amberleigh House sparkled.

Amberleigh House had been circling the paddock for a short time when our jockey, Graham Lee, approached in the file of forty riders emptying out from the weighing room. Graham was twenty-eight and about to ride in his first Grand National. I went to have a word with him, but then I looked at Graham and Donald and said, 'There is no point me saying too much because you two buggers have already made your own arrangements, haven't you?' I said this light-heartedly because I knew from Donald that everything had been talked out in depth. I have that much confidence in my son – he has had such a thorough grounding – and what more could I say to Graham other than to wish him good luck?

After they had left the paddock, I went to take my usual spot with Sean Byrne. The senior security man allows us the privilege of standing opposite the winning post on a stairwell some ten or twelve feet up. As I've said before, it's not easy to find somewhere to watch from if you have been in the paddock, as the owners' and trainers' box fills so quickly. It is the same with the car park – every bugger and his wife seems to park there.

I had with me the same binoculars that I used to watch Red Rum with. It's nothing to do with having them for sentimental value – well, not entirely. You get used to them on your hip in their old case with a long strap that goes over your head. You pick them up to watch a race and it's the same sense of familiarity you get from handling a favourite gun. You just know that the balance and focus are right. If I went racing without those glasses I'd feel naked.

In fact, I thought I had lost them when I went to see our little mare Calomeria run at the Welsh Grand National meeting at Chepstow just after Christmas 2004. The day started unpromisingly when we came off the Severn Bridge to get stuck in a traffic jam. It irked me that I had to pay £4.60 to get over the bridge. To my way of thinking they should give you a tenner to go into bloody Wales and charge you to come back to England! Anyway, we paid, but once on the Welsh side we hit gridlock.

Apparently, a horse called Bindaree that was running in the Welsh National was taken out of his horsebox and trotted up the road for something like a mile and a half to get to the racecourse. Our little mare, who had won three hurdle races as a four-year-old, was already at Chepstow, but as her race drew nearer Beryl left me in the traffic and walked the last three-quarters of a mile to be certain one of us was present. I arrived with a bit of a hump on my back – then my mare ran abysmally. I am convinced that she was footsore after trouble with one of her shoes a couple of days earlier.

I was not in the best of moods as I headed for lunch as a guest of one of the bookmakers. I was sitting next to a plain-looking fellow with not the best-looking girl in the world. We introduced ourselves and I asked him his line of business. He told me he was an MP. I asked him for his opinion on hunting. 'Oh, I oppose it,' he said. His partner chipped in as well. 'I oppose hunting, too,' she said. 'Why should people ride round in pink coats?' I should have known better than to involve myself in a debate with them. She had a stud in her nose – and she was getting up my nose a little bit. I asked them if they had seen a hunt. He said that he had not, but likewise he said that he had not seen an execution and he knew that he opposed executions. I thought it was a typical politician's practised quip. As for the woman, she looked like she had been a protester all her life and probably never done a stroke of bloody work. You could say that by now we were not getting on very well! But before we left I had to have the last word. I looked at the woman and said, straight-faced: 'I must tell you this. When I was in India ladies that wore a stud in their nose were of a certain profession. What's yours?'

I have never been to India in my life, but she wasn't to know that.

A couple of days later we were going racing and as I threw my coat in the boot I looked to see that my binoculars were where I always kept them. Nope. I began to wonder if I'd left them on top of the car before we had driven away from Chepstow. I was not a very happy man, I can tell you, as I'd had them over forty years. We telephoned the racecourse and they said that they would check if my glasses had been handed in and give me a call back.

They were true to their word. They found the glasses in the dining room. For that, I am eternally grateful to the people at Chepstow. But that MP and his woman partner did not impress me at all. What was he doing in a bookmaker's marquee watching jump racing? Because the next step down the road from banning hunting is to ban shooting . . . and then how long will it be before they try to ban National Hunt racing? He was nothing but a freeloading hypocrite – but that's the type of people that we vote into Parliament.

Excuse the interlude – but these glasses I go racing with have a rich heritage, and that's why I was so pleased to have them back. Anyway, at Aintree twenty months earlier I took those glasses from their weather-beaten old case to follow the progress of Amberleigh House. He came over the second last in touch with Monty's Pass and Supreme Glory. It was fabulous – but I was just delighted to see him running a big race. Honestly, if he had been anywhere in the first six I would have been equally pleased.

As they crossed the line with Monty's Pass winning from Supreme Glory and my little horse in third place, I rushed down to be at the unsaddling enclosure to meet Amberleigh House. He'd run his heart out. As reporters gathered round me, I don't mind admitting I was lit up. 'I'll tell you something,' I said. 'If he'd had a proper trainer he would have won.' Amberleigh House had brought back a lot of memories. I believe that Mike Flutter had landed a million-pound gamble with Monty's Pass, and good luck to him. But I had much to celebrate as well. I knew that I had another pro on my hands – and horses like him are hard to find.

I went to John's box and had a jar or two with him. Obviously, he was delighted to have a horse in the frame in the Grand National. It was past six o'clock when I left him and made my way out on to the course. I was smiling as I walked towards Red Rum's grave. I wanted a few words with the old horse on my own. In the old days, I used to go into his box at night and spend a quiet ten minutes with him. Sometimes, I'd have a piddle before I left. It was something old horsemen did. Why? They just did. You'll be glad to know I didn't repeat that old tradition this time round, but as I stood over his grave I let him know what I thought about the day. I shall be for ever grateful to the old lad for where he put me in the racing world and what he did for me – and that's what I told him. It was a special moment.

But perhaps John had his tail up even more than I did. After the National, we returned to Aintree in November for a third crack at the Becher Chase. This time Amberleigh House was beaten by a whisker by Jonjo O'Neill's Clan Royal. Graham Lee and Liam Cooper had their sticks singing as they raced one another in a thrilling finish. The horses had their heads down and battled it out like they are bred to do. People who want to abolish that kind of riding are utterly wrong. As I've said, I don't like to see any horse of mine come back with marks all over him, but at the same time there is nothing wrong with a jockey using his stick to bring the best out of his horse.

John's reaction to the narrow defeat was to become even more bullish about what we could achieve. There were plenty of nights when the phone rang at two or three o'clock in the morning with John on the other end of the line. Usually, he had been watching a video of Amberleigh House and he was telling me how we were going to win next year's Grand National. I have dozed off listening to him – and have woken up with John still talking excitedly. I tried to suggest that although Amberleigh House was a good little horse, you still had to arrive there fit on the day – and then there was the matter of having to negotiate thirty fences while having the luck in running. He kicked all such logic into touch. We were just going to win a National: simple as that. I didn't always appreciate the timing of his calls, as my work demands that I make an early start. But I do admit his enthusiasm and conviction were grand.

Still, I didn't allow him to put me under pressure. If he wanted to make daft predictions, well, bugger him, he could. Imagine me being the one playing a straight bat . . .

Chapter Twenty-one

FROM RED TO AMBER

EVEN THOUGH JOHN Halewood had faith in Amberleigh House, it did not dissuade him from showing an interest in acquiring another high-quality horse with the National in mind.

I had taken notice of a French-bred horse called Joly Bey, trained by Paul Nicholls. My horse Ebony Light had beaten him at Carlisle, but he was clearly a strong, good type. He was owned by a syndicate that at that time always sold their horses at the end of the season. I could knock Joly Bey on a couple of little points, but he was a tough, hard fellow and I thought he could make a Liverpool horse. So I called John and told him that I thought Joly Bey might do for us.

Joly Bey was to go to the sales in Doncaster in 2003. Auctioneer Harry Beeby estimated that he would make between £100,000 and £140,000. I asked John to be at the sale because, knowing what a competitive man he is, I thought if he was present he wouldn't get beat. But several days before the sale he rang and said that he had forgotten he was going to his home in Barbados. John's instructions to me were to go ahead and buy the horse in the ring.

Hang on a minute, I thought. You're in the West Indies and if I buy him and you pop your bloody clogs I'm stuck and I'm sunk. I said that I'd call him in Barbados a few minutes before the horse went in the ring.

On the day of the sale I stood in my usual place. I opened the bidding at 80,000 guineas – giving them a right crack in the ribs from the start. The price kept rising and rising until an Irish friend of mine turned to another Irishman I knew and whispered, 'For fuck's sake get hold of Ginger, I think he's pissed.' Well, you could see their point: I usually dealt in horses worth no more than 10,000 guineas. My last bid for Joly Bey was 200,000 guineas. John didn't say stop – but I thought that was plenty. The horse made 240,000 guineas.

Afterwards, I went to the champagne bar and ordered a bottle. Put it down to Mr Ken Oliver, I said. Ken had been dead for some time and, truthfully, I was going to pay for the champagne. But Harry walked in said, 'Ginger, you can order as many bottles as you like!' He appreciated the way I'd driven the price up, I suppose.

I'd been unsuccessful in buying Joly Bey, but both John and I knew we still had a star-in-waiting in Amberleigh House. Yet I was more conscious than anyone about what it took to get a horse right for the big day at Aintree.

Amberleigh House's next race after his superb run in the Becher Chase was in February 2004, a two-mile four-furlong hurdle at Haydock: but he didn't sparkle and Graham Lee pulled him up. The ground was a little bit on the soft side for him, but I think he was treating the race flippantly. For such a good, good jumper, the hurdles just weren't enough to motivate him. Graham was right to look after him in the circumstances, but I admit to being a bit despondent. You just have that slight nagging feeling, you look at your horse with a cautious eye. Has he started to deteriorate? At twelve years old, is his age just starting to catch up with him? Yet I also understood that the driving finish in the Becher had to have taken something out of him and that he had not yet fully recovered, despite his lay-off.

Three weeks later we sent him out in a steeplechase at Doncaster over three miles. He finished fifth behind Grey Abbey and I left the course with some reservations. I tend to go to the races thinking we can win everything – even with bad horses, never mind the best in the yard. But again the ground was softish, and Donald was still quite chirpy about the horse. And so was Graham. Our job now was to give the horse that 'edge' that I have talked about. We took him back on the racecourse just once more, galloping him over two and a half miles at Bangor after the day's racing had ended. As Graham was nursing a small injury, Tony Dobbin rode him, and he told us that in his opinion the horse felt absolutely spot-on.

With the National precisely one week away, this was the news we wanted to hear. Amberleigh House came away from Bangor cock-a-hoop, and when he got home he ate up his food and seemed full of himself. From then on the job was basically done: all we needed to do was to keep him safe and sound. To some trainers that means keeping someone with your horse around the clock. I have never felt a need to mount a twenty-four-hour guard on my horses – not even when Red Rum was in his Aintree prime. I prefer to keep the horse's routine as unchanged as possible. You just tick off the days until the big day arrives.

RACE MORNING, SATURDAY 3 April 2004. I shared a light breakfast with our friend Sean Byrne, who has stayed with us for the Grand National meeting for years. Sean, of course, was largely responsible for our buying Amberleigh House, so he anticipated the day ahead with even greater enthusiasm than ever – if that could be remotely possible.

At around nine o'clock Amberleigh House was loaded up for the journey to Aintree, driven by Wizard and accompanied by Donald and Sian. Once there, the drill is for our horse to have a gentle walk around the stable yard before being taken into his box – Red Rum's old box, again. He's an old pro and he doesn't get steamed up.

Beryl, Sean and I arrived in my car around noon. As a courtesy, I looked in at John's box in the Queen Mother Stand. It was packed with his friends being entertained to lunch. It is not my scene, if I am honest. Racing for me is about horses and meeting friends and having a scoop, not about sitting down for a meal. Yet John is a generous host, of course. He arranged for Richard Pitman to come to his box to tell a few stories and go through the card for the benefit of John's guests. I know Richard is a friend, but I am not being biased when I say that he does this awfully well.

After my traditional drink with Derek, the stable manager, I watched the early races. In recent years, Aintree's management has created an area where complimentary drinks are available to winning owners and trainers in a room alongside the weighing room, so Sean and I had a glass of champagne as we watched video reruns of the races before the National. It is not a privilege that I abuse, but it is an excellent facility. I missed the race before the National, though. I like to be with my horse by then, although I'd leave Amberleigh House to be saddled by Donald and Wizard.

Tradition was broken, however, when to my horror, John arrived with a small army of his guests to see Amberleigh House in the saddling box beside the paddock. There had to be at least a dozen people with him. I didn't want all these people disturbing our horse by patting him or fussing all around him. It had bugger all to do with them. He's a professional athlete about to do a professional job. I am sure they were all nice people, but I am always starting to get on my toes at this time and I had no desire to be going through niceties with John's friends. It had been a twelve-month job to get Amberleigh House to Aintree for this National; twelve months of slog to prepare him to run the race of his life in the next half-hour. John's a big-hearted man and I know that his motive was honourable and that he just wanted to share his horse with as many of his friends as he could. But this was the wrong place – and the wrong time.

Look, John had given me this great opportunity late in life and he could do whatever he wanted. Yet even at the risk of being thought a grumpy old bugger, I still felt a sense of responsibility to our horse – and on Grand National day the horse has to be the first consideration.

Once we headed into the paddock I felt better as we waited for Graham to make the short journey from the weighing room. All the jockeys are wound up – in the old days some would probably have taken a sharp nip of brandy or whisky to steady the nerves – as they think about riding in the greatest steeplechase in the world. Graham is the ultimate professional, quiet and focused. And he is ambitious almost to a fault. After he had finished third in the National the previous year, I was tickled pink for him as well as me. Graham said that he was gutted. I told him that he should be skipping and jumping as he'd had a brilliant ride. But third was not acceptable to him. He takes the job very, very seriously. I mean, for a jockey to say he was third in a National is a calling card to carry through life. But this was not sufficient for Graham and I liked that.

As he joined us in the paddock to accompany Amberleigh House in the National for a second time, Graham was a man already looking to the task ahead. He and Donald had talked in depth about the race, and he certainly knew the horse like the back of his hand. I watched Graham leave the paddock on Amberleigh House with a sense of optimism, but also with a sense of trepidation. Had we got the horse fit enough? I went to my usual pitch to watch with Sean. As the horses shuffled past one another at the start in front of the stands, the buzz was electric, as it always is. The race is never won at the first fence, but it can be lost here.

As the thirty-nine horses lined up, with jockeys seeking some fresh air in the crowd, or looking to get close to the horse they have decided to track, all I could see of them now was their rumps. Five or six from the outside I spotted the little backside of Amberleigh House. His bottom was four or five inches below that of any of the horses lined either side of him. For a second I felt bad. Was it fair to ask a little, light horse like him to go out to do the job we were asking of him? As that thought flashed through my mind, the starter released the tape and the 2004 Grand National was on.

I tried to follow the field with my binoculars, but I lost sight of my horse and switched my attention to the huge diamond screen in front of the grandstands. You try to look at the overall picture, but that you are focusing on your own fellow goes without saying. All I could see was that John Halewood's other runner in the race, Kelami – trained by Frenchman François Doumen – was unluckily brought down at the first. At least

John had only to trace the fortunes of Amberleigh House now. Graham had him placed towards the back and was hunting down the outside.

At Becher's – the most infamous fence in the world and the sixth to be jumped on the first circuit – there was carnage as the hopes of nine horses vanished: Akarus (fell), Bounce Back (fell), Montreal (fell), Bindaree (unseated rider), Skycab (unseated rider), Risk Assessor (unseated rider), What's Up Boys (brought down), Blowing Wind (refused) and Bramblehill Duke (refused). Somehow, Graham negotiated a route through what looked like a battlefield. Later, he explained how Amberleigh House had got himself out of trouble. 'He's so tough because we had a nightmare passage over the first six fences,' said Graham. 'At that point, I could just imagine Ginger throwing himself off the stands. The horse had a bit of a fright, too. Plan A went out the window after three fences. He jumped Becher's from almost a standstill first time around and I promise you eight out of ten horses wouldn't have been able to do it. That was when I lost my position – but this horse would jump these big fences blindfolded.'

By the time the field reached the water jump in front of the stands, Graham had our horse creeping into the race. He was jumping flawlessly. And what you tend to forget at Liverpool is that when you go out into the country for the second circuit you've still got two and a quarter miles to race. The theory for a jockey is to hunt the first circuit, then start race riding on the second. I believe Amberleigh House was sixth or thereabouts at the Canal Turn second time around. He was getting into the race.

He was still a long way back, but it truly didn't matter to me. We'd run a big race again – and that was magic. I am quite serious when I say that. If you finish in the first half-dozen of the Grand National that has justified all the work and expense, all the sweat and the tears. As the horses came back across the Melling Road, Graham had gone fourth, but there was still plenty of ground between him and the leaders. The front three – Hedgehunter, Clan Royal and Lord Atterbury – were racing one another hammer and tongs. At the last, Amberleigh House was still fourth.

Then Hedgehunter fell . . . and Graham landed safely and started to get after the two in front. We were going to be third . . . but wait . . . as they cleared the Elbow, Clan Royal and Lord Atterbury both gave the impression that they were drunk. One hundred and fifty yards to go . . . one hundred now. Oh shit, we're going to be second.

When we were going to be third, and then second, I felt content. But hang on! Graham had brought Amberleigh House on to the shoulder of Clan Royal, and then, moving in a rhythm that neither of the other horses could get close to matching, he moved past him. Bloody magic! Our little horse had the Grand National at his mercy.

Sean was behind me and he was thumping me on the back and jumping up and down. To be quite honest, from the second last, I was completely relaxed, not edgy or wound up. I was just satisfied that our horse had given a great account of himself. As Amberleigh House galloped to the line I thought to myself, 'Jesus that's great!'

But here's a confession: I never did see him win the race. Suddenly this Irishman – my good friend Sean, in fact – knocks my trilby over my bloody eyes and I missed him crossing the line. Sean was still thumping me as Graham brought Amberleigh House to a halt, before he turned to walk back to receive an ovation from the crowd. I confess to having a tear or two. We took off down the stairs, but I'm getting too old to run, so I kicked the silly bloody Irishman to slow him down!

I headed for the winner's enclosure, and by this time Amberleigh House was being shepherded through the crowd by some horsemen from the Liverpool Mounted Police and there was bedlam. Jonjo O'Neill and J. P. McManus were already there, and both gave me a warm handshake and offered their congratulations. To show you what this race does to you, I was too thick or overwhelmed to remember that Jonjo had trained Clan Royal for JP, and Jonjo must have been gutted as the race had been taken from his horse almost on the line. It was almost an echo of Red Rum's first win in the National, when he caught Crisp just before the winning post. I look on Jonjo as a friend and I felt for him. I'd given him his first ride in the Grand National on Glenkiln, and now I'd deprived him of training the winner. But one day he will win this race, no doubt about it.

As for me, I'd shown that, given a horse with the Aintree Factor, I could get the job done as well as any other trainer in the land, if not better. I'd never given up my belief that I could win the race again; but after so many years it had become something of a forlorn hope. Then Amberleigh House came along and the belief burned bright again, it really did.

In these moments that will live with me for the rest of my days I knew that I had to be thankful to Donald and Graham, as well as all those who had played their part at home, like Sian and Wizard and, of course, Beryl. Donald deserved so much praise. He had barely left Amberleigh House's side. And Graham had given the horse the most fantastic, intelligent ride possible. He gave us a public masterclass in horsemanship. Let him tell you what ran through his mind as he began to stalk the three horses that were a long way in front of him:

'When I thought I should have been going for Amberleigh House I thought, "I'll count to ten, because he only has one run." I remember thinking when we were turning into the straight, "Christ, there's a strong headwind", so I didn't want to go after them and I thought I'd wait for them to come back to me. Luckily, they did.'

I think that is what is meant when writers talk about performing with grace under pressure.

I was just made up for John and Judy, too: they had placed their faith in me and we had made their dreams come true. No matter how much money you have, you cannot buy a moment like this. You just have to have a great deal of patience and a lot of luck. John had waited twenty-one years to stand in the winner's enclosure on Grand National day. He will never forget the sensation, or that immense feeling of pride. It simply added to the sense of occasion that the Princess Royal presented the trophies.

In the midst of the emotion of the occasion, I blurted out to the media: 'You can have your Gold Cup days at Ascot with all those formal, up-nosed people, and you can have your Cheltenham with all your county types and the tweeds and whatever. This is the people's place and this is the people's race.' Once again, what I may have lacked in diplomacy I think I made up for in honesty! This is the race where the little old lady has her one bet of the year; this is the race where they run a sweepstake in offices all over the country – and the television viewing figures speak for themselves.

To win the Grand National for a fourth time was very, very special. You could have taken me round the corner and shot me right there and then. It wouldn't have bothered me one bit.

But the day was not without poignancy. In the press interview room, I noticed my lovely friend Emlyn Hughes had managed to sneak inside. He stuck up a thumb and whispered, 'Great, Ginge.' He was a poorly man, but he'd had a share in an outsider in the National and he did not want to miss the day. He loved the Grand National like he loved Liverpool Football Club. I still miss his infectious smile, his enthusiasm and his sportsmanship.

John, naturally, was invited to the media conference. 'It's the best day of my life,' he pronounced. 'I'm a local lad, born in Liverpool, and after I saw Red Rum win I vowed I'd come back one day and win the race. I told everyone it would win and as I've got a big drinks firm there will be no shortage of celebrations tonight.'

After I'd finished with the media, I popped up to join John in his box with his guests. A party was in full flow, but I still heard my phone above the noise.

It was Jonjo. 'Boss,' he said. 'We're on our way home and just wanted to call to say well done, great job. But will you do one thing for me?'

I said, 'Sure, Jonjo, what's that?

'Now that you're back at the top where you should be, hand in your licence and let Donald take over. He'll make a far better trainer than you anyway!'

I laughed, because it was pure Jonjo. But I admit that doing that very thing had crossed my mind. You have to be very grateful, don't you? To win the Grand National once is grand, but to win four is a bit greedy. You're not entitled to do that – but by gosh we did. I was reminded that I had equalled Fred Rimell's record of training the winner of the race four times, and I reckoned I would have a run at claiming a fifth. Donald was still only thirty-three. He had time to wait just a little longer. I thought that I had two more Nationals in me and then I would call it a day. Then Donald can have the licence and I'll be his assistant. The programme will be much as it is now, and he will unquestionably make a better trainer than me. And he will win his own National – it's bred into him.

While the party in John's box rocked on, Donald and Wizard prepared Amberleigh House for his journey home. Sponsors Martell decorated his horsebox with banners proclaiming Amberleigh House the winner of the 2004 Grand National, and as Donald, Sian and Wizard and a couple of lads drove through Liverpool, drivers hooted horns and people waved and cheered. Wizard told me later: 'I wouldn't have minded driving round Liverpool all night, the reception we got was just fantastic.'

As the course slowly emptied – and that takes a time at Aintree, as the bars are not quick to shut – I walked down the steps and through the little gate leading on to the racetrack. I strolled down the course in my trench coat and trilby, alone with my thoughts. I passed the water jump and continued down to The Chair, where the spruce still lay scattered on the ground. I just wanted to savour the moment – as I had last done in 1977. Then I went to Red's grave, thinking over the events of the last few extraordinary hours.

I looked down at his headstone and said: 'What do you think about that, then, old lad?'

'Well, Boss,' I heard the old horse reply. 'When he's done it twice more ask me again.'

THAT NIGHT WE went to the Poacher, a pub about a mile and a half down the road from Bankhouse. It's the one the boys from the yard use, so it was the natural place for us to celebrate – and the pub was already heaving when I arrived with Sean and Beryl. The landlady had promised to put on a spread if Amberleigh House won the Grand National, and she was as good as her word. I asked her to serve people whatever they wanted to drink. But I had decided I wasn't going to stay and get pickled, so around 10.30 p.m. I slid away. It had been a special, special day, but I am getting a bit long in the tooth for these long drinking thrashes. I only had £500 in my pocket and I gave that to Donald to pass to the landlady, with the promise that I would return the next day to straighten up with her. She refused to take any money at all, and thanked us for the custom – which I thought was a very nice gesture. I just went home to bed to gather my thoughts in peace. I slept like a log.

The next morning we opened the yard to the media, as tradition dictates. Five cases of champagne arrived from Aintree for us to distribute among the newspaper reporters and television crews. Before long, the yard resembled an NCP car park. Lady Cholmondeley accepted an invitation to join us and, of course, John and Judy came to share the occasion that they had done so much to create.

We brought Amberleigh House out of his box and you really wouldn't have known that he'd had a race. He was bright, perky and posing for the photographers. The only time he put a foot wrong was when, standing next to me, he trod on my toes with all his weight. I made a noise between a howl and a laugh – but I could hardly be cross with the winner of the Grand National! The reception seemed to go down well with the press, and it was an enjoyable end to the weekend. I can't say that I had any real flashbacks to Red Rum for the simple reason that the old horse is never far from my mind. After everyone had left I had a quiet evening with Beryl and Sean over dinner and a bottle of wine. We went to bed very early, as it had been a hard three days. I really must be getting old. The job was done.

AT THE END of the week John and Judy hosted a great party at Tree Tops, a country house hotel at Woodvale, just outside Southport. It was a stylish occasion and from a personal perspective it was a good feeling to return to Southport. I confess that as we left Aintree I felt it was wrong turning left to go to Cheshire when on these occasions in the past we had always turned right for Southport. It was only a momentary feeling . . . but it was good all the same to be able to see all our friends from Southport again. Thoughtfully, Judy had invited all my old pals. It was as good a party as I have ever attended.

At short notice, Judy had arranged for a marquee to be erected in the grounds of Tree Tops – and there were a few gasps of surprise when I led Amberleigh House into it. We had dressed him in exactly the way he had been dressed to go into the paddock before the Grand National. With no disrespect to Amberleigh, he isn't Red Rum. You could do that with the old horse because he was the absolute ultimate star. He just posed for one and all. But I must say Amberleigh House was well behaved, and didn't object to being made a fuss over.

My percentage of the prize money worked out at around £27,000, and Graham Lee received the same. Each of us had also received a large bottle of Martell's most exclusive cognac – as had John – which, they tell me, would cost more than £1,000 over the counter. Sean signed for them – but mine never made it home. Who knows where it went . . . but I reckon a big bottle like that would have been too much of a temptation for someone celebrating at the track. You know what they say about Liverpool: you can get a Persian rug or a brand new car at the right price if you ask. The trouble is, these days they won't let you state what colour you would like!

I believe that John gave Donald and Graham a good cash bonus. Mr

Le Mare used to double our percentage and send a present for the boys, but that was the way the Guv'nor thought. In actual fact, I had seen the perfect 'bonus' that John might have given me. Some weeks prior to the National I'd been to John's home and among his collection of expensive cars was an Aston Martin. The car had been driven less than 1,000 miles before John had garaged it months earlier. I said to him with a grin, 'If I win you the National, you can give me that car.' John didn't say yes, but I got the impression that he might. So when we won the race, I gave him a bit of a nudge. 'What about that Aston Martin, John?' I said. John replied, 'Blast! I sold it six weeks ago, Ginger.' It all worked out well, though. For everyone. John had made sure that Donald and Graham were given a decent token of his appreciation, but I reckon I was luckier than either of them with the gift I received: a limited edition of Amberleigh House whisky – only one bottle, mind!

When the celebrations had died down, we eased Amberleigh House out of his work. Donald hacked him for a week or so, and we accepted just two or three of the many invitations requesting him to make personal appearances. John wanted his horse to attend an occasional charity event, but he didn't make demands as he could so easily have done. After all, he owns the horse.

To be quite honest, personally I didn't want to go down that road again with this horse. As I say, he's not a Red Rum – and he was still an athlete in training. So Amberleigh House was turned out to graze the spring grass for ten or twelve weeks. Then, about a fortnight before he was due to come in, we started to give him one hard feed a day, just to start priming his system. It's about striking a balance with diet and exercise. I know corners are cut all the time one way or another in a lot of places, but there is a way to do it sensibly and correctly. Everything with Amberleigh House was done by the book. But he is the most straightforward little horse.

He came back in at the end of June – once the flies start to get troublesome, you are better with your horses in. Quietly, he was reintroduced to light work, and Donald would initially take him through the woods adjoining our land. Then Donald returned to the gallops with him, going out with the first lot. His countdown to the 2005 Grand National was under way.

IN THE HOME STRAIGHT

WHAT HAPPENED IN the 2005 Grand National is history now: our little horse ran a highly respectable race, and we could ask no more than that. He's spent this past spring and early summer out to grass as usual, and the plan is to keep him in training for another year.

We will aim Amberleigh House at the Becher Chase at Aintree in November, then see what unfolds. I do not rule out his having one more crack at the National. He's sound – touch wood – and he is a horse who loves his training. You wouldn't go to Liverpool with any great expectations of winning, but if he was fit he could go back with 10st 5lb or thereabouts and run a creditable race; and he could even be a danger, despite being fourteen years old. Jockey Graham Lee came out with a lovely expression to describe what a safe ride he has proved round those big fences at Aintree: 'Amberleigh House could land on an egg and not break it.'

We have another horse in the yard, called Ebony Light, who has the potential to challenge for the Grand National. He was placed high enough in the ratings to have got into the handicap in 2004, but his owner Roger Bellamy and Donald both thought that we would be better waiting for another year. The horse hasn't won since, although he has scarcely been out of the frame. To me, he is a horse that wants all of four and a half miles, as he is a big, old-fashioned chaser. He is prone to making a mistake, and has disappointed when he has started favourite in good races – but he is one with some real promise.

It is not impossible that an owner could instruct us to buy him a horse to run in the National, but I wouldn't be inclined to pay too much money for one. And I say that even though the 2006 Grand National will be my last one as a trainer. As I have already told you, I am a firm believer in Fred Winter's maxim: 'You don't buy good horses, they arrive.'

The future is now clearly mapped out at Bankhouse. I have made up my mind to hand the licence over to my son Donald in the spring of next year. I will retire from training with no regrets. There have been moments when I've been down, there has even been the odd occasion when I was totally gutted and thought the job was not worth continuing with. But those moments never lasted long, and they never festered or broke me. Something always came along that offered a little shaft of daylight, and that was all it took to restore my faith in the old game. I've had a longer innings than most, haven't I? They say that one of the most difficult decisions a sportsman faces in his career is timing his retirement. Go too soon and you spend years resenting the fact that you took your leave prematurely. Hang around too long and you become a figure of ridicule. Yet for me, training racehorses has never been a job; it's been a way of life.

In reaching my decision this summer, I remembered the advice another trainer, Peter Easterby, offered me not too long ago. Peter, a much-respected man, said, 'Ginger, when you go, make sure that Donald has a good platform to launch himself. Don't put the boy into bat when the job is on the floor.' And at this moment, the job has never been better. We won fifteen races last season, and this year we began with a flourish of winners through May. We have more horses – and better horses – than we have ever done.

It is time for Donald to take the reins. I say that with a great deal of confidence, knowing that it is not always easy for a son to follow in his father's footsteps. Some are beaten before they start, and you can only sympathize. Donald Bradman's son changed his name rather than have to confront walking through life as the son of the man many would regard as the greatest batsman of all time; Sir Stanley Matthews' boy tried to make a career in tennis, rather than be compared to his father on the football field; and George Best's son Calum soon abandoned football as a bad idea because it was depressing to be reminded every day what a genius his father had been with a ball at his feet. There are other examples that we can all recite – only this past June, Pele woke up to hear allegations that his son Edson Cholbi Nascimento was involved with a gang of cocaine traffickers arrested in Santos in Brazil. Pele's son had been a second-string goalkeeper for eight years.

I am not for a second placing myself in the same company as those great sportsmen – but there is no denying that similar principles are involved. For over thirty years the name McCain has been in the headlines. I know that my manner has not always won universal approval. To some, I was an upstart. To others, I railed too readily against the established order. I did not always tell people what they wanted to hear. I know that now, but do I want to apologize? Not really, as all I could ever be accused of doing was speaking my mind. When I last checked that wasn't a crime.

But with the passing of time I suppose I've mellowed, and I like to think that people have come to realize that I am not talking a complete load of cobblers. Not all the time, at any rate. It's lovely to be afforded some kind of respect. I am not talking in an egotistical way. It's just grand that after all these years I am able to move among titled people, or to be around immensely successful businessmen, and to speak with them on level terms. To think that Ginger McCain, a broken-down old taxi driver, can speak to people like that is rather nice.

So, I have bequeathed Donald a name that is well known in the circles he works in. But I am certain that he will have no difficulty with that. He has learned the job not just from me, but from others like Luca Cumani, Sir Michael Stoute and Oliver Sherwood. His manner with owners is totally different from mine when I started out; he is forward-thinking and he is becoming an outstanding judge of horses. If I were an owner, I'd have no qualms sending a horse, and a good horse, to Donald to train. With Donald the job is done correctly, the only way that is acceptable to my mind, and it is done without bullshit and with utter honesty. The breeding's coming out in him!

The transfer of the licence from me to Donald will be a smooth transition and won't mean a great deal of change in the way things run in the yard now. This time next year, he will simply have an even better platform to make his mark. We have been building a house in the yard for Donald and Sian and their daughters, Abbie, now aged six, and Ella, who is four, and when we have upgraded elements of our house it will be a truly beautiful training establishment. At the moment, we have forty-plus boxes, but we will have to build a barn for another half a dozen horses.

There is nowhere in the world that I would rather be. On a summer's evening I take a glass of wine into the garden and look out over a lake on to fields that fill the eye for as far as you can see. If they are playing cricket at the local club, you can hear the odd shouted appeal. It is the very essence of the English countryside. I would have loved to buy this place, but that was never an option.

I don't like being a tenant. I've had a thing all my life about owning a piece of land, and I will before I die. I'm English and I feel a need to own somewhere. I don't mean to live in, but just to say I own my little part of England. We do own properties at Southport, but we do not own the land on which they stand. They are on what we call three nines – a lease requiring you to pay a nominal ground rent for 999 years. But somewhere down the line something is going to come up and I am going to buy that piece of land I can call my own. Not that I have ever envied another man his money; his horses, perhaps, but never his money. I have never been bothered by money, although I admit a lack of it at times has been a problem.

But I can say we have never been more financially secure at any other period in our lives than we are today. Recently we were made an offer on the stable block at Southport, but Beryl wasn't keen to sell and there was no compelling need to realize the capital, so we turned the proposal down. Even though the place is a run-down shell of how it was in Red Rum's day, when we kept it in immaculate condition, I still hold the old yard in great affection. So many great times, so many great memories.

I feel a fortunate man. Out in the fields surrounding Bankhouse I look at some of the nice young horses we have and I hope I last long enough to see them run. I said to Donald just this past summer that I don't know why we look at other people's horses, because we have some of our own now that years ago I'd have given my back teeth to get my hands on. Some are still unbroken, but they are from good jumping families and there is every reason to hope that they can become competitive. I have ten or twelve brood mares of my own, too, and I have always begrudged selling any of my horses to anyone else in case they did any good with them! But it's coming to crunch time where horses are going to have to go the sales, and I know I must sell some of my home-breds, probably eight or ten each year.

One of the pleasures I have taken in this job is the wheeling and dealing. And as I've said, I do love horse sales; I love just looking at horses and evaluating them. I have never tired of the craic, never wearied of trying to buy a decent horse for sensible money and then having lunch with some good people and talking horses over a bottle of champagne or wine. Horses have always been my reason for getting up every morning.

Our owners now include Trevor Hemmings, who brought a couple of horses to us after he won his Grand National with Hedgehunter this year. I'd love to get a good Liverpool horse off him. Another of our owners, John Glews, has eight in the yard and in the summer asked us to find him another, as well as one for his accountant, at Fairyhouse sales. John would love to have horses to be aimed at big races.

It remains a hard game to win at. Mr Hemmings had thrown fortunes at horses before he won the Grand National. Other rich men are hooked on achieving the same success – among them Graham Wylie in County Durham, David Johnson, who has a lot of horses with Martin Pipe, and, of course, J. P. McManus. Money alone is no guarantee of fulfilling the ambition. The Rank family tried and failed; so did the Earl of Sefton. But such is the magnetic appeal of the National that prosperous men will go on investing heavily in the hope that one day they might stand in the winner's enclosure at Aintree.

My dreams are different now. I wish to see Donald win the National and I hope that I survive long enough to watch one of Joanne and Andrew's boys, Noah and Toby (now aged six and four), or Donald's girls for that matter, ride round Liverpool. It's a grandfather's privilege to spoil his grandchildren and they are grand, they really are (though I am never so happy as when they go home!). But they are in the right environment to have a happy childhood – and a far more comfortable environment than either Beryl or I had. Yet, kids being kids, they are just as likely to kick horses into touch and decide to be footballers or artists or actors. They have to find their own way, of course; but they are being brought up with space and horses and fresh air, and that is not a bad start to life, is it?

Joanne is studying to become a teacher, and in the summer of 2005 completed the third year of her degree. If I am honest, at first I didn't appreciate why she should want to be a teacher when she already had serious responsibilities as a mother and farmer's wife. But then I thought about it and I understand that she felt the need for some independence. She is a talented woman and I admire her bravery in creating a new career for herself.

I am still out on the gallops at 8 a.m., and that won't change. But a sign of age is that I do want to go to bed earlier, and unless there is something special on the television I am upstairs before 10 p.m. I like to read – biographies, mainly, as I like to learn about other people's real-life experiences – and this winter I will accept more invitations to go shooting with my old dog Tilly, a Springer. I will argue for ever in favour of the right of an Englishman to hunt, shoot and fish.

It was perhaps no coincidence that I received a request from the local hunt to meet at our yard in late winter this year. I invited them, of course; but it was only afterwards that I realized the meet was scheduled to take place after Tony Blair's government had officially banned hunting. I suppose the local huntsmen and women realized they would receive a sympathetic response from me – and they were right. I suspect this is a battle the Prime Minister is going to have a hard time winning; and rightly so.

As for my health, I feel good and my precautionary radiotherapy finished just after the Grand National. I did give Beryl cause for some concern, though, when I had excruciating toothache over the May Bank Holiday. I saw a dentist who was operating an emergency clinic, but, regrettably, the pain didn't subside, and the next day I saw my own dentist. I had an abscess – and no amount of painkillers gave me any relief. On the fourth day of suffering I saw a dental consultant and he sent me straight to the A&E department at Chester hospital. As Beryl was going to see one of our horses run that afternoon at the Chester Cup meeting, we drove to the hospital in separate cars. She saw me in, then left for the races. Beryl has lived with me so long now, it's hardly surprising she puts horses before the old man, is it? Seriously, there was nothing she could do for me and it was important for one of us to see the owners. When she called the hospital later the same afternoon to ask where she had to come to visit, she was told at first that they had no record of me. She suspected that I'd checked out and sneaked back to the racecourse. If only . . .

After some tests it was decided that I needed to have an operation that night, and I was admitted on the spot. Beryl did eventually trace me and came to see me before I had surgery. The next morning I felt less than brilliant, but after examining me the doctors suggested that I could go home some time the following day. Beryl was given this information and she made arrangements for Joanne to accompany her to the hospital on Saturday to drive my car back. But when I awoke early on Saturday all I wanted to do was get home. So I discharged myself and walked out to the car park, unlocked my car and drove home. I think Beryl was quite surprised when she saw my car draw up in the yard mid-morning – and even more surprised when she watched me get out in my pyjamas and slippers! In actual fact it took me a good couple of weeks to feel fully recovered, as I was completely run down from the poison in the abscess.

Within a couple of weeks of that episode we had one of those moments that is surreal. We could not find our way to Aintree. Perhaps I need to say that again – after all these years, the McCains couldn't find their way to Aintree. It was utterly embarrassing and utterly true. We had driven to the home of our friends Tony and Elsie Stannard to go to a night meeting, and headed for the course from Knutsford, close to where they live. Coming into Liverpool from that direction totally threw my internal compass out of sync. Not one of us knew where we were. Beryl was leaning over from the back seat trying to make the navigational satellite system work – but that proved a dead loss. As the traffic increased, the more steamed up we became. Eventually, we pulled against the kerb to ask someone on the street for directions.

He took one look in the car, then asked incredulously: 'Are you Ginger McCain? You want to know how to find *Aintree*? You must be fucking joking!'

It was so ridiculous we had to laugh aloud with him. So that's what they mean by a senior moment, I suppose. I don't imagine I will ever live that down now.

AS I SIT in my corner of England and reflect, it is hard not to think that life is pretty good. I suspect that Beryl privately wonders, and perhaps even worries, what will become of me in retirement. But I know she won't let me curl up my toes until she is ready. I am not going to vegetate, but I am going to do what I want to do rather than what I have to do. It will make only the subtlest of differences. I will never lose my interest in the horses and I will be there for whenever Donald needs me.

Beryl and I will soon have our forty-fifth wedding anniversary. Let me tell you, there isn't a man in the country who has suffered as much as I have! It says a lot for my character that I have put up with it. She would no doubt make the same argument; indeed, she reckons that if her father had not been so stubbornly against her going out with me, she would probably have lost interest right at the beginning. In truthfulness, I admit she has been a star – but a self-opinionated star. I am a Lancashireman and the old Lancashireman's expression was that women should be seen and not heard. The world has moved on a long way from those sentiments, but just occasionally I do remind Beryl that I have limits. After all, I was fond of Red Rum but I still had him shot!

I can say with complete honesty that there isn't a day when Red doesn't flash through my mind, not a day when his name isn't mentioned in conversation. We had him with us for twenty-three years, very intense years even when he was retired, and that is a big lump out of anyone's life. I can never be anything but eternally grateful to the old lad for what he did for me. I was very fortunate – and honoured – to be associated with him. I still miss him. Always will.

In my lifetime I have seen the start and end of many incredible careers in racing. I saw Fred Winter become champion jockey, then champion trainer; I watched men like Stan Mellor and Terry Biddlecombe ride with brilliance and courage when the levels of safety were nowhere near today's standards. Behind them came jockeys like Richard Pitman and Johnny Francome, a class act. I gave Jonjo O'Neill his first ride in the National, and we struck up a friendship that has lasted for ever; and then first Peter Scudamore, then Richard Dunwoody, illustrated an obsession in the saddle before Tony McCoy raised the stakes and the standards to an incredible level. I observed with fascination, like the rest of the country, the riding phenomenon known as Lester Piggott. The

Oscars awarded each year to the outstanding jockeys are known to everybody as the 'Lesters'. It says all you need know about his place within the game.

Perhaps the one change in racing that I actively hate – and for the main, all the other changes have been for the better – is the introduction of all-weather tracks at courses like Wolverhampton, Southwell and Lingfield. I think there is a grave danger that we are going to go down the American road and I hate every minute of it. Soon, they're not going to be calling out the names of horses; they are going to be calling out bloody numbers. That has no appeal to me.

But it will be for others to object; not me any more. I have almost had my day, and I know that I have timed my departure to the second. I truly do. I will leave others to write my epitaph if they should so desire. It is not something that concerns me. But if I have left a small mark it is that my name will always crop up as long as there is a Grand National. All records are there to be broken, and one day someone will come along and train five winners of this greatest of all horse races. But with four I will still be up there with the best of them, and that's a satisfying thought.

I cannot end this trawl through my life without thanking everybody who has given me a horse to train, good or bad. It has been an eventful ride from the sands of Southport Beach to the rural idyll of Cheshire. There have been a few bruises, but mostly it has been one grand craic. Nobody has enjoyed it more than me.

In the final analysis, perhaps people will remember Ginger McCain wasn't quite the prat he tried to be.

EPILOGUE

SEVENTEEN DAYS BEFORE the 2006 Grand National I went to the Doncaster Sales on a mission for John Halewood. Before the sale began I had a quiet word with auctioneer Henry Beeby and told him that I intended to bid for the star of the day, a horse called Inca Trail, a full brother to the late, triple Cheltenham Gold Cup hero Best Mate. As I have explained earlier there are times when it pays to be seen, but not heard in the sales ring. Consequently, I arranged with Henry that I could be considered still to be in the bidding for Inca Trail until such time as I shook my head. In due course, the horse that had been in training with Paul Nicholls was paraded for sale. His price kept rising, as I knew it would – 80,000 guineas . . . 90,000 . . . 100,000. I never moved and no one present had an inkling that I was interested in the horse. At 110,000 guineas the room went silent. Then, the auctioneer said, 'Going once, going twice . . . sold to Ginger McCain.' I'd surprised everyone – again. As a ten-year-old, I reckoned that with a clean bill of health Inca Trail could give John a decent shot at three Nationals.

So, for my last ever Grand National as a licensed trainer, I took three horses to Aintree: Amberleigh House, my sparkling little old horse who held the record for Grand National fences jumped; Ebony Light, an old fashioned chaser, a bit of an ignorant bugger who growls all the time; and Inca Trail, who had won nine races from 25 starts, and been in the frame on six other occasions.

Naturally, on the morning of the race, 8 April, I was in the yard to watch the horses loaded into the box for the journey from Cheshire to Aintree. All three are good old professionals and I felt a contented man as I watched the box disappear slowly down the drive. Each horse carried a lock of Red's hair in his bridal. My daughter Joanne went with them, as did Donald's wife Sian, travelling head lad Wiz and a couple of lads.

I went indoors to open a good bottle of champagne, after all it was nearly 9.30 a.m.! I poured the champagne into crystal glasses as I thought my retirement warranted getting out the Waterford. Beryl, Donald, my old friend Sean Byrne, over from Ireland as usual, and Malcolm Folley, chronicling events for his newspaper the *Mail on Sunday* and for this book, all raised a glass in my direction. I had determined this was a day to be celebrated, not mourned.

When I arrived at Aintree I couldn't help but think that the place looked a picture with a spanking new winner's enclosure and paddock. I was particularly tickled pink to see that the old steward's room had been turned into a toilet!

Everywhere I went, people kept saying nice things to me and that was grand, if unwarranted. But the most humbling moment occurred when Aintree's managing director Charles Barnett requested my presence as he unveiled a plaque on a stairwell of the Queen Mother Stand to denote this was the place where I traditionally watched the Grand National. He said, 'Ginger, you've done such a tremendous amount for the National. In those terrible days 20-odd years ago, it was very much down to you and Red Rum that the race survived.' As hard as it might be to believe, I was lost for words. In its own way, it was a gesture that meant as much to me as winning my four Grand Nationals. The only other people who have earned this kind of award at Aintree are the Earl of Derby and the Earl of Sefton. I was very touched that it had been given to a broken-down old taxi driver like me. I now have the right to stand at that spot on

Grand National Day until my dying day – I plan to make use of it for years to come.

Sean stood next to me on the stairwell to watch the race. Ebony Light fell at the fifth fence, and unfortunately my stable jockey Steve Craine, having his first ride in the National, fractured his collarbone in the fall. Amberleigh House, 14 years young, galloped one-paced as gamely as ever, yet Graham Lee felt the need to pull him up on the second circuit before the 21st of the 30 fences. Age had caught up with him, if not with me! Graham looked forlorn as he dismounted from Amberleigh away from the clamour rightly surrounding the winner, Numbersixvalverde, and his jubilant connections. 'It was just one year too many, but he's still a superstar,' said Graham. And after giving Amberleigh an affectionate, final pat on his neck, he offered me his gloved hand. 'Thanks, Ginger,' he said. We both knew that we had so much to be grateful for to the little horse now headed for a well-deserved retirement.

As for Inca Trail, he looked to be travelling as well as any of them as they crossed the Melling Road for the last time, but he ran out of steam and came home eighth of the nine finishers. Still, it was another lovely, lovely Liverpool.

I had a final appointment to keep, of course. As the sun dipped in the sky, it was only right and proper that my day ended with a visit to Red's grave. As I stood beside the old lad, I admit to feeling wistful. My Aintrees were behind me - but I knew that I could not harbour any real regrets. Who knows, I could yet return as an owner or breeder on Grand National day and that would be grand.

But as the National Hunt season ended on 29 April – my most successful ever – my trainer's licence was soon to be destined for Donald. My role as his assistant would grant me a few more days on the golf course in the summer, but otherwise not too much was going to change. It was around this time that I had a taste of what is in store for the future, however.

Donald said that we had runners at Ludlow and Sedgefield, so I informed that I'd go to Ludlow. He looked at me and smiled, 'All right . . . but when I have the licence you'll go where you're told!'

Like father like son, after all?

INDEX

Note: Horses' names are in italics.